Eat, Fast, Feast

A TRIBAL COOKBOOK by the True Light Beavers

Doubleday & Company, Inc.
Garden City, New York

1972

Eat,

Not a book, but a process

DEDICATION

To the Diggers, who, in the Summer of Love of 1967,
fed 1,000,000 Street Saints without spending a penny

To the Hog Farm, who kept 400,000 people well-fed and
together at the Woodstock Festival against all odds

To all cooks of all the families who are standing at the door
of the new culture saying, "Come on in"

And to everyone who realizes that   .   .   .

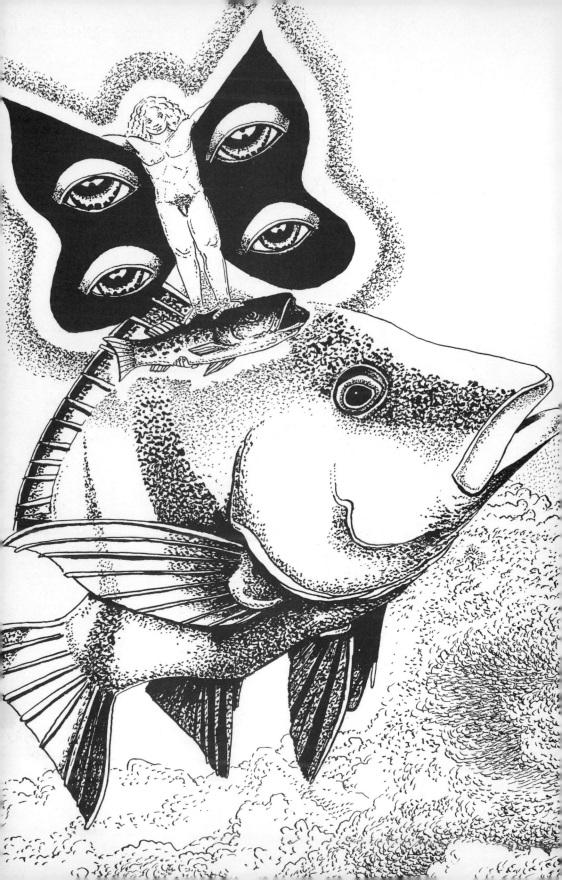

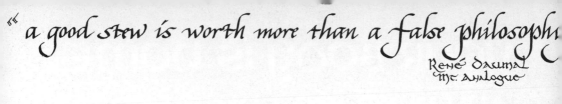

AS WE PASS

FROM ONE AGE

TO ANOTHER...

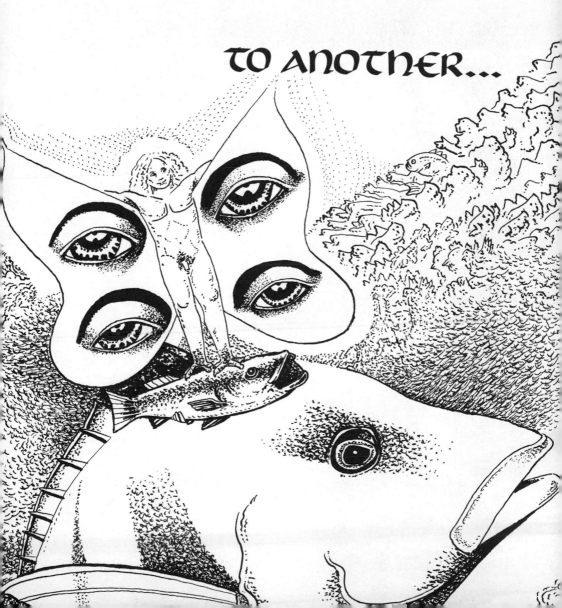

YOUR BODY IS HOME.
ANY PLACE ON THIS SPINNING
GEO-CREATURE EARTH
IS PART OF THE SKIN THAT
GROWS US ALL.

CONTENTS

† *Recipe sections*

xiii   Contents

FROM ZEN BASKETBALL TEAM TO MOUNTAINTOP TRIBE—
The True Light Beaver Story

*Back in the Summer of '66, when family still meant nuclear, and our
heads were into dope, and reclaiming the city streets with flowers, love,
and costumes, the True Light Beavers were born, delivered on a back
shelf of Moe's Discount Mart. Susan Beaver used to shop at Moe's for old
football jerseys, basketball shirts, and the like, finding the beautiful colors
and nice slogans (Courtesy Taxi) just right for decorating body and soul.
Her real find was a batch of nine basketball jerseys, white and shiny
green, with the words True Light Beavers emblazoned on the front. (The
True Light Beavers, we discovered years later, were a defunct Zen Buddhist
Basketball team from Chinatown.) We found the name fitting and
symbolic of just about everything. Instantly, the shirts were passed
out among friends, and True Light Beavers started showing up at
sweep-ins, ESSO meetings, psychedelic showcases, be-ins, and finally, at
the raising of the Pentagon. When the Pentagon was raised, so were
many consciousnesses, and flowers and costumes started being replaced by
flags and overalls. A big exodus started taking place: some flower kids
took off for Chicago (Yippie!), others for the woods; some dropping
out, some digging in.*

*¶ The True Light Beavers dug in! From a nuclear family of four in
New York and three in Boston, the True Light Beavers became seven in
the woods of New Hampshire. Brothers and sisters moving together, we
became a clan of ignorant Indians, learning, that first year, how much
we didn't know. Life-art is where we're at, and that year in New
Hampshire meant a lot of life-art dealing with heating a house, making
a garden, stringing beads, doing some movies, and a lot of drawing. We
grew close in New Hampshire, brothers rediscovering each other, sisters
working it out, all of us, with the kids, making it work. We learned
a little bit to read the seasons and interpret the messages, we learned a
bit that to make the revolutionary alternative first meant getting our shit
together. . . . New Hampshire got the clan together, a new order came
into being, and we flashed that we were at the beginning of the biggest
trip we've ever taken.*

¶ *To Woodstock! And we become more of what we are: energy artists! The new lessons that began in New Hampshire are continued here: we learn new shills, develop new tools. The progession of the seasons now forms a strong rhythm for our lives, with spring devoted to gardens, chickens, a new baby, and plans; summer busy building new systems; fall, harvesting and getting ready for winter, which becomes less isolating because of the new community of many clans growing and living around us. We find new needs and meet them with a school, a switchboard, new medicine, food sharing, trading, new communication systems, more land, earth people buildings, and suddenly we find ourselves a tribe expanded to eighteen on a mountaintop. And going further! We find, as we build, builders all around us: a tribe on every mountaintop. The years of digging in and learning are now producing so many new life ways that are just now beginning to trade and expand and be together cooperatively.*

¶ *So here it is from us to you: our first collection of many ways from many tribes: new tools, workable systems, shared thoughts, and warm foods which have nourished and fed us all for many years; which will give us all the energy to go further.*

GARDEN OF EATIN'

Harvest —THE FIRST SACRAMENT

Lightning —THE FIRST COOK

Fruits and Vegetables

Recipes for the Health of Your Garden

Growing your own food is fun. But sometimes gardens are troubled with insects and other invaders. Here's a collection of ways that will help you keep your garden healthy, without pesticides.

¶ Snails (slugs) can be dealt with by hand-picking and squashing, or by placing small flat containers (bottle tops) full of stale beer near the susceptible plants. Morning will find the slugs drowned in the brew.

¶ Garlic is a potent repellent. Plant it near troubled plants, and it will help ward off insects. The juice from crushed cloves kills mosquito larvae and other insect pests. Garlic powder can be diluted and sprayed as an effective agent against powdery mildew, and some bacterial blights.

¶ Green onions help keep aphids away from roses. Chop the onions, add water, and strain. Then spray the mixture over the affected rose bush. And remember, rose-hips are a rich source of vitamin C.

¶ Fungi kill nematodes. So, keep your garden rich in humus (see the compost recipe) and you'll encourage these helpful fungi, which will ward off the minute worms that damage crops without being seen.

¶ Tansy, coriander, and mint are helpful in keeping ants from your kitchen. Plant them near the back door, and the ants will stay away. Marigolds also work.

¶ Try marigolds in between your tomato and pepper plants. It keeps the damaging bugs away, and you'll have lovely flowers through the fall.

¶ Flea beetles can be discouraged from devouring tomato and eggplant leaves by sprinkling lime or wood ashes over the plants after each rain.

¶ Protect young tomato and pepper plants from cutworm damage by placing a small paper collar around each plant. Make it extend one inch below the soil and one inch above.

¶ Wood ashes are efficient protectors of plants from snails. They can also be used to replace lime in sweetening the soil.

¶ Blood meal will help deter small animals from eating your garden up. Sprinkle it about the growing rows.

¶ Lime is essential for aiding alkaline-loving plants such as beans and peas. Others, like radishes and strawberries, thrive in acidic soil, so before you sprinkle lime everywhere, plan your garden.

¶ *Companion crops:* Some crops thrive next to one another and would do well to be planted in conjunction. A partial list of pairings follows:

> *Tomatoes and parsley and asparagus*
> *Cabbage and hemp, mint, or tomatoes*
> *Carrots and peas*
> *Celery and bush beans*
> *Cucumbers and beans or corn*
> *Beets and Kohlrabi*
> *Beans and onions*
> *Potatoes and corn*
> *Radishes and lettuce*
> *Peas and turnips*

¶ Mulch your crops with about five or six inches of hay, grass clippings, or leaves. This will keep the ground moist and keep weeds down.

¶ Encourage ladybugs, mantids, dragonflies, wasps, tiger beetles, and damselflies to visit your garden and eat all the harmful pests.

¶ Aphids (brought by ants) will be checked by mulching, since ants desire dry ground. Bone meal also protects against ants.

¶ Collars should also be used for young cabbage, broccoli, and cauliflower plants to protect them from cutworms.

¶ Cabbage family and radishes and turnips that are bothered by maggots can be protected by a mulch of oak leaves.

¶ Ground-up hot peppers protects tomatoes from the green hornworm, which will strip foliage if left alive.

¶ Corn: when it is beginning to mature, squeeze the wilting silks and crush the earworms. Drop a bit of mineral oil into the tip of the silk to kill the worms.

¶ Always check the undersides of leaves for insects or egg clusters.

¶ Japanese beetles will be lured from plants by marigolds and geraniums. Pick them off and drown them in water with a thin film of kerosene.

¶ Wood ash helps keep plants clean of red spiders.

¶ Keep your plants and soil healthy . . . a healthy garden will be much less susceptible to insect damage.

¶ From October 1 on (in the North), there is usually a danger of frost. At the beginning of the month start making a habit of covering your tomato plants with blankets or sheets of plastic at night. This will protect them from the hardest frosts, and give you an additional two weeks to a month of tomatoes. Just cover them at dusk, and remove the protection in the morning.

¶ Cabbage can be protected from predators by sprinkling confectioners' sugar around and on them.

¶ Burlap is an effective mulch around eggplants.

¶ To help a new garden get started, and to enrich any garden soil, plant rye in the fall, and plow it under before the hard frost.

¶ Remember that with a little care and some ingenious solutions, your garden can be relatively pest-free and healthy enough to provide good organic food for the table over the entire summer and through most of the winter. By using the suggestions above, you'll save headaches as well as your garden. And you'll be able to do it all without resorting to harmful poisons.

¶ Planting Swiss chard is a quick way to improve garden soil, add abundant iron, vitamins A and C to your diet, and have a carefree, huge, summer-long greens supply. Chard likes an alkaline soil. A little liming to encourage the chard's fullest growth will give your garden great rewards in soil aeration; Swiss chard's roots can go down 6 feet in a season. And no more July wilt problems. It will supply greens for salads and cooking, over and above any temperamental, wilting spinach.

¶ Plant thickly and eat all the thinnings in salads. Pick the outside leaves when the stalks are long and white and the leaves big and full. When you've got a big pile of leaves, wash them off, and drain off the excess water. Sauté a lot of garlic—three or four cloves—in a little oil. You should use a 6–8-quart pot with a lid. Plunge all the chard into the hot oil. Stand back for spattering, and then cover. Keep the flame down low and let the greens cook down slowly. A huge potful wilts down to a medium-sized bowlful. Cook until the white stalks are limp, sweet, and tender. This yields an iron rich, strong but sweet-tasting, sort of oriental-flavored, mess of greens: really good counterpoint to brown rice, squashes, or fish. My grandmother reveres Swiss chard and beet greens as promoters of longevity.

Longevity Tied to Gardening

LONDON (AP) — Want to live longer? Take up gardening. David Hessayon, doctor of biology and horticultural expert, told the Royal Horticultural Society: Gardening has prevented more nervous breakdowns and has prolonged more lives than any other single activity.

Shushi's Zucchini and Onions

Serves 10

Zucchini tastes good with just about everything, and most people love
onions. For about 10 people, buy about 5 zucchinis and 2 onions and slice
everything very thin. Put some oil or margarine in a huge skillet or 2 large
pans, and sauté over a low heat until done. The zucchini will be moist
and the onions will be golden. Add salt and pepper to taste.

Paul and Lisa's Great Sandwiches

2 cups tahini
1 cup miso
Raw onions, diced
Bean sprouts

Lettuce
Mushrooms, sliced
Bread

Mix tahini, miso, and raw onions to make a spread, adding water if too
thick. Place bean sprouts, lettuce, mushrooms, and spread on thick bread
slices and eat.

White Gazpacho (*in blender*)

Serves 10

4 medium cucumbers
2 cloves garlic
3 cups chicken or vegetable broth
2 cups sour cream

2 teaspoons salt
4 tablespoons lemon juice, or to
  taste

**Condiments: Chopped tomatoes, fresh parsley, sliced scallions or chopped
chives, slivered almonds, chopped egg, freshly grated Parmesan or Cheddar
cheese.**

Combine cucumbers, garlic, and a little of the broth in blender container
and whirl till smooth. In a large bowl, blend cucumber mixture, remaining
broth, sour cream, salt, and lemon juice.
Chill.
Serve with condiments in separate bowls so that each person may choose
his own combination.

Delicious Golden Delicious Squash

Serves 8

When Steve and I left New York City, we left behind all our old eating habits. Outside one of our favorite towns, Missoula, Montana, we wandered into a supermarket the like of which we had never seen. Oranges were the size of cantaloupes, and zucchini looked as fat as cucumbers. We wandered around getting high from the smells and colors, buying our week's supply of food. That night we steamed a golden delicious squash the size of a small pumpkin. We steamed it in a big pot over our campfire with a little margarine and water. We ate it with honey, salt, and pepper. About 8 people could have filled their bellies on that squash, and it cost only about 40 cents.

Onion Pie

Serves 4

1½ cups dry bread crumbs
¼ teaspoon curry powder
¼ teaspoon salt
6 tablespoons melted butter or
   margarine
1½ cups sliced or chopped onion
2 tablespoons butter

1¼ cups milk
1 teaspoon salt
¼ teaspoon paprika
½ teaspoon curry powder
Dash of cayenne
1¼ cups grated sharp cheese
2 eggs, beaten

Combine first 4 ingredients and line a deep pie pan, reserving ¼ cup of the crumb mixture. Sauté the onions in butter, and add milk. When it's hot, stir in the remaining seasonings and the cheese. Allow to cool a bit, and then add the eggs. Pour the filling into the crust and sprinkle remaining crumbs on top. Bake until set—35–40 minutes—at 325°. One of these pies serves 4 people, so make several for a feast day.

Butternut Squash with Apples and Raisins

Serves 10–12

2 or 3 butternut squash, peeled,
cut into ½-inch slices
3 pounds apples, peeled, sliced
Sugar or honey
Raisins

¼ pound butter
Allspice to taste
Lemon juice to taste
Cinnamon to taste

Steam squash till tender but not falling apart. In a casserole, put a layer of squash and a layer of apple slices. Put sugar or honey on each layer. Sprinkle with raisins. Melt 1 stick of butter and pour some butter over layer. Sprinkle with allspice, lemon juice, and cinnamon.
Continue layering, ending with layer of squash.
Bake in 350° oven until apples are tender—about 20 minutes. Fantastic with pork roast.

Rich Resplendent Ratatouille (c'est French) Lizzie

Serves 10–12

(Can use any number of
vegetables)
1 large eggplant, peeled, diced
2 large onions, sliced
5 cloves garlic, crushed
Olive oil
1 green pepper, diced

2 pounds zucchini, sliced
1 pound summer squash, sliced
Fresh mushrooms, sliced
5 or 6 tomatoes, peeled, chopped
(or 1 large can, undrained)
Lots of basil, thyme, pepper,
oregano

Sauté onions and garlic in small amount olive oil till golden. Add eggplant and sauté a few minutes. Add the other vegetables (can sauté them in olive oil before, to make it extra rich), stir a couple of minutes, add seasonings (can add capers too), and simmer 45 minutes to an hour.
Yummy either hot or cold.

Baked Onions

This is a simple but really tasty dish.
Peel onions.
Wrap in foil with butter or margarine; add salt, pepper, celery seeds.
Bake at 375° until done.
The onions turn out very sweet.

Billie's Cauliflower Pie

Serves 10–12

4 ounces butter	½ cup strong grated cheese
2 tablespoons flour	Head of 1 small cauliflower,
Enough milk to make a white	cooked, strained, mashed
sauce with above	3 egg whites, stiffly beaten
3 egg yolks, beaten	(peaked)

Combine the first 3 ingredients to make a light white sauce. Mix in
the beaten egg yolks. Add the grated cheese. Add the mashed (or puréed)
cauliflower. Turn the whole mixture into an ungreased 9-inch round
baking dish. Bake in a moderate oven until the top is gold-brown. A
9-inch pie yields 8–10 small wedges. Double all ingredients for a very
large head of cauliflower (or 2 small ones). Turn mix into 2 9-inch
baking dishes. Two small ones bake better than 1 giant one. Top with
stiffly beaten egg whites. This pie may be eaten hot or cold; good both
ways.

Mara's Super Spinach

Serves 10–12

Take a big pot that has a tight-fitting lid. Put in a clump of butter and
some peanut oil—get it really hot. Put in a few cloves of garlic, sliced
up. When the garlic is a little brown—this should take half a minute if
it's hot enough—put in a lot of washed spinach. Fill the pot with it. Clap
the cover on tight. When steam comes out, stir the spinach, and put the
lid back on fast. Wait a minute, put it into a bowl. Eat it real quick.

Hershey's Interstellar Cellar Stew
or *Chopped Slop Shit Green Tomato Chutney*

Green tomatoes are easy to find at harvest time in Vermont, and chutney
becomes a delicacy that even beans and rice get off on. If you're walking
through any hardwood areas, check the ground late in the fall for a vine
of heart-shaped flowers . . . wild ginger root looks like this. I found mine
this year along an old maple sugar road on the way to fell wood for the
winter. Clean it with a vegetable brush and dry it above the stove. It's
really strong and delicious. Vinegar: I made from pressing apples with a

metal squisher instead of a wooden one, which turned the apple juice to vinegar within 4 days.

2 cloves garlic	2 teaspoons cloves
2 tablespoons salt	1 4-inch piece cinnamon stick
4 teaspoons cayenne or red chili	60 whole peppercorns
8 tablespoons ginger root	2 pounds honey
3 cups vinegar	4 teaspoons cumin
8 cardamom pods with seeds	4 pounds green tomatoes

All of these goodies can be chopped, ground, or broken up into a large pot. Don't boil it away, but keep it over a moderate flame for about an hour. Stir it once in a while, and when it's cooked, cool it out, or place it in jars to can. It gets better the longer it keeps. Store in a cool dark place.

Apple Wine

3 pounds apples, chopped up	1 lemon
1 gallon cold water	3 pounds sugar

Cover chopped apples with water and the juice and skin of 1 lemon. Leave for 3 weeks in a loosely covered stone crock, stirring each day. Then, strain pulp and add sugar. Leave for 3 days with cheesecloth over it. Bottle and keep for 6 months before using.

THE JAMESTOWN WEED

". . . The Jamestown weed (or thorn-apple). This, being an early plant, was gathered very young for a boiled salad, by some of the soldiers sent thither [i.e., to Virginia] to quell the rebellion of Bacon; and some of them ate plentifully of it, to the effect of which was a very pleasant comedy, for they turned natural fools upon it for several days: one would blow up a feather in the air; another would dart straws at it with much fury; and another, stark naked, was sitting up in a corner like a monkey, grinning and making mows at them; a fourth would fondly kiss and paw his companions, and sneer in their faces, with a countenance more antic than any in a Dutch droll. In this frantic condition they were confined, lest they should, in their folly, destroy themselves—though it was observed that all their actions were full of innocence and good nature. Indeed, they were not very cleanly. A thousand such simple tricks they played, and after eleven days returned to themselves again, not remembering anything that had passed." (Beverley's *History of Virginia*, p. 120)

From Robert Beverley, *The History and Present State of Virginia,* edited by David Freeman Hawkes. Copyright © 1971 by The Bobbs-Merrill Company, Inc. Reprinted by permission of the publisher.

Willie & Carol's Fruits au Rhum (The Seven-month Rhum Pot)

In June swirl boiling water in a rum pot or glazed stoneware or glass crock. Let it dry completely and set it in a cool dry place. (It will remain here until the contents are ready to be eaten, in December.) Arrange a layer of 1 pound hulled strawberries in the pot. They must be ripe but not overripe; they must be clean and perfectly dry. Sun-drying is recommended. All bruised and blemished fruit must be discarded, as it will ferment and spoil the rum pot. Sprinkle 1¼ cups sugar over the strawberries and pour 1 quart rum slowly down the inside wall of the pot, being careful not to disturb the berries. The level of the rum must always be maintained at least 1¾ inches above the fruit. As the lighter berries are likely to rise to the surface until they have absorbed enough rum to sink of their own weight, it may be necessary to place a light plate on the berries. Cover the rum pot with plastic wrap to completely seal it, and adjust the cover. Since plastic wrap is available, it is no longer necessary to seal down the rum pot cover. After 3 or 4 days, remove the plate and shake the rum pot gently to dissolve any remaining sugar. Add rum, if necessary, to maintain the proper level. If, at any period, there is no ripe fruit available within 2 weeks of the last addition, shake the pot gently, add rum if necessary, and seal it tight.

As soon as *cherries* are in season, add 1 pound perfectly clean stemmed ripe cherries and sprinkle them with 1/2 pound (1 1/8 cups) sugar. Add rum, if necessary. If sour cherries are available, before or after the strawberries, add 1 pound ripe *sour cherries* and 1/2 pound sugar. Use both sweet and sour cherries. A 6-quart rum pot should be filled with 1-pound layers of fruit and 1/2 pound sugar per pound of fruit. The sugar can be increased to 1 1/4 cups for *sour currants* or *gooseberries* and decreased to 1 cup for very sweet fruit.

To prepare *peaches* and *apricots* for the rum pot, scald them and draw off the skins. Halve the fruits, remove the stones (pits), and add the fruit to the rum pot. *Plums* and *greengages,* which cannot be peeled, should be split and stoned (pitted). *Small hard pears* have to be scalded and peeled.

Large pears have to be scalded, peeled, quartered, and cored. *Blueberries, blackberries,* and *raspberries* must be carefully picked over and *currants* and *gooseberries* have to be stemmed and individually pricked with a pin. Apples are unsuitable for the rum pot, and owners stand divided over bananas and grapes. If *grapes* are added, they must be halved and seeded. Very large grapes must be peeled. *Pineapple* has to be peeled, sliced, all blemishes removed, and fruit cut into wedges.

Add the last fruit in October. Then seal the rum pot with plastic wrap and let it stand undisturbed for 1 month. Open it and add another 2 cups rum, or enough to bring the level up to 2 inches above the fruit. Seal the pot again and wait for the Christmas holidays. Set the rum pot on the table, provide each guest with a pointed stick, or skewer, and let each help himself. Or serve the rum fruit in bowls with whipped cream.

Susan's Homemade Peanut Butter
(*It seems you can never make enough*)

5 cups shelled roasted peanuts
2 teaspoons salt

7 tablespoons peanut (or any other kind) oil

You should get about 3 pounds of roasted peanuts. This will give you enough for about a quart of peanut butter, with enough peanuts left around for nibbling. A quart will cost you about $1.50, roughly what health-food peanut butter costs.
Place shelled peanuts, oil, and salt in blender. Blend, stirring, until it is well mixed, with some chunks. Turn out into quart jar, and stand back while all the peanut butter fans have their peanut butter holiday.

Note: You may want to blend the peanut butter using a cup of peanuts at a time, depending on the ability of your blender to handle big, chunky loads.
And remember, you asked for it!

Mike's Cole Slaw

Serves 75–100

6 large cabbages, 3 red, 3 white,
   totaling 20 pounds
1 pound carrots
2 green peppers, diced
2 large onions, diced

4 quarts mayonnaise
½ cup sugar
Juice of 5 lemons
Salt and pepper to taste

Shred cabbages, carrots; mix with peppers and onions. Mix mayonnaise, sugar, lemon juice, salt and pepper to taste. Pour dressing over cabbage-onion-carrot-pepper mixture. Mix and chill.

Sweet and Sour Cabbage

Serves 12–16

5 pounds red cabbage
¼ cup fat
1 teaspoon salt
¼ teaspoon pepper
8 cloves

1 teaspoon allspice
1 cup sugar
Boiling water
6 tart apples
⅔ cup vinegar or lemon juice

Slice the cabbage fine and place in a pan. Add the fat, salt, pepper, spices, sugar, and boiling water to just cover. Place on fire, cover, and bring to boil. Pare and slice apples, add to cabbage, and cook ½ hour. Add vinegar or lemon juice and simmer for about ¾ hour longer. Serve over rice.

Stuffed Cabbage

Serves 12–16

2 heads cabbage
  Stuffing:
4 pounds ground meat
2 onions, grated
2 eggs
½ cup motzah meal
1 cup hot water
Salt and pepper to taste

  Sauce:
2 14-ounce cans tomato juice
1 8-ounce jar apple jelly
1 8-ounce jar grape jelly
4 medium onions, sliced
2–4 lemon slices

Mix all stuffing ingredients together and set aside. Tear apart 2 heads of cabbage, and place leaves in a kettle of boiling water. Boil for 10 minutes, drain, and rinse with cold water. Roll a portion of the stuffing in each leaf of cabbage. Mix together all the sauce ingredients, and bring to a boil. Place the stuffed cabbage rolls into the pot of boiling sauce and cook, covered, at a simmer for 1½ hours. Then bake in a slow oven, uncovered, until brown.

Cabbage and Raisins

Serves 8–10

1 large savoy cabbage   **Salt**
1½ cups raisins

Slice and sauté cabbage lightly in a little corn oil. Salt to taste. Add 1½ cups raisins and enough water to cover bottom of pan. Cover tightly and steam till done.

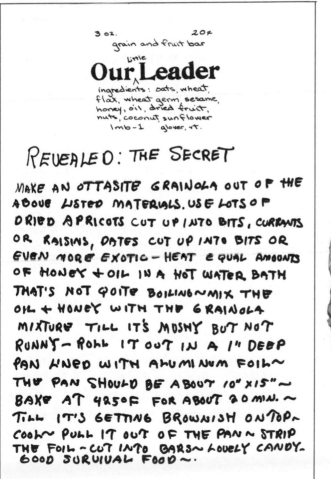

3 oz.   20¢
grain and fruit bar

Our little Leader

ingredients: oats, wheat,
flax, wheat germ, sesame,
honey, oil, dried fruit,
nuts, coconut, sunflower
lmb-1   glover, vt.

REVEALED: THE SECRET

MAKE AN OTTASITE GRAINOLA OUT OF THE ABOVE LISTED MATERIALS. USE LOTS OF DRIED APRICOTS CUT UP INTO BITS, CURRANTS OR RAISINS, DATES CUT UP INTO BITS OR EVEN MORE EXOTIC — HEAT EQUAL AMOUNTS OF HONEY + OIL IN A HOT WATER BATH THAT'S NOT QUITE BOILING~MIX THE OIL + HONEY WITH THE GRAINOLA MIXTURE TILL IT'S MUSHY BUT NOT RUNNY — ROLL IT OUT IN A 1" DEEP PAN LINED WITH ALUMINUM FOIL~ THE PAN SHOULD BE ABOUT 10"X15"~ BAKE AT 425°F FOR ABOUT 20 MIN. ~ TILL IT'S GETTING BROWNISH ON TOP~ COOL~ PULL IT OUT OF THE PAN ~ STRIP THE FOIL — CUT INTO BARS~ LOVELY CANDY. GOOD SURVIVAL FOOD ~.

Future Feast

PRESERVING FOOD

The more you get into feasting (good, healthful food cooked and eaten together with your group of family/friends), the more aware you'll become of the need for good methods of preserving the food that you grow and eat. To feed large numbers of people good food inexpensively, you should grow and preserve your own. Fortunately, the largest number of people to be fed also make up a good work force. Lots of people working together can, in a short amount of time, preserve a winter's worth of vegetables, fruit, jams, and meats; dry enough herbs for all the teas, soups, and sauces you can cook, and construct and fill a beautiful root cellar.

¶ Here are some notes on home preserving, as we do it. Take what information and hints you need, and work with them. The methods that suit your family/group needs best will be the methods that you find quickest, easiest, most fun, and most satisfying. Eat and enjoy your own homegrown, home-preserved food any time of the year.

¶ Our family prefers freezing vegetables to any other kind of preserving method available. We find it to be a quick, easy, and safe method for preserving large quantities of vegetables and meats. We were fortunate to inherit a freezer with the house we now occupy. If you don't have a freezer, though, try buying a freezer (and later, a cow, or side of beef) communally. It works out to be not much money, and a real saving after you've got it stocked with your home-frozen goods. Some people object to freezing for fear that, should the electricity fail, all the food will be ruined. From our experience in freezing food (we live in the Northeastern United States), the electricity only goes out for long periods of time during the winter; if the food is in danger of thawing, we simply move it outside, where nature keeps it frozen for us.

¶ A freezer that has stopped because of some mechanical failure or power shortage will keep food frozen for at least 48 hours. If, after 48 hours, you want to do something to ensure that the food won't spoil, simply spread about 25 pounds of dry ice on top of the food, and close the freezer. If, by some chance, your food has thawed, there are still some things that can be done to prevent spoilage or waste. So long as ice crystals remain in a package of frozen food, it can be safely refrozen. Even some foods that have thawed completely can be refrozen. Fruits can be refrozen if you catch them just after they have been thawed. Meats, poultry, and fish can be refrozen if careful examination shows that they still smell fresh. Shellfish and vegetables cannot be refrozen if they have become thawed. I just figure that freezing is the easiest way to preserve food, and that if your freezer breaks, and all else fails you can *then* begin to think of another way of preserving the thawed food.

¶ Almost anything can be frozen: milk, butter, hard cheeses, bread, pastries, piecrusts, cucumbers, eggs, pimientos, etc. You may freeze, as leftovers, soups, casseroles, main dishes, sauces, vegetables, noodles, stuffed cabbages. Most fruits can be frozen in sugar syrup, plain, puréed, as jams, or cooked. Meats, poultry, and fish need only be cleaned and fresh, or can be frozen after they've been cooked, to be reheated. All food that is put in the freezer should be wrapped or packaged tightly, to keep ice crystals from forming on the food itself.

¶ To freeze in quantity, for long-term storage, you should follow a specific method. All vegetables and fruits that are to be frozen should be young, tender, and without bruises. Most vegetables should be cooked before freezing for maximum flavor. You should plan to freeze your produce as soon after picking as possible; that way you'll be pretty sure of getting all the nutrients that they have to offer. (Corn, for instance, contains natural sugar while it is on the stalk. Once it has been picked, that natural sugar changes within 3 hours to starch.) The whole process should be done quickly: we've found that 3 or 4 people working together can freeze an incredible amount of food within a couple of hours. We usually have one person out in the garden collecting the produce, another in the kitchen cutting and preparing it for cooking, another doing the actual cooking and quick-cooling, and another doing the draining, drying, and packing.

¶ The method that you use to cook the vegetables for the freezer— steaming or boiling—will depend upon the vegetable to be frozen. In both methods quick cooling is of the utmost importance. To stop the cooking process, you should cool the vegetables in cold water (50°); using ice cubes in the water ensures rapid cooling. The vegetables should be allowed to cool about two times as long as they were cooked, or until the center of the vegetable is cool. The vegetables, once cooled, should be drained well on toweling, and completely dry before being packed. Pack the vegetables in freezer cartons, plastic bags, etc., keeping all air and moisture out (the air and moisture won't cause the vegetable to spoil; it will just lose some of its flavor and freshness).

Steam Method

Put 1½–2 inches of water on the bottom of a large pot. Bring the water to a boil. Place vegetables (don't steam more than a pound at a time) in a steaming basket or colander in the pot. Cover, starting to time when the water begins to boil again.

Asparagus	3½–4½ minutes (depending on size)
Beans, green shell	105 seconds
Beets	3½ minutes
Kohlrabi	100 seconds
Mushrooms	3½–4½ minutes (cool first in 2% citric acid solution, then cold water)
Okra	3–5 minutes
Parsnips	3 minutes
Turnips	70 seconds

Boiling Water Method

Put 1 gallon of water in a large pot (don't cook more than a pound of vegetables at a time; for greens, use 2 gallons of water per pound), and bring to a rolling boil. Place vegetables in a wire basket or colander, and then in the water. Bring to a boil immediately and start timing. Agitate from time to time by moving the basket back and forth.

Beans, green	2 minutes
Beans, lima	1–2 minutes (depending on size)
Beans, soy	4 minutes
Beans, wax	2 minutes
Beet greens	2 minutes
Broccoli	3–5 minutes (depending on size)
Brussels sprouts	4 minutes
Carrots	3 minutes
Cauliflower	3–4 minutes (depending on size)
Corn, cut	5–7 minutes
Corn on the cob	7–11 minutes (wrap each piece for freezer in individual wrapper, then wrap 6 of the individually wrapped pieces in another wrapper)
Eggplant	4 minutes (cool first in 2% citric acid solution, then in cold water)
Kale	70 seconds
Mustard greens, dandelion greens, lamb's quarter, etc.	2–3 minutes
Peas, black-eyed	2 minutes
Peas, green	1 minute
Peppers	3–4 minutes
Pumpkin	Bake. It can be made as a pie mixture with all of the ingredients except cloves, and frozen. Add cloves when ready to use.
Spinach	2½ minutes
Squash	3½ minutes
Swiss chard	2 minutes
Turnip greens	1 minute

Although our family prefers freezing food, your family may want to try other methods of preserving foods. Another method for preserving large quantities of food for a long period of time is canning. There are three methods of canning, each suitable for a different type of food. In all methods, you must use fresh, unmarred produce, good, unchipped jars, and clean, unused tops. It is important to use the right method with the right type of food, as some foods spoil and can become toxic if the wrong method is used to can them.

¶ The simplest method, and one that we use a lot, is the *open-kettle method*. It is used only to preserve fruit jams, jellies, preserves, conserves, marmalades, relishes, and some pickles. We also use it to can tomatoes and applesauce, both acidic. To preserve these foods, you will be performing two operations at the same time. While you are cooking the food to be canned (and keeping it hot) you will also be sterilizing the jars that the food is to be placed in. To sterilize, place clean jars on a rack at the bottom of a large pot. Jars should not touch each other or the sides or bottom of the pot. Fill the pot with water until the jars are covered. Bring to boil, and continue to boil for 20 minutes, adding boiling water as the water in the pot evaporates. Sterilize the lids by boiling them for 5 minutes.

¶ Remove the jars. Into the hot jars place hot food to be preserved to within 1–1½ inches of the top. Place hot, dry lid on the top of the jar, and seal as tightly as you can. Allow the jars to cool, on a level spot, for 12 hours. If, after 12 hours, the lid has not flattened, or makes a hollow rather than a tinny sound when a spoon is bounced on it (compare the sound to the sound made of a newly set up batch that has not been sealed), the batch has not sealed and should be redone. If you're uncertain, let it be. If it has not taken, you'll be able to tell when you're ready to eat it . . . there will be a mold on top. Either throw it away or, before eating, boil for 15 minutes, then eat it.

Tomatoes

Peel tomatoes. (A quick way of peeling tomatoes, peaches, etc., is to place in boiling water for 30 seconds, until the skin cracks. Put immediately into cold water, then peel.)
Cut tomatoes into quarters, and place in a large pot.
Boil for 20 minutes, add salt to taste.
Place hot tomatoes into hot, sterile jars, and seal tightly.

Jams

Jams are very quick, easy and cheap to make. They require only one step in cooking, and can be preserved either by the open-kettle method of preserving, or by putting hot paraffin on the top of the jar. To use hot paraffin: melt the paraffin over very low heat or hot water (it's extremely flammable). Don't let the paraffin get too hot, or it won't cover the jam sufficiently. Pour the paraffin slowly, from a small container, covering the jam with a thin film. Allow to set a bit, then cover a second time, tilting glass to make sure it's all covered.

Berry Jam

Put fruit pulp into a heavy enamel pot, crushing the bottom layers to make sure there's enough moisture. If you think it should be moister, add water, ¼ cup at a time. Simmer fruit until it is soft. Add warmed sugar (¾–1 cup of sugar per cup of berries), stirring until sugar dissolves. Bring to a boil, stirring with a wooden spoon. Reduce heat, and simmer until jam thickens (we remove the scum as it floats to the top, making for a smoother jam). It's thick enough when a little bit dropped on a plate stays in one place. At this point, you may add a bit of lemon juice to taste. Pour jam into hot, dry, sterile jars, and seal as you prefer.

Rhubarb Jam

Combine:

5 cups rhubarb, peeled, chopped small   **4 cups sugar**

Let stand overnight. Next day, stir well, adding 1 teaspoon butter. Boil 5 minutes. Add 1½ packages strawberry Jell-O. Turn into jars.

Rose Hip Jam

Collect hips after first frost.
Place 1 pound of hips and 1 cup water into heavy pot.
Simmer until tender.
Rub the pulp through a fine sieve.
To each pound of pulp, add 1 pound heated sugar.
Simmer until thick.   Turn into jars.

Preserves and Conserves

Preserves and conserves are like jam, in that they require only one cooking step. There are two methods of preparing preserves and conserves. The first method is to place in a large crock or stainless steel pan equal amounts of fruit and sugar, layered alternately. Allow this to sit, covered, for 24 hours. Then, bring the mixture slowly to a boil and simmer until the fruit is clear. Turn into jars. The second method is quicker. Place the fruit with a very small amount of water into a heavy stainless or enamel pan. Add ½–¾ cup of sugar per cup of fruit. Bring slowly to a boil until the fruit is clear. Seal and store.

Strawberry-Rhubarb Preserves

Cut into small pieces 1 quart rhubarb.
Sprinkle over it 8 cups of sugar.
Let sit for 12 hours.
Bring quickly to a boil.
Add 2 quarts hulled strawberries.
Simmer until thick—about 15 minutes.
Turn into jars.

¶ The method most commonly preferred in canning tomatoes and fruits (both contain enough acidity to be processed at boiling temperatures) is the *hot-water-bath method*. To can using the water-bath method, you will need a large kettle or pail that is deep enough to cover jars at least 1 inch over the tops, with a little extra space beyond that for boiling. As in the open-kettle method, a rack should be placed at the bottom for the jars to rest on to keep them from cracking when they come in contact with the heat.

¶ Fill the kettle with water to about jar height. When the water is boiling, lower filled, tighly covered jars onto the rack in the water, not allowing them to be closer than 2 inches to each other or the sides of the kettle. Add more boiling water to cover them at least 1 inch above the top. Process at a rolling boil (placing a cover on the kettle will keep the boil constant), continuing to add boiling water as the water in the kettle evaporates. Continue to process the required length of time for the particular food you are canning.

¶ Most glass jar manufacturers provide free brochures which give good recipes for canned fruits, along with the proper amount of time to process each fruit. You can get such brochures by writing:

Kerr Canning Book	*Ball Blue Book*
Kerr Glass Mfg. Corp.	*Ball Bros., Inc.*
Consumer Products Division	*Muncie, Indiana 47302*
Sand Springs, Oklahoma 74063	

Vegetables and meats are nonacid foods, and, as such, should be processed only in a *pressure canner*. Pressure canners come complete with instructions for use, recommendations for jar types and lids to be used, and recipes for preparing the food to be processed. You should follow the instructions carefully; these foods improperly processed might become contaminated by the germ that causes botulism, a fatal food poisoning. Botulinus may be present even if there is no odor, discoloring, or softening of the food. Therefore, all home-canned, nonacidic food should be cooked, stirring frequently, in boiling liquid, uncovered for 15 minutes before serving. **Don't even taste the food before you cook it that way!**
¶ Many foods may be kept for a long period of time by simply drying them, or wrapping them and keeping them in a cool place. All herbs, spices,

and teas may be dried, and saved in jars for future use. Simply cut the herb or tea when it's grown, wrap several in a bunch with string, and hang upside down from any part of the kitchen. For herbs or teas that are hard to wrap in a bunch, simply place them in a piece of cheesecloth, and hang the cheesecloth in the kitchen. When dried, they may be placed in jars to be used when needed.

¶ Green tomatoes and apples may be kept all winter and used when needed by following a simple process. For tomatoes, pick all green tomatoes before they have been killed by frost, and wrap each perfect green tomato individually in newspaper. Place in a basket, and store in a cool dry place (you don't have to have a root cellar to store them in). When you want red tomatoes, simply unwrap a few green ones, and place them in a sunny window. Within a couple of days, you'll have warm, red tomatoes, ready to eat. Apples, green or red, may be saved the same way. Be sure to use perfect, firm apples, and you'll have fresh apples all winter long. (For water glass eggs, see page 25.)

¶ Root cellars are good for storing a wide variety of food all year round. The most sophisticated type of root cellars will keep even lettuce fresh for many months. But you can devise a simple root cellar that can be used to store squash, apples, pears, carrots, tomatoes, etc., with very little trouble. One way of having a root cellar is to build one in your own cellar. In the coldest part of your cellar (usually the north or northeast corner is best), build a cinderblock box. Insulate it against freezing, and make sure that the floor is not too damp. Place your produce to be stored into boxes, without crowding, and place the boxes in the root cellar. If you have no cellar, or if your cellar isn't suitable, you may also construct a bank root cellar. Dig deep enough into the bank to be beyond the frost line (sometimes as much as 6 feet below the surface) and build your storage box there. Cinderblocks are good, as are sturdy barrels. If you want to be able to use the cellar throughout the winter, you'll have to rig up an access to the cellar somehow. Finally, if you just want to store things over the winter, with no thought of being able to get at them until spring, simply get a sturdy barrel. Wrap each piece of produce to be saved in newspaper, with newspaper between the layers of produce in the barrel. Dig a deep hole, and sink the barrel into it below the frost line. In the spring, dig it up, and you'll have seemingly fresh produce.

Water Glass (for Keeping Eggs)

For 15 dozen eggs, you will need:

9 quarts water

¾ quart water glass (soluble sodium silicate)

1 8-gallon earthen or glass jar, or several smaller jars

1. Boil water, allow to cool, then pour into jar.
2. Add water glass.
3. Add eggs with a long-handled spoon. Only good, clean eggs should be used. Any eggs that are cracked, or crack easily, should not be used.
Any dirty eggs should be cleaned before placing them into the solution.
The eggs can be added daily, as you collect them, but the water glass eggs should always be kept covered, in a cool spot.
Water glass eggs will keep for 6–8 months. Before using a water glass egg, wash it carefully. If you're going to boil it, poke a small hole in the large end with a pin, to allow the air to escape.

Sauerkraut

100 pounds cabbage (fall cabbage preferably)

1 pound uniodized salt

1. Grate cabbage and place in stone crock. Sprinkle in salt with grated cabbage.
2. Stomp the hell out of the cabbage in the crock. The key to good sauerkraut is stomping.
3. Place several large cabbage leaves over sauerkraut, place plate on top of leaves, then 1-gallon *glass* jar full of water on top of plate to weight it down.
4. Since working juice will spew over, place crock where this won't create problems.
5. Let it sit for 30 days.
6. Warm sauerkraut and place in hot sterile quart jars. As kraut cools, it will seal the jar tops.
7. Makes 30 quarts of dynamite sauerkraut.

PERSONAL TESTIMONY

It is with bemused resignation that I stroll around the streets of my native
Woodstock these days, watching the health-food stores spring up like
damnable weeds, hearing the incessant chatter about "crunchy granola,"
"lentils," and "organic gardening." If the unisex legions of the world want
to bring these foods with them to their nude-ins, I, for one, will not gainsay
their right to do so. However, I do feel that it is time that the wit and
beauty of mass-produced American food be celebrated, that the
hamburgers, french fries, milk shakes and assorted comestibles freely
available to this country receive their rightful homage.
¶ My first effort at describing the wonders of this fare came the first time
I sampled a McDonald's hamburger. Thrown into a hallucinatory reverie,
dazzled with the beauty of it, I composed the following lines:

> Tentative, yet with a luminous
>   sheen of red,
> twisting fumes of mustard—yet
>   not the gas that
> harassed our boys, German-sent
>   World War One;
> picklefunny, yet dour with
>   sliced onions, I
> eat you.

Yet do not you, simultaneous,
    eat me? I fear 'tis so,
O unsanctified ambrosia. I fear
    I subsume myself
to your glory.
'Sblood! I have no hoary oath
    to hurl at those who hate
you, no reproach for the
    pimply scoffers;
to their twice-barbed venom;
to their barbarous complaints
    I offer only you,
round, warm, final.

¶ I submitted this poem to many major magazines, who refused to publish
it. The reasons they gave for the rejection were such obvious lies that I had
to laugh out loud. "Pretentious trash," they called it. Read it and join with
me at laughing at the big-magazine idiots! Ho-ho-ho! Jackals! Buffoons!
¶ I did not let their effrontery dismay me, for within my heart I knew the
real reason for their refusal: the subject matter of my ode was simply too
controversial for them. Pornography they rush to print—decent poetry they
shrink from. I hope you will not follow their mistake.

ROSÉ-TERHUNE
SHOWING HIS
FIRST JUNGLE
OYSTER TO
TRACE-PURCELL.

¶ After completing this poem—which, incidentally, I polished and refined for four torturous weeks, in the manner of Keats—I entered into a meditation period. For days I sat, before a sack crammed with White Tower french fries. The result:

TO FRENCH FRIES

(*With apologies to Dylan Thomas*)

> The force that through the
>   greasy griddle fries these strips
> fries my green youth;
>   that stirs the malted shakes,
>   stirs my heart's blood.

¶ A short poem, yes. It pointed the way for much of my future work, which is too abstract and inaccessible for me to publish here.

¶ Since the completion of that poem, which was eight years ago, I have eaten nothing but 20-cent hamburgers, 20-cent french fries greased up right, and 35-cent thick jumbo shakes. My health is excellent. I suffer none of the nagging backaches of my friends. My teeth—checked twice a month by a crackerjack dentist-poet—are without fault. I continue to pour out a flood of gastropoetical masterpieces totally unacknowledged, a prophet without honor in his own country.

¶ But I am not bitter. I have found the "something greater" that so many of today's youth are looking for. I stumbled across that something greater that first day I sampled a McDonald's hamburger. I will continue to sing my hamburger songs until my breath stops in my chest. And then, I have arranged to be cremated, and my ashes sprinkled over a dozen burgers to go.

¶ I have nothing more to say, really. By printing the true story of an old man's search and discovery, perhaps you can inspire some poor, deluded health-food faddist to put away his childish beans and join the crowd down at Carrol's, McDonald's, Burger King, or the White Tower. One can worship the god of mass-hamburgers at many shrines.

Have a Turkey for Dinner

and

Serve It Corn

SIMPLE VEGETARIAN SURVIVAL

Someday, perhaps, we will absorb our energy directly from the Source; for now we take life to maintain our own. If you can't or won't take the life of a sentient being, you may find varied good eating and excellent health a bit harder to come by at the start.

You need protein—one half your proper weight indicates how many grams of protein you need daily. If you should weigh 150 pounds, you need 75 grams of protein to maintain a healthy body. Kids and pregnant women need more. Whole grains, eggs, dairy products, nuts, and beans provide the vegetarian with proteins, and if you are sure to include a wide selection of these foods in your daily diet, you will have no trouble getting *all* the essential amino acids. For an idea of grammage: 1 quart milk = 32 grams; 1 egg = 7 grams; 1 tablespoon peanut butter = 9 grams; 1 cup cooked dried beans = 12–20 grams (depending on the variety of the bean); ½ cup wheat germ = 20 grams; whole grains = approximately 10–15 grams per cup; 1 cup cottage cheese = 30 grams.

For some weird reason, vegetarians often lack iron. Iron is abundant in dark green or yellow vegetables, prunes and apricots, and egg yolks. Eat the vegetables raw sometimes.

The B-vitamin complex gets heavier and heavier. It keeps hormones straightened out, pretty well controls your state of joy or lack thereof, and keeps various segments of the body in proper functioning order. Recently there has been evidence showing that B_{17} keeps healthy cells from becoming cancerous. You can get vitamin B_{17} from eating almonds or prune or apricot pits (see the Last Whole Earth Catalog, p. 49). The B complex is in whole grains, eggs, milk fat, butter, green vegetables.

Vitamin A is in green, red, and yellow vegetables and fruits. It keeps mucous membranes happy.

Vitamin C is in raw citrus fruits, berries, greenery. It provides energy, helps metabolize iron, prevents scurvy.

Vitamin D is in milk fats, egg yolk, sunshine. Without it your bones, teeth, skin, and so on cannot obtain calcium (which is in milk products and turnip greens).

Vitamin E is in wheat germ and is useful to heart, blood, and hormones.

Clearly, some grains, raw fruits and vegetables, and dairy products or egg are needed daily, and your diet will more or less take care of itself. One thing to watch for, especially when you first become a vegetarian, is a tendency to overdo starches. The first few weeks are not always easy, regardless of the depth of your convictions. You'll miss textures in particular, and you are bound to feel vaguely unsatisfied. So you eat bread, noodles, pastries, and filling, starchy foods —and you get fat and gray. It is wise to strictly limit starches for a month or two, and the starches you do eat should be whole grain. Allow one large portion a day for a while. If you feel the need to chew something tough and stringy, a piece of cold yesterday's pizza may help.

If you have a main meal low in protein—chop suey or stew, for instance—follow it with a custard or pudding. Use parsley and cress, which are incredibly good for you, as more than mere garnish; put them in sandwiches instead of lettuce, chop into casseroles, and so on. Cheese and fruit make a much better munch than pastries. In a short while common sense will balance your diet, but make the effort at the start. If you feel soggy and pooped, you aren't good for much.

When you make bread, toss in lots of wheat germ, which will give it a wonderful nutty flavor. The best wheat germ available comes from Deaf Smith County, Texas, and it is not hard to find it organically grown. It is exceedingly high in minerals, vitamins, proteins, etc., which proves that food is only as good as the earth it grows from. Use peanut butter all you wish; it is higher in protein in proportion to amount and calories than cheese, eggs, or grains.

It can't be said too often: Don't drown things when you cook! For vegetables, use a heavy pan with a cover and just enough water to keep things from scorching. Bring water to boil, turn heat to very low, cover tightly, and steam. It helps to add a good chunk of butter. Add salt after cooking to avoid toughness. Save any leftover water and use in soup (some vegetable waters darken when cool—like spinach, potatoes, etc.). If you haven't a pepperpot soup going, don't bother saving juices that turn dark. Several brands of vegetarian bouillon cubes are available, and they are indispensable for soups, grain dishes, and gravies. All they are is concentrated vegetable broth, but they add a richness to things.

If you are bringing up vegetarian children, see that they get extra dairy and egg protein, like eggnogs, milkshakes, etc. *And,* they should be informed, when old enough to understand, that if they ever do decide to eat meat, they must start with a very tiny bit—like a teaspoon—and work up to a full amount very gradually. If they were to eat a normal portion of meat the first time, they would incur a form of food poisoning, because their bodies would be overdosed with forms of bacteria and toxins they are unprepared to handle. I assume this may be true of older persons who have done without meat for several years. So, if your body has not handled meat in years, or ever, do not risk hospitalization. Treat the food as if you were giving it to a baby for the first time. This is partly because meat is aged prior to use—once the fibers begin to break down, the meat is more tender, but it is also loaded with bacteria.

Recipes

Don't get hung up on noodles, although it is now fairly easy to get organic noodles of weird varieties that are full of nourishment. A plate of vegetables staring at you every meal is no more exciting than it sounds, but neither is a life of casseroles. There is no need to give up your favorite dishes—here comes sledgehammer enlightenment—just leave out the meat (told me by a true Chinese grocerman sage). Substitute vegetables or cheese or eggs; mushrooms are especially helpful. I used to crave Chinese vegetable soup, and admit I deliberately cheated a few months after first giving up meat (it's usually made with chicken broth). Now I just simmer celery, mushrooms, and some onion in water until it gets to look like old dishwater, salt it up good, and have my broth. No problem. Fill your wontons with the vegetables you make the broth out of. Clobber your nonvegetarian company with these recipes:

Cheese Pie

Serves 4

4 eggs
1½ cups evaporated milk or
   cream
½ pound Swiss cheese, grated
   coarsely

1 tablespoon minced onion
Thyme, salt, pepper
1 unbaked piecrust

Beat eggs and milk well, stir in cheese, onion, thyme, etc. Pour into crust. Garnish with mushrooms. Bake at 425° for 15 minutes, lower to 350° till golden brown and set—20–30 minutes. Or use slightly diluted cream of asparagus soup, and garnish with asparagus spears.

Mushroom Stroganoff

Serves 10

1 large onion, sliced
Butter
4 pounds sliced mushrooms
⅔ teaspoon nutmeg

Salt and pepper to taste
Red wine (optional)
3–4 pints sour cream

Sauté onion in lots of butter until yellow. Add mushrooms, cover, and simmer 5 minutes. Grate in nutmeg, add salt and pepper. Add in whatever amount of wine you want, up to a cup. Stir in sour cream over very low heat. Do not let it boil, just keep it hot. Serve at once over brown rice or noodles.

Gravy

Sauté some onions and/or mushrooms in butter. To each cup of water add 1½ vegetable bouillon cubes. Add to sauté mixture, stirring till cubes are dissolved. Make a smooth mixture of flour and water, 1 heaping tablespoon of flour per cup of gravy desired. Stir into hot broth over medium-high heat until thickened.

Blintzes

Serve 10–12

Batter:
8 eggs
4 cups water
4 cups unbleached white flour
Salt and pepper
Oil

Filling:
3 cups mashed potatoes
1 cup sharp Cheddar cheese
1 egg, mixed well
Salt and pepper

or:
2 pounds cottage cheese
1 large package cream cheese
2 eggs
2–3 tablespoons sugar
Hefty dash of cinnamon

Beat eggs, water, flour, till very smooth. Salt and pepper lightly. Put a little oil in a frying pan—a small one is best. When oil is hot, put in batter, just covering the bottom of the pan. Fry till the top is dry-looking. Turn out of pan, unfried side down. Cook all the batter that way. Put a spoonful of filling on each pancake, roll up, tucking in edges. Fry in butter till golden brown. Serve with fruits, sour cream, applesauce.

Spinach Soufflé

Serves 4 or 5

4 tablespoons butter
4 tablespoons flour
2 cups milk

6 eggs, separated
2 cups cooked, puréed spinach

Melt butter in a saucepan. Stir in flour to make a very smooth paste.
Gradually add warm milk, stirring over low heat, till smooth and thick.
Turn off heat. Add egg yolks, beating one by one. Heat again till mix is
warm, add spinach, and set aside. Beat egg whites till peaks are fluffy but
not stiff. Salt lightly. Beat 1 tablespoon beaten egg white into sauce
mixture. Have ready a 3-quart casserole, buttered well. Preheat oven to
375°. Fold rest of whites into sauce carefully. Put the whole thing very
gently into casserole and put into center of oven. Bake about 35 minutes.
You cannot make a soufflé larger than a 3-quart-dish-size. It won't soufflé.
For lots of people, make several small ones.

Solyanka

Serves 10

4 pounds white cabbage, shredded
1 bay leaf
Butter
3 pounds mushrooms, sliced
4 teaspoons brown sugar

2 onions, sliced, fried
2 or 3 tomatoes, sliced thick
Basil
Salt and pepper
Bread crumbs

Sauté cabbage and bay leaf in butter till tender. Likewise do mushrooms.
In a large buttered casserole, lay half of cabbage mixture in bottom,
sprinkled with a little brown sugar. Lay on sliced onions, then mushrooms,
then tomatoes. Sprinkle with basil and salt and pepper. Sprinkle with bread
crumbs, dot with butter, and bake in medium-high oven till golden brown.

Stew

Serves 8

12 vegetable bouillon cubes
3 quarts water
1½ pounds pearl onions
6 cups peeled carrot chunks

5 potatoes, peeled and sliced
Peas (optional)
6 tablespoons flour
1½ cups water

Put everything except flour and 1½ cups water together in a large pot and simmer until carrots are not quite tender. Mix the flour with the 1½ cups water, making a smooth thick liquid. Stir into soup till evenly blended. Bring to boil, stirring constantly till it begins to thicken slightly. Let it stand at least a couple of hours before reheating and serving. Of course, add salt, pepper, herbs, and additional vegetables as you wish.

Corn Peppers

Use, per person:
2 cups sweet corn
¾ cup Cheddar cheese
1 tablespoon diced onion
washed and cored
2 large sweet green peppers,

Mix all ingredients except peppers together. Place mixture into peppers, which have been prepared for stuffing. Dot with butter. Put extra stuffing into a buttered baking dish. Set peppers in, bake at 350° for about ½ hour.

Custard

Serves 12

6 cups milk
⅔–1 cup sugar

8 eggs
1 tablespoon vanilla extract

In a pot put milk and sugar. Scald the milk. Beat eggs and blend into hot milk. Stir in vanilla. Bake in 1-quart casserole at 350° until a knife stuck into it comes out clean—about 15 minutes.

Heavy Soup

Serves 10–12

4 large sweet onions, sliced
1 pound mushrooms, sliced
Marjoram
6 tablespoons butter
2 quarts milk

6 tablespoons whole wheat flour
Salt and pepper to taste
1 pound sharp Cheddar cheese, grated

Sauté onions and mushrooms with a pinch of marjoram in butter. Scald milk. Mix flour with ½ cup of the milk till smooth, beating well to keep from lumping. Add flour, rest of scalded milk, salt, pepper, and mushroom stuff in a large pot. Cook over medium heat, stirring, until it begins to thicken. Add cheese. Serve when cheese has melted.

Pilaf

Serves 10

5 cups cracked wheat
3 vegetable bouillon cubes
8 cups water
1 head red cabbage, sliced
1 onion, sliced

1 pepper, sliced
¾–1 pound mushrooms
1 tablespoon brown sugar
Basil

Sauté wheat in butter till coated. Mash cubes, add to water, stir. Cook wheat in water over low heat for 20–30 minutes, covered. Meanwhile, sauté sliced cabbage, onion, pepper, and mushrooms with sugar and basil. Serve over hot wheat pilaf.

Rice Cutlets

Serves 10

5 cups cooked rice (cook in stock)
6 hard-boiled eggs, mashed
Parsley, salt, pepper

Chopped peppers or tomatoes
4 eggs
1 cup flour

Mix it all together. Form patties and refrigerate till set. Fry in butter till brown. Serve with lemon or lime wedges.

Stuffed Onion Stuff

Allow one onion per person

5 cups rice
¾ cup parsley
5 cloves garlic, minced
1 tablespoon sage
5 bouillon cubes

Basil, oregano
Salt, pepper
4 large Spanish onions
¼ cup chopped onion

Boil rice normally. When half cooked, put in parsley, garlic, sage, bouillon cubes, a dash of basil, oregano, salt, pepper. Peel onions and slice thickly. Pour boiling water over them and let cool. When rice is almost done, mix in ¼ cup raw chopped onion. In a casserole, lay drained onion slices, then rice. Top with the rest of the onions and grated cheese, if desired. Bake ½ hour at 350°.

Yorkshire Pudding

Serves 8–10

6 eggs
3 cups flour
3 cups milk

Dash of nutmeg
Oil
3 vegetable bouillon cubes

Beat eggs, flour, milk, nutmeg. In a large pan, heat oil to cover bottom ¼ inch thick, with cubes thoroughly crushed in. When oil is very hot, pour in egg mixture, and put in 450° preheated oven. Bake till puffy and golden brown—15–20 minutes. Serve with gravy.

Curry

Serves 10

Celery, broccoli, mushrooms,
    tomatoes, beans, peas, or
    whatever you have
6 hard-boiled eggs
2 potatoes, diced
3 peppers, diced
2 large onions, sliced

Butter
4 cups water
4–5 cloves garlic, crushed
3 vegetable bouillon cubes
6–10 tablespoons curry spices
2 cups yogurt

Sauté any hard-textured vegetables in some butter. Add eggs and other vegetables. Pour on water, crushed garlic, bouillon cubes, and curry spices to taste. Simmer till vegetables are tender. Add yogurt. Let stand while you cook up brown rice. Heat and pour over rice.

Bread

2 packages yeast	1 tablespoon salt
2½ cups water and milk, mixed to taste	½ cup honey
2 eggs	1½ cups wheat germ
½ cup melted butter	7–8 cups unbleached flour

Sprinkle yeast over ½ cup warm water, let sit 5 minutes. Mix in hot milk and water, eggs, butter, salt, honey, and wheat germ. Beat in flour until kneadable. Knead at least 5 minutes. Let rise, covered, in a warm place. After 1½–2 hours, punch down dough, flatten to rectangle, divide in two, and roll tightly. Tuck ends under; put seam on bottom. Place in well-greased loaf pans. Place in cold oven. Turn heat to 400° for 15 minutes, lower to 350° until bread is hollow-sounding when tapped—20–30 minutes more. Brush with butter and set loaves on sides.

Egg Manicotti

Serves 10–12

Shells:
12 eggs
2 cups milk
Salt and pepper to taste

Filling:
2 pounds cottage cheese
2 eggs
1 pound mozzarella or provolone, grated
1 cup grated Parmesan
½ cup parsley
Salt and pepper to taste

To make shells, beat eggs, and mix with milk and salt and pepper. Cover fry pan ¼–½ inch deep with oil, and fry batter, a bit at a time, till set. Cook all mixture thus. Mix together all filling ingredients. Put filling on one side of each "pancake" and roll up. Put filled pancakes in baking dish with spaghetti sauce, slice on the cheapest provolone you can find (it's gooier) and bake ½ hour in medium oven.

Stuffed Cabbage for 4

1 large head cabbage
Butter
1 medium onion, sliced
1 pound mushrooms, sliced
1 teaspoon thyme
2–3 cloves garlic, pressed

Salt and pepper to taste
1 pound spinach, chopped
½ pound Graddost cheese (or
   strong Swiss, or ½ Swiss,
   ½ Cheddar), grated

Steam cabbage leaves till tender; set aside. In lots of butter, sauté onion
and mushrooms till juicy and tender. Douse with thyme and garlic. Add salt
and pepper. Add chopped fresh spinach; cook and stir. Throw in grated
cheese. Stir till cheese is melted. Put a dollop on each cabbage leaf, roll up,
place in casserole. Pour juice over rolled-up things, cover, and bake 15
minutes in a moderate oven.

Vanilla Milk

Vanilla milk is very relaxing: it soothes overfeasted bellies. Per cup of
milk, put in 1 scant teaspoon of vanilla (or 2 inches of vanilla bean) and 1
teaspoon honey or sugar. Heat in pan till sugar is dissolved, and serve.

Yogurt Thing

If you're going to do a yogurt thing, you'll need a dairy thermometer. Most
yogurt-making kits are little more than a heating pad and plastic quart
containers. Don't get ripped off. The bacteria which produce yogurt will
clean toxins out of your intestines. But they are not natural to the body.
Acidophilus culture is, but it takes 12 hours at 90° to culture.

Whatever you eat is fine and holy, prepare and eat it with joy and much
love.

Miscellaneous Thoughts on Some Miscellaneous Food

Honey: Honey is the only nonalkaline sweetener known to man. It is a good relaxer. It is good for sore throats: mix with garlic (an antibiotic) and lemon (citrus . . . vitamin C) and spoon it into your mouth.
Honey is sterile, so germs cannot live in it. If you get a bad burn, slap some honey on it until you can get to the old doc.

Lemonade: Float a few lemon balms on top in the pitcher.

Peppermint: Peppermint is good for upset stomachs, and good for morning sickness.

Marjoram: Hang it in the window to keep bad witches away. Also use it as a good accent in sour cream. As a tea, it is good for tension headaches.

Tansy, basil, rue: They are good fly repellents. Tansy sprinkled around the cracks in the floor, or in the cellar, will keep ants away.

Camomile tea: Use it for headaches, stomachaches, worms. It's also good as a hair rinse.

Rue and thrift (called sea pinks): Worms.

Milk and meat of coconut: Coconut is a terrific laxative and is good for hemorrhoids. It is more effective than prunes, which give some people gas. By the way, if you have hemorrhoids, don't eat nuts or anything with small seeds (raspberries, blueberries, strawberries, etc.).

Cranberry juice: Add to your cranberry juice a touch of ginger and some fruit sherbet . . . it's dynamite.

Ginger: It's good for your stomach.

Potatoes, onions, apples, and carrots: Do not store them together with each other. They give off gases which make other foods spoil faster.

Dandelions: Boil them in water, and use them for your skin. They're very good for it.

Oatmeal: Wash your face really well. Put oatmeal on your face. (You don't even have to cook it. Just add water.) Leave on your face until dry. Wash off with water and a tiny bit of milk. It makes your skin soft and smooth; it tightens it; it removes oils.

Cloves: Cloves are good to chew on for healthy teeth.

Bees: Bees are enraged by the smell of new blue denim. Always wash any clothing made of new blue denim first before wearing outside, otherwise you run a big risk of being (bee-ing) stung. Beekeepers never wear denim on the job—most beekeepers wear white.

Anise: Mix with lard or shortening for lice.

Ajuga reptans: Also known as bugleweed; it is a common rock garden thing, often used in California as a ground cover. Mildly narcotic, resembles digitalis in action. Good for circulation.

Burnet: Used to control hemorrhages.

Garlic: Antiseptic and antibiotic. Allicin is derived from it. It is said to be useful against scarlet fever, tuberculosis, dysentery, and diphtheria.

Catnip: As a tea, it is mildly sedative.

Calendula: The flowers applied to wounds act as antiseptic.

Wormwood: Good for parasitic worms; moderately useful for fevers and upset bellies.

Feverfew: Infusion repels insects.

Horehound: Good for coughs and colds.

Oil of lavender: Repels ticks.

Mints: Good for colic and stomachaches, headaches; spearmint keeps mice away, peppermint repels moths.

Black mustard: Laxative, good for headaches.

Anemone: Some help in asthma, coughs, and syphilis.

Thrift (Armeria): Useful for urinary troubles.

Yarrow: Is used for uterine diseases.

Note: Most information here was obtained from *Herbs: Their Culture and Usage* by Rosetta E. Clarkson, published by Macmillan.

Buried
IN dirt
Hobbit
Essie

Debby's Bull's-eye Egg

Cut a hole in the center of a slice of bread. Brown the bread in butter on both sides in a frying pan. Drop egg in hole. Cook until done to taste.

Cinnamon Bread for Poached Eggs—An Added Dimension

Put cinnamon and sugar on buttered toast. Drop poached eggs on it. It smells great as well as tastes great.

Chris's Eggs Poached in Milk

Pour ½ cup milk into a frying pan. Add paprika, basil, parsley, thyme, salt, and pepper to taste. Heat to simmering. Into simmering milk, crack an egg. Cook slowly, spooning milk over egg until done to your liking. Turn eggs onto plate or toast, and spoon milk over it. It is especially delicious using goat's milk.

COMMUNAL CLUSTER EXTRAVAGANZA OF EGGIES

FULLY EQUIPED
EGGIE WITH
LASER —
FOR CUTTING WOOD

Silver Hollow Rainy Morning Eggs

Serves 6–10

6 tablespoons butter
2 large Spanish onions, minced
2 cups grated sharp cheese

Salt and butter as needed
½ pound grated sharp cheese

Sauté onions in 4 tablespoons of the butter for 6 or 7 minutes. Butter a
baking dish (or two) and put the onions in the bottom of it. Sprinkle lightly
with cheese, salt, and pepper. Break eggs carefully and place them on top of
onions. Add more seasonings, dot with remaining butter, add a thick layer
of cheese, and bake in a very moderate oven (300°–350°) for 15 minutes.

Cold Night Deviled Eggs

Serves 6

12 hard-boiled eggs
½ teaspoon dry mustard
2 tablespoons butter
1 heaping teaspoon grated
  horseradish

3 tablespoons mayonnaise
Grated black pepper
Sliced bread as needed
Salt and butter as needed
½ pound grated sharp cheese

Halve boiled eggs lengthwise and remove the yolks. Mash yolks with
mustard, 2 tablespoons butter, horseradish, and mayonnaise. Add grated
black pepper to taste and a little bit of salt, if needed. Put mixture back into
whites. Cut appropriate number of bread slices. Toast bread on one side,
then butter on the other. Put 3 egg halves on each slice, sprinkle with
cheese, and brown under grill.

FOUNDATION FREE SAUCER EGGIE

JOEY TISSUE SEZ DONT FORGET MISTER SCHMAGEGGIE HE BUYS THE EGGIES

Flamenco Eggs—Like They Eat in Spain!

Serves at least 10 hungry people

This is a delicious, fairly cheap recipe that's easier to make than it looks or tastes.

10 potatoes
10 ounces butter
10 franks (kosher ones work well) or smoked sausages
Salt, pepper, and hot mustard
10 tablespoons cooked peas
10 fresh or canned sweet red peppers, cut into shreds

20–25 tomatoes, skinned, seeded, quartered (canned work fine)
Chopped parsley
20 eggs
10 tablespoons milk or single cream
Cayenne pepper

Peel the potatoes, cover with cold water, and bring to boil. Cook for 4 minutes, strain, and dice. Melt butter in a pan, add the potatoes and franks or sausages. Cook until the potatoes begin to brown. Keeping the pan over heat, add seasonings, peas, and sweet peppers. After 4 or 5 minutes, add the tomatoes and a generous sprinkling of parsley. Turn the mixture into 3 or 4 ovenproof pans, and break the eggs on top.
Season again with salt and pepper, and pour the milk or cream on top.
Cook in a moderate oven (350°) until the eggs are set—about 8 minutes.
If you prefer your eggs less liquidy, leave them in a little longer. Sprinkle with cayenne pepper and serve.
This makes a very satisfying main course that will result in several compliments from everyone eating—even the people who made it!

Yogurt

3 cups milk (skimmed, whole, or raw)
1 cup evaporated milk, or
½ cup spray-dried non-instant milk (can't use regular instant milk . . . all in all, evaporated milk is best)

2 tablespoons plain yogurt

Scald milk. Set aside, covered, to cool off. (If you use spray-dried milk, cook it with 4 cups of water, and stir to thoroughly dissolve it.) When warm, not hot, add evaporated milk (don't need it if you used the dry milk method). You want the milk between 105°–110°, no hotter, no cooler, although better on the cool side than hot. Stir in 2 tablespoons yogurt thoroughly. Do not use metal containers; use glass, porcelain, or wood. Set on a heating pad on low setting (medium, if you lay on a towel), cover with towels to keep warmth even. Check in 4 hours, though it can take 8 hours, depending on heat. When it has jelled to custard texture, refrigerate. To make cheese, let it get very thick—at least 8 hours—hang in cheesecloth bag overnight. Save whey for baking. It is wise to save a few tablespoons of yogurt out in a separate container to avoid contamination of your starter.

Colleen's Macaroni and Cheese

1½–2 pounds elbow macaroni
8 tablespoons butter or margarine
8 tablespoons flour
3½–4 teaspoons salt
¼ teaspoon pepper
1–1¼ teaspoons garlic powder
4–4½ cups milk

1 small onion, diced
4½–5 cups grated Cheddar cheese (4 cups for sauce, ½–1 cup for top), 1½ pounds
½ cup bread crumbs or grated Parmesan cheese

Cook macaroni in pot of water. Drain, set aside. Melt butter over low heat. Add flour gradually, stirring so it doesn't lump. Add salt, pepper, garlic powder. Gradually pour in milk, stirring constantly to keep mixture smooth. Cook, stirring, over medium low heat until mixture thickens. Add onion. Add 4 cups of grated cheese, stirring, until cheese melts and mixture becomes smooth. In large casserole, place macaroni. Pour cheese sauce over macaroni, and mix well. Top with bread crumbs dotted with butter, and/or Parmesan cheese. Bake in preheated 350° oven until golden brown and bubbly—about 30 minutes.

Note: The basic cheese sauce, in smaller proportions, is a great sauce for broccoli, cauliflower, asparagus.

Egg and Cheese Dish to Eat with Beer

Serves 8–10

3 large onions
½ pound mushrooms
1 quart sour cream
1 dozen eggs
1 teaspoon salt
¼ teaspoon pepper
1 teaspoon dill
Paprika
½ pound cheese

Cut onions into rings, cut mushrooms into slices. Sauté in butter for 15 minutes in large skillet. Cover with a quart of sour cream. **Do not stir or mix.** After about 5 minutes, make small depressions on top of sour cream and break 1 dozen eggs into the depressions. Sprinkle with salt, pepper, dill on top, and cover with paprika. (It's the paprika that gives it the flavor, so don't skimp.) Cover and cook over medium flame until eggs are firm but not hard. Remove from heat, place strips of cheese (mozzarella, Cheddar, any kind) over the top and place under the broiler until brown and bubbly—about 2 minutes.
Eat with beer.

POTATOES

Coffee Can Hash Browns

Serves 10–12

In coffee cans put alternate layers of peeled, sliced potatoes and sliced onions. Sprinkle salt as you go, until you are within a few inches from the top. Fill the can to the top with water. Cover, and let sit overnight. When you open the can in the morning, the aroma will start your mouth to watering. Cook in a wok, if possible; if not, a heavy fry pan. Drop the potatoes and onions into the hot pan with a spoon. Let the water that has clung to the potatoes and onions cook off, then start adding butter to prevent them from burning. Keep stirring to prevent burning. Allow at least 20 minutes for the cooking. If you have a few 2-pound coffee cans full of potatoes and onions to cook, allow even more time. As some get cooked, keep warm in the oven while others cook. Fry until a deep golden brown.

June's Luscious Baked Potato Casserole

Serves 12

6 tablespoons fine bread crumbs
2 cups sour cream
2 cups mayonnaise
4 tablespoons flour
4 tablespoons minced scallions or chives

12 medium cooked potatoes
Salt to taste
8 hard-boiled eggs, sliced
½ cup melted butter or grated Cheddar cheese

Put 2 tablespoons of the bread crumbs in greased casserole. Combine sour cream, mayonnaise, flour, and scallions. Blend well. Place layer of potatoes in casserole. Salt to taste. Top with egg slices and half of cream mixture. Repeat layers. Sprinkle rest of crumbs on top. Pour melted butter over top, or top with grated Cheddar cheese. Bake in a 350° oven for 25 minutes.

Billie's Potato Gratin

Serves 12

4 pounds potatoes
2 pounds sliced, cooked smoked ham
1 pound sliced Gruyère, Swiss, or Munster cheese

6 teaspoons fresh ground black pepper
1 cup strong grated cheese
2 cups milk

Boil and slice the potatoes thin (leave their skins on). Put into a large casserole layers of ham, sliced potatoes, and sliced cheese. Sprinkle the grated cheese and some of the pepper on top of each layer of sliced cheese. Repeat until you use up all your ingredients. Top with grated cheese and some bread crumbs. Pour the milk into the casserole. Bake, covered, in a slow oven for 15 minutes. Uncover and bake until the top is bubbly and gold-brown. I put in tarragon leaves when I have them with the cheese layers as well as pepper.

PANCAKES

Hungarian Pancakes—a Great Late Breakfast! ! ! !

Makes 10 pancakes

Try whipping up a batch of Hungary's answer to the crepe and Live a Little.

20 eggs
2½ teaspoons salt
20 teaspoons sugar

2½ cups flour
5 cups milk
Oil

Mix eggs, salt, sugar, and flour together in a large bowl. Add milk gradually, stirring until batter is smooth. Heat oil in large skillet and pour batter in, forming individual-sized pancakes or crepes. You'll either need more than one skillet, or fewer people, or you can make them in batches. Cook the pancakes quickly on both sides. They should be thin. When pancakes are done to taste, remove from pan and spread with jelly, preserves, cream cheese, or anything else you think would make a good filling. Start from any edge and roll into thin cone. Serve hot.

Whole Wheat Cinnamon Pancakes

Serves 10–12

4 cups whole wheat flour
10 teaspoons baking powdeer
2 teaspoons salt
2 teaspoons cinnamon

4 cups milk
4 eggs
⅔ cup corn oil
1 cup honey

Mix. Cook in oil on heat from pan.

Pumpkin Fritters

Serves 10

2 cups mashed pumpkin or squash
2 eggs
Salt
8 teaspoons sugar

½ cup milk
1 cup flour
Dash nutmeg and vanilla

Mix all ingredients together until the texture of pancake batter. Fry like griddlecakes . . . they will be creamy inside. Sprinkle with raw sugar and serve.

RICE

Mai's Brown Rice

There Are Many Ways

1. Bring 1½–2 cups water and ½ teaspoon sea salt to boil. Add 1 cup rice. Cover and lower flame to low for 30–40 minutes.
2. Toast the rice in a pan over a medium flame. Then cook in the usual way using equal portions rice and water.
3. In a covered casserole dish put 1 cup rice and 3 cups water and ½ teaspoon salt. Cook for 1–1½ hours in medium oven (a little oil may be added before cooking).
4. To the water in method 1: Add one teaspoon tamari or miso, and cook in usual way.
5. Rice and lentils: Add to 3–4 cups boiling water: 1cup lentils, 1 cup rice, ½ teaspoon salt. Reduce heat and cook 30–45 minutes.
5a. Vegetables may be added to rice after 20 minutes, provided a little extra water is used.
6. Add to cooked rice ½ cup caraway or cumin seeds. Serve with:

Vegetable Dish

Heat at least 1 inch butter or cooking oil in a deep saucepan with a lid. Add thyme, pepper, turmeric, garlic, ginger, etc. Then add vegetables in order of longest cooking time, letting each vegetable cook before adding next type. Be sure to add enough turmeric.

Mai's Rice Cakes

Mix cooked rice and whole wheat flour in equal parts. Cooked vegetables and/or onions can also be added. Add water and a little salt until pancakes can be made in hand. Fry or deep-fry.

True Light Beaver Wok Fried Rice

Serves 10–12

1¼ cups peanut oil
2 bunches scallions, chopped
2 green peppers, diced
2 cups sprouts
5 eggs, beaten with 2 tablespoons
   tamari
6 bouillon cubes

4 cups raw brown rice, cooked in
   7 cups water
¼ cup tamari
½ teaspoon ginger
½ teaspoon garlic powder
¼ teaspoon pepper

In a wok, place ¼ cup of the oil and allow to get very hot. In oil, sauté scallions, peppers, and at end, sprouts. Remove from wok, leaving about 1 tablespoon of oil. In remaining oil, scramble eggs until dry and separating. Remove from wok. Drain leftover oil from vegetables, and add enough more to make ¾ cup. Place in wok, and crush bouillon cubes into it. Heat, add rice, stirring until well coated with oil-bouillon mixture. Add tamari, spices, vegetables, and cook, stirring until fried throughout. At end, add eggs, mix well, and serve garnished with more scallions.

True Light Beaver Pilaf

Serves 10

¾ cup cooking oil
4½ cups fine egg noodles, broken
   small
4½ cups uncooked white rice

11 cups boiling water
10–12 bouillon cubes
2½ teaspoons salt
½ teaspoon pepper

In oil, brown noodles and rice until noodles are golden brown. Add boiling water and bouillon cubes, stirring till cubes are dissolved. Add salt and pepper and cook, covered, at low boil for 30 minutes. Serve topped with sour cream.

June's Fried Rice

2 cups rice
4 cups chopped cooked pork, ham,
   shrimp, or chicken
½ cup oil

4 eggs, lightly beaten
½ teaspoon black pepper
4 tablespoons soy sauce
1 cup chopped scallions

Cook rice. Fry meat in oil until coated and heated (1 minute), stirring constantly. Add eggs and pepper and fry over medium heat for 5 minutes. Add cooked rice and soy sauce. Fry, stirring frequently, about 5 minutes. Sprinkle green scallions on top.

June's Pearllu (Chicken and Ham Rice)

1 4–5-pound chicken
1 pound salt pork
1 pound ham or bacon
4 medium onions, quartered
1 teaspoon salt

1 small dried red pepper
3½–4 cups tomatoes (1 large can)
4 cups water
4 cups uncooked rice

Cut chicken and put in heavy covered pot with salt pork, ham, onions, salt, and pepper. Add tomatoes and water. Cook gently 2 hours or more in lightly covered pot, stirring from time to time, until meats are tender and water boiled down. Place rice around meat. There should be enough liquid in pot to cover rice; if not, add water. Cook gently, loosening rice with fork, keeping lid on as much as possible. When rice is done, and meats are done, remove pot to warm oven so that rice can steam until dry.

Curried Lentils and Rice

4 cups uncooked brown rice
1 pound lentils
Bouillon cubes
6 teaspoons honey

4 teaspoons chutney
Raisins
1–2 teaspoons curry powder
½ cup shredded coconut

Cook the rice and the lentils separately, adding chicken, beef, or vegetable bouillon cubes to each, if you have them. When they are done, mix together, adding the honey, chutney, and raisins, making sure they are well blended throughout. Add the curry powder a little at a time until it tastes right to you. Add the shredded coconut and blend that, leaving a little on top. If 12 people are expected to gather for eating and happy times and only half the group decide they're up for it, you never have to worry with curried lentils and rice. Both ingredients can be used in various other dishes and combinations.

Arleen's Rice, Chicken Livers, and Mushrooms

Serves 10–12

3 cups sliced onions
1 stick margarine
1½–2 pounds chicken livers
1 pound sliced mushrooms

5 cups cooked brown rice (cook in
  bouillon)
Salt and pepper to taste

Sauté onions in some margarine until golden and soft. Remove from skillet. Leaving remaining margarine, add livers, and sauté until done. Remove from skillet and add mushrooms with onions (add a little more margarine if needed). When mushrooms are soft, add rice and livers, salt, and pepper. Heat till heated through.

Balkan Rice

Serves 10–12

4 large Spanish onions
8 tablespoons olive oil
6 ounces chopped nuts
1 pound long-grain rice, uncooked
4 ounces currants
2–4 large ripe tomatoes, sliced

4 pints vegetable water or stock
Salt to taste
2 teaspoons black pepper
2 teaspoons mixed spice
2 teaspoons each sage and parsley
2 ounces brown sugar

Peel and slice onions and cook in oil until soft. Add the nuts and uncooked rice. Fry them for 5–6 minutes, stirring continuously with a wooden spoon. Add currants, sliced tomatoes, boiling stock or water, and season with salt and pepper. Put a tight lid on the pan. Cook over a low heat until all the liquid has been absorbed. Remove from heat and, keeping the lid on, let stand for 15 minutes before adding herbs, spices, and brown sugar.

Chicken with Rice

½ cup olive oil
2 small onions, chopped
2 cloves garlic, mashed
1 bay leaf
Salt and pepper
2 4-pound broiler-fryers

4 cups uncooked rice
2 teaspoons saffron
8 cups chicken broth
4 cups cooked green peas
4 pimientos, cut into strips
Pinch of cayenne

Heat oil in a heavy skillet and sauté onions lightly, adding garlic, bay leaf, salt, and pepper. When onions have just started to take color, push aside and brown chicken pieces in oil, turning till golden brown all over. Put chicken on paper towel in another pan for a few minutes while you brown the rice in the same oil. Stir the rice constantly until it is yellow, and add the saffron if you like the flavor and deep yellow tone. Pour rice and onion mixture into a large deep casserole. Pour chicken broth into the skillet to clean out the brown glaze and add this to the casserole. Lay chicken pieces on the top, cover tightly, and bake in a moderate oven (350°) 45 minutes to an hour. Take off some of the chicken, stir rice to release the steam, and add hot peas and strips of pimiento and serve.

. HSU.

WAITING NOURISHMENT

ABOVE—K'AN, THE ABYSMAL WATER
BELOW—CHIEN, THE CREATIVE, HEAVEN

All things have need of nourishment from above. But the gift of food comes in its own time, and for this one must wait. This hexagram shows the clouds in the heavens, giving rain to refresh all that grows and to provide mankind with food and drink. The rain will come in its own time. We cannot make it come; we have to wait for it. The idea of waiting is further suggested by the attributes of the 2 trigrams—strength within, danger in front. Strength in the face of danger does not plunge ahead but bides its time, whereas weakness in the face of danger grows agitated and has not the patience to wait.

THE IMAGE

Clouds rise up to heaven:
The image of WAITING.
Thus the superior man eats and drinks,
Is joyous and of good cheer.

When clouds rise in the sky, it is a sign that it will rain. There is nothing to do but to wait until the rain falls. It is the same in life when destiny is at work. We should not worry and seek to shape the future by interfering in things before the time is ripe. We should quietly fortify the body with food and drink and the mind with gladness and good cheer. Fate comes when it will, and thus we are ready.

5 ROCK CITY ROAD

No one could ever agree on a name for the restaurant; so it just got called by its address. I guess that's pretty cosmic because the number 5 hexagram in the *I Ching* means *waiting* (nourishment); so it will be *5 Rock City Road*. I don't really know how to put a restaurant together from scratch; I only try to keep turning out food that people can get feeling high from, and it's not hard when you use the food I do. It is all good whole grains and as much organic produce as we can find or grow ourselves.

¶ The restaurant family has fluctuated a lot in the year that I've been here and every new person who comes to help brings strong energy to continue the work the family has started; and those who don't really want to contribute, well, they usually get bored and leave; or if they can't seem to make the move, someone in the family gives a nudge to them to help them along. I know this restaurant can't work unless everyone involved is consciously aware of the work necessary to keep flowing smoothly. We have had so many meetings about this, and it is the biggest problem for everyone to work out. The hardest role to play in these family games is the decision maker or foreman or whatever you want to call it (maybe wagonmaster). You've got to work out a way to keep your spiritual self alive, strong enough to order people, and still be detached from the role of ordering. Staying high has been the hardest thing to work out for all of us. We have the dualism of wanting to split for the woods and yet we don't know enough to live out there very long without the society which has so heavily imprinted us—it's not good or bad, it just is. We keep trying to confront each other when a personality "wiggle" happens; but sometimes you can get real knotted up inside and the trouble builds pressure—you want to say something about something to someone, but all of a sudden you wonder if maybe it's not your ego coloring your perception of a friend's actions, and you keep it inside to protect yourself from being wrong—well, that's when it's got to blow, so you can get it out of your head where you can see it. And that's what we're doing; and when we're not doing that, we have this restaurant.

¶ Now there's something I really like to do and that is cook; and I can do as much as I like at the restaurant. When I started cooking, I didn't know the first thing about the food—I knew how to cook brown rice and beans (pretty basic); but I read a whole bunch of books and pamphlets that people had lying around and got an understanding of what was going on. I could never, hardly ever, use the books directly, though, because we never had a lot of things in the recipes; so I had to sort of alter things until I finally got more into altering than into reading, which is just like making it up as you go along. Everyone who cooked at 5 Rock City got great at doing just about anything in the world with carrots and onions and squash. Anyway, enough of this rambling; what I really want to say is I'm a cook and I dig it, and I've found some things I'd like to pass on. And if you don't cook, I'd just like to mention that it isn't hard to make really good food; so I've tried to make it all as simple to understand as it really is— and these things don't taste bad either. All the recipes are from the *5 Rock*

City Road Cooks' Book, which is not yet published in its entirety mainly because it hasn't been in its entirety yet, but which is slowly being published in fragments in different literary works. At any rate, here is a cross section of secret recipes never before revealed to the public:

From the FIVE ROCK CITY ROAD COOKS' BOOK: Let's begin with soup; it's good for you and it is cheap, two admirable qualities.

Miso Soup

Serves 8

1 large carrot, cut into matchsticks
1 stalk celery, cut in diagonal U's
1 large onion, cut in moon slivers
¼ head cabbage, shredded
Oil

¼ pound whole almonds
1½ quarts water
Fistful of miso
Tamari

Cut veggies, heat 1 tablespoon oil, and toss in onion, stirring until it begins to get soft. Add carrot and simmer with cover in their own juice 1–2 minutes. Throw in celery, cabbage, and almonds and stir together a minute. Add 1½ quarts of water and bring to a simmering boil for about 15 minutes. Make a smooth paste from miso by adding a little water and mixing. Turn off soup and cool slightly, then add miso and tamari to taste. (Miso has natural digestive agents which shouldn't be boiled because it destroys their properties.)

Also: Soak a long strand of wakame seaweed for 20 minutes, cut it into strips, and sauté with vegetables before adding water. Seaweed is a natural source of calcium, vitamin D, some vitamin A, K, and over 30 essential minerals necessary for feeling and being healthy.

Autumn Vegetable Soup

Serves 8

1 large carrot
1 butternut squash
1 acorn squash
1 large onion
2 stalks celery
Oil

3 quarts water
2 teaspoons salt
¼ pound buckwheat soba
 (noodles)
Tamari to taste

Cut carrot and butternut squash into matchsticks; dice acorn squash, cut onion in moon slivers and celery in diagonal U's. Heat a little oil (not more than 1 tablespoon) and toss in onion, stir-frying until slightly softened. Add other vegetables and stir-fry about 2 minutes, adding 3 quarts of water then. Bring to simmering boil, add salt, and cook for 10 minutes, covered. Add buckwheat noodles and bubble for 5 more minutes. Add tamari to taste.

Split-Pea Tahini Cream Soup with Wakame

Serves 8

1 cup split peas
1½ quarts boiling water
1 long piece wakame seaweed, soaked and cut into little pieces

1 medium onion, cut into moon slivers
Salt to taste
2 tablespoons tahini

Add split peas to boiling water, cover, and let simmer 1 hour. Add wakame and onion and salt and let simmer, covered, until of creamy consistency—about 30 more minutes. Turn off flame and add tahini, stirring it in until smooth. That's all. Unless you want to add tamari for a little different flavor.
After soup come a few simple grain dishes.

Autumn Hash

Serves 8

Oil
1 large onion, cut into moon slivers
½ butternut squash, diced fine
1 medium sweet potato, diced fine

1 small yellow squash, cut into little matchsticks
4 cups cooked kasha
Tamari

In 1 tablespoon oil, sauté onion until slightly soft; add other vegetables and steam over low heat for 5 minutes with cover on. Mix in kasha, 1 more tablespoon oil, and tamari to taste, and press into lightly oiled baking dish. Bake at 350° for 20 minutes.

Millet Burgers

Serves 4–8

2 cups cooked millet
3 tablespoons tahini
1 large onion, chopped

1 cup buckwheat flour
3 tablespoons tamari

Mix all ingredients together and add enough water to make a sticky batter. Spread enough batter on lightly greased skilled to make desired size of patties. Cook over medium flame until golden on both sides and done in middle. Eat hot or cold. They are great for traveling.

Crispy Barley Balls

Serves 4–8

2 cups cooked barley
2 tablespoons sesame seeds
Tamari

½ cup whole wheat pastry flour
1 teaspoon summer savory
Water

Mix all ingredients and add enough water to make somewhat sticky dough. Dip hands into cold water, shape dough into little balls, and fry in deep oil until crisp and golden. These are good to take on trips, too. When forming balls, add a sliver of umeboshi (Japanese salted plums), chopped, to each; this acts as a natural preservative which will enable you to keep the food for days.

Cornmeal Mush

Serves 4

This is something not many people eat or even know about; so I want to bring it up so more people will try it.

1 cup yellow cornmeal
1 cup cold water

¼ teaspoon salt
3 cups boiling water

Mix cornmeal with cold water and drop into salted boiling water, stirring until smooth. Turn flame as low as possible, cover, and let bubble until creamy—10–15 minutes. Serve it sweet with honey and butter if you are into that, or with sesame salt if you are not into sweets.

Next come some vegetables and salad.

Vegetable Pie

Makes 1 pie

Pie dough*
Oil
2 onions, cut into thin rings
2 carrots, cut into diagonal ovals
1 small butternut squash, diced

2 parsnips, cut same as carrots
3 or 4 sprigs parsley, chopped
2 tablespoons tamari
Roasted or raw sesame seeds

Roll half of pie dough to fit 9-inch pie pan. Heat about 1 tablespoon oil and toss in onions, stirring until they begin to get soft; add other vegetables, stir together, turn flame to low, cover and steam 2–3 minutes. Add tamari and pile into bottom crust. Roll out second crust and cover pie, pressing edges with thumbs for sealing. Sprinkle top with sesame seeds, after brushing crust with oil. Bake in 350° oven until crust is golden brown— about 30 minutes.

* Pie Dough: Measure 3 cups whole wheat pastry flour into bowl; add 1 teaspoon salt and 3 tablespoons oil. A little at a time, add cold water and mix with hands until a firm but workable dough forms. Roll on floured surface.

Dulse-Carrot-Apple Salad

Serves 8

1 3-ounce package dulse seaweed
2 fresh apples, sliced, or ⅛ pound dried apples, chopped
1 handful currants

3 large carrots, grated
1 cup sprouts (alfalfa or wheat are good)

Wash dulse well, as it is salty, and chop. Mix all ingredients together and add dressing:

Dressing: ½ cup oil (sesame and sunflower are best and unfortunately also most expensive; but use what you've got), juice of ½ lemon, ½ cup water and 2 tablespoons tamari. Mix and pour over salad; toss.

5 Rock City Road Dressing #3

Makes 1 quart

1 cup oil
1½ cups water
1 tablespoon dill weed
2 fat cloves garlic, minced

3 umeboshi plums, pitted
¼ cup tahini—a good ¼ cup
1 tablespoon paprika

Either toss everything in a blender and whip about 30 seconds, or put in bowl and whip with egg beater or wire whip.

During the winter we make vegetable tempura at the restaurant; one of the favorite ways to make it is what we call "vegetananda."

Vegetananda Tempura

Serves many; just add more vegetables

1 onion, finely chopped
Pieces of any uncooked leftover
  vegetables, chopped fine
  (broccoli, cauliflower, corn,
  green beans, parsley . . .)

1 carrot, finely chopped
Piece of acorn or butternut
  squash, chopped
Basic Tempura Batter
Enough oil to deep-fry

Mix vegetables with tempura batter and drop into oil heated to 350°. Never let oil smoke; it is much too hot then. Use a large wooden spoon for dropping, allow to get golden on one side, then turn and do same to other. Remove from oil and drain well to remove excess oil. Serve with Ginger-Tamari Sauce.*

Basic Tempura Batter (eggless): Mix together 2 cups soy powder, 1 cup whole wheat pastry flour, 1 cup corn flour or finely ground cornmeal, salt to taste, and 5 cups water. Batter should be as cold as possible for best tempura.

*__**Ginger-Tamari Sauce:**__ 1 cup water, 3 tablespoons tamari, and 1 tablespoon grated ginger. Whip together in blender or shake together in jar and sit in refrig an hour or two. Dip vegetanandas in sauce and eat.

5 Rock City Road Overnight Bread

3 cups cooked grain (rice is always
  good, but for a change, barley
  is great and so is millet)
1 cup whole wheat flour
1 cup buckwheat flour

2 cups cornmeal
¼ cup oil
1 rounded teaspoon salt
Water

Mix everything but water together until well blended. Add water until dough is sticky and feels like patting a fat stomach. Cover and let sit in warm place overnight. Put in oiled bread pan and run knife around edges to keep from sticking. Put in cold oven and turn on to 350°, baking until done through—1–1½ hours. (It should look golden and not feel soft when pressed on with your fingers.) Remove from pan by hitting end of bread pan flat on hard surface and turning bread out into other hand. Cool before cutting. Serve with miso-tahini spread: walnut-sized piece miso softened with a little water, about 3 times as much tahini (it's up to you how strongly miso you want it); mix together to smooth paste. This is a basic recipe to which can be added minced onions or parsley, or garlic, sprouts, grated carrots, any number of things.

Corn Balls

2 cups cornmeal
½ cup buckwheat flour
3 cloves garlic, minced
1 teaspoon tamari
1 cup whole wheat pastry flour

1 onion, chopped fine
1 teaspoon salt
3 tablespoons oil
Water

Mix all ingredients but water until blended; add water until dough is sticky enough to roll into little ping-pong ball-sized pieces. Do this by dipping your hands in cold water and rolling in palms. Bake in 375° oven for 20–25 minutes. Until golden.

Eggless French Toast

4 tablespoons soy powder   4 tablespoons tahini
2 cups water   ½ teaspoon salt

Mix ingredients together in blender or with beater or wire whip. Soak yeast bread in batter and cook on lightly greased griddle until done on both sides. Serve with apple butter.

SAUCES

Basic White Sauce

Makes 1 cup

2 tablespoons sesame seeds   2 tablespoons oil
3 tablespoons whole wheat   1 cup water
   pastry flour or barley flour   Tamari

Dry-roast sesame seeds until golden and crumbly when rubbed between fingers. Add flour and oil and roast flour, stirring constantly, about 5 minutes over medium heat. Slowly add water, whipping all the time with a wire whip (this is the best tool I know to get unlumpy sauce, and they're cheap). Stir with whip until sauce comes to boil and is thick. Turn off and allow to cool a few minutes before adding tamari to taste. This is one of the best grain sauces, vegetable sauces, and just about everything sauces I've found.

Tahini-Onion Sauce

1 medium onion, chopped fine   1 cup water
1 teaspoon oil   Tamari to taste
2 tablespoons tahini

Sauté onion lightly in oil; add tahini and mix; then add water, slowly beating with wire whip until smooth and thick. If too thick for you, add more water; if too thin, add more tahini. Put in tamari to taste and serve on grain or vegetables.

Lynn's Adzuki Pizza

(As opposed to the many other ones I've seen written somewhere)

4 cups adzuki beans (cover them with water and soak several hours, preferably overnight)	½ cup oil
	1 tablespoon oregano
	1 teaspoon marjoram
2 good-sized onions, chopped	2 teaspoons salt
½ green pepper, minced	1 teaspoon basil
Several cloves garlic, minced	Tamari to taste
Favorite cheese (about ½ pound)	Pizza Dough*

Drain adzuki beans, saving juice. While they drain, chop vegetables and grate cheese. Grind beans through a meat grinder (it's really worth it to get a meat grinder to make your own meat substitutes because the canned stuff is usually garbage). Put 1 tablespoon of the oil into pan and sauté garlic, onion, and green pepper slightly; add ground adzuki beans and remaining oil and also herbs, salt, and tamari to taste. Stir together a few minutes over medium high flame; add about 2 cups of water from soaked adzukis, stir, turn down flame, and cover, letting it cook until water is absorbed. If beans still seem a little hard, add another cup of water and cook a little longer; they should have a rough texture, not be mushy. Spread this mixture onto cookie sheet lined with pizza dough. Top with grated cheese and bake at 375° for 20 minutes.

*Pizza Dough: Soften ½ teaspoon dry yeast in 1 cup warm water and add 1 teaspoon salt and 2 tablespoons oil. Mix in 3–4 cups whole wheat flour until soft and elastic. Knead a short while and set in warm place, covered, to rise—about 1 hour. When risen, punch down, let it rest 10–20 minutes, and press onto greased cookie sheet or pizza pan or large iron skillet.

IF you're not into pizza, use the same dough and filling, only roll or press balls of dough into circles and fill with the bean stuff and cheese, fold over, press edges with fork, put on greased cookie sheet, brush with oil and bake 20–35 minutes at 350°.

Nori Rice Rolls

4 cups cooked rice
1 large chopped onion
2 stalks celery, diced fine
½ cup sunflower seeds
2 carrots, finely chopped

4 or 5 sprigs chopped parsley
½ cup currants
Tamari
2 tablespoons oil
1 package nori seaweed

Mix all ingredients except nori together with tamari to taste. Roll up in squares of nori and place on oiled sheet to bake for 25 minutes at 400°. Cool and eat, or eat hot. If you want to take these traveling, chop umeboshi slivers in each roll as a preservative.

Green and Feta Cheese Pie

Makes 1 pie

½ pound of your favorite greens
  (mustard greens are fantastic)
1 pound feta cheese, crumbled
1 large onion, diced
3 or 4 sprigs parsley, chopped

Tamari
1 carrot, grated
1 tablespoon oil
½ cup water
1 piecrust

Chop greens well and mix with cheese, onion, parsley, and tamari to taste. Fill pie shell very full with mixture and sprinkle top with grated carrot. Mix oil with water and sprinkle over top of pie. Bake 20–25 minutes in 350° oven.

SEAWEED Very Important

Baked Wakame Casserole

Serves many

1 package wakame seaweed,
  soaked, drained, and chopped
4 tablespoons tahini

1 large onion, cut into moon slivers
4 tablespoons tamari
¼ cup roasted or raw sesame seeds

Save water from soaked seaweed for soup stock. Mix first 4 ingredients together and wet with some of wakame water. Put in casserole and sprinkle with sesame seeds. Bake 25 minutes in 375° oven.

Hiziki and Carrots

½ small package hiziki

3 carrots, cut into matchsticks

1 tablespoon oil

Tamari

Soak hiziki about 30 minutes. Drain, saving water for stock. Sauté carrots for a few minutes in oil and add seaweed. Stir a few minutes, turn down flame, and cover. Steam about 15 minutes and add tamari to taste.

TO THE WOODS

Wild Animals and Mother Nature

To start with basics: If you're going to shoot a deer for food, normally you don't get a chance to bleed that deer the same as you would beef—to cut its throat. The deer may run off and it'd be 3–4 minutes before you get up to it. By then the deer is completely dead and your chance of getting it to pump its blood out by cutting its throat isn't very good.

¶ The most practical shot is in the lung cavity, because that way the deer bleeds to death. It dies from hemorrhage. It drowns in its own blood and dies just about as quick as from a heart shot. It may run 50–100 yards but when it drops, it's dead. In the meantime, practically all the blood is pumped out into the lung cavity, so when you open the deer the blood just falls out in great quantities. The deer is completely bled out and the meat is in good condition. Also, if you shoot it through the ribs, you have one little hole going in one side and out the other and there's no wasted meat. You should shoot all game through the lungs, although when you shoot a rabbit or squirrel you don't often get a chance to place the shot.

¶ The next step is to cool the meat as quickly as possible, which means to gut the deer. Normally, you roll the deer over on its back, prop it up, then slit the hide from the anus right up through to the brisket (that's between the ribs). Normally I don't carry a big hunting knife; I just carry a pocket knife. I find it just as practical as a big hunting knife. If you have a big hunting knife, you can split the pelvis with it. But if you don't have a knife that's heavy enough to split the pelvis, then the thing to do is, when you open the skin up to the anus, go around the anus and loosen that completely. That way when you pull the big gut out, you can pull the anus out with it. It all comes out at once, including the bladder and everything in it. Then you just proceed to open the belly in such a way that you don't cut the gut, or the paunch. Usually you run two fingers up ahead of your knife and cut after them to keep the belly skin up away from the guts. Just open it up to the brisket. Then it's just a matter of reaching in and rolling the guts out. They're loose, so just pull them out.

¶ Wipe the deer out with ferns or grass or whatever you have to get all the blood out of it. *But don't use water on it.* For some reason, if you wash meat, it doesn't save as well. That's true of any wild meat. I suppose it's true of most meats. Normally, even if I'm near a stream, I never wash a deer out. I'll take ferns or grass or whatever I have and wipe all the blood out. Whatever I can't get, I don't worry about. Then I'll dry it on the outside.

¶ As soon as you can, get the deer someplace where you can hang it up. Prop the rib cage open and let it cool as quickly as possible. A deer, properly dressed and properly cooled—especially in the fall, when the weather's right—can hang for two weeks. Many times, when we've had fairly cool weather, I've let a deer hang for two weeks before I've started to use it for food. By then it was just starting to tenderize and get good.

¶ You can use practically all the methods on venison that you use on beef to cut it up, except that you have to remove every bit of fat that you can. The fat on venison is similar to mutton: when you cook it and it gets cold, it sticks to the roof of your mouth. It's not very palatable. When I prepare meat for the freezer, I go over it very carefully and take every speck of fat off.

¶ You hear so much about all these fancy recipes. If you like wild meat, I think the more you dress it up, the more harm you do to it, the less it tastes like wild meat. You hear of all this marinating and these fancy sauces and everything. Of course, I've cultivated a taste for wild meat. I crave the taste of the wild flavor in it. If I don't get that I may as well have beef as far as the flavor is concerned. If the flavor isn't *too* strong, that is. Now an old buck shot in rutting season when it's ready can be a little bit more even than *I* like.

¶ Cook it to taste. I don't like it overly done. Venison normally needs to be cooked a little bit more than beef. For instance, if you enjoy a real rare roast of beef, I would say to cook the venison more than beef. That's my own personal taste. You know, I don't like it quite as raw. I like beef really red raw, but venison I like cooked a little more than beef. It's very good broiled or fried.

¶ I almost believe that venison will last longer (in storage), under the same conditions, than beef would—if it's properly bled out, butchered, and killed. If an animal is killed instantly, and it isn't bled—if its throat isn't cut or its arteries aren't cut or something—blood congeals in the muscles. Meat has a tendency to spoil much, much faster than the meat that's properly bled out. If you shoot a deer and have some pieces that are full of blood, it's good to soak them overnight in salt water. The salt will draw some of the blood out. Otherwise, when you cook it, it just turns black.

¶ Now, rabbits and squirrels, you almost always leave them sit overnight in salt water. Porcupines: delicious. Young porcupine is good. It's quite a dark, coarse meat, but very tender. They're strictly vegetarians. There's no reason why their meat wouldn't be good. They live on practically the same diet as a rabbit or any other vegetarian. They're not hard to skin, although you might think so. If you lay them on their back, and rip them up the belly, the skin pulls off almost as easily as a rabbit. On the other hand, the woodchuck is very hard to skin. Young woodchucks are very good. They have the same season as porcupines. For instance, one born this spring would be about half grown late this summer, and would be delicious. Woodchucks and porcupines are quite gamy. I would say to parboil them in salt and baking soda water (½ teaspoon baking soda) until they're nearly done. Then brown them down, either in an iron pot or in a frying pan. Flour them, a few onions thrown in, that sort of thing.

¶ Porcupines are very useful. Quills left over are good for decorative things. My wife makes earrings out of them; the Indians used to do quill work from them. Porcupines will eat anything with salt or any kind of like mineral on it. It doesn't even have to be salt. I once set a cast iron frying pan out in the woods and forgot about it. I went back for it later and the porcupines had gnawed their way half through it. A friend of mine put their taste for salt to really good use. He used to man the fire tower up on that mountain over there, when the tower was first built, and there were a lot of stumps around the tower that he wanted to get rid of. So every time he had to go to the bathroom, he went out and urinated on the stumps. By the end of the summer, there wasn't a single stump standing. The porcupines had chewed them all away.

¶ Now, to take quills out of dogs' mouths and noses: there's a theory that if you put vinegar on the quills, it softens them. I've tried it and couldn't see that it helped any. There's another theory that if you clip the ends off it lets the air out and they'll come out easier. But I haven't found anything that's really worked. You only can try to hold the dog as quiet as possible and pull them out as gently as you can. There isn't very much that's gentle about it; they stick so you really have to give a quick sudden yank to get them out. Normally if you pull them slowly, there's too much pain, the dog can't stand it.

¶ *Game birds:* Some of the game birds tend to be dry. It's a good idea, if you're going to roast them, to put bacon across them, or something to moisten the meat. And wild duck, there's a type of orange-flavored sauce that's very good. I don't know the ingredients that go into it, but it's very good; the orange sauce complements the flavor of the wild duck. Pheasant you would cook the same as chicken. Pheasant is a fairly domestic flavor; the wild flavor is very slight. Best of all, to my taste, is the grouse. They're a real delicacy. They're small, but have a very sweet, nutty flavor.

¶*Fish:* You can use deer tails and some parts of the porcupine quills to tie flies. Bass and pickerel and carp are good pond fish. Trout are good stream fish. Even suckers, if you catch them in the spring, have good flavor. They're sort of bony, but have good flavor. Later on into the summer, they'll start to taste sort of muddy, but you can still eat them.

¶ Of course, you can eat snakes. Just cut off their heads, and skin them down the belly, then cook them like you would a porcupine. Parboil them and then fry them. Turtles are good in soups and stews. I don't know if many people realize this, but most turtles except snapping turtles are protected by law. Of course if it were a matter of survival, you wouldn't think of that, but as it is, snapping turtles can be cooked. Just shell them and cut them into chunks, and cook them in a soup or stew.

¶ I've shot carp with a bow and arrow and then salted and smoked them. I always salt the fish before I smoke them. I grew up on a farm and I remember watching my dad make a brine for salting pork and beef. His rule to tell if the brine was heavy enough was, he'd keep adding salt to soft water until there was enough salt to float a potato. Now, this brine is a heavier solution than what you use to soak a rabbit or squirrel in. You make your brine heavy enough to float a potato, and put your fish in it for 24 hours. You'd put meat in for longer, and keep adding to your brine. I think, if I remember right, my father used to salt meat for as long as a month. I don't remember the exact process, but he used to fill a barrel with the brine, hold the meat down in it with a rock, cover it up, and let it set for a month, it seemed.

¶ Once you've salted your fish (or meat), you can smoke it. Every farm, when I was growing up, had its own smokehouse. But you can use a barrel. Build a smoke. I put a pan down, and get good coals going, then I cover it with another pan so it's almost smothered. I put sawdust or green wood on the coals to keep the smoke up. Put racks in the barrel, with a smoke under them. Smoke until the meat or fish turns brown.

¶ You can make jerky by cutting your meat into thin strips and hanging them over a slow heat until all the moisture is out of the meat and it breaks into dry chips. This is done outside, of course.

¶ You use an outside fire to make maple syrup, too. Collect the sap from the maple trees in the early spring. Be sure to collect the sap at least once a day, more when the weather gets warmer. If the sap isn't collected soon enough, or if too much outside stuff falls into the pails, the sap will sour. There's enough sugar in it to cause it to ferment and go sour. If it turns milky in color, it's gone sour. Don't add it to the other sap; it'll just make the syrup sour. If it's milky, or if it tastes sour, don't use it. Boil the sap down to about 1 gallon of syrup for 40 gallons of sap collected. You can boil the sap like crazy while it's still thin, but once it starts to get thick, watch it really carefully. The boiling sap, when it starts to thicken, can boil up right in front of you and turn to sugar. So once it starts to get thick, keep the heat low, and don't let it go to sugar.

¶ I guess you could even make sap wine; there's enough sugar in it. I only made dandelion wine once in my whole life, and I'm kicking myself today because I didn't write down the recipe. What I did was collect about 2 bucketfuls of dandelion flowers and throw them on the bottom of a stone crock. I threw in some water, a couple of packages of yeast I got at the hardware store, and some fistfuls of sugar. I put the top on it, and put the crock under the stairs. Then, I actually forgot about it. Around September or October, my wife got after me to get the crock out and clean it out so we could use it for some apples or something. So I took the crock out back and opened it up. On top was this layer of film, real thick and cloudy. I was starting to pour it all out onto the ground, when the layer of film shifted, and under it was the clearest, most golden liquid I've ever seen. Well, when my wife got home, I was so crocked on that dandelion wine . . . I just bottled the rest of it up and put it away. Once it's worked itself out like that, just put it into bottles and cork it up, and it'll keep just fine.

An Interview with Aaron Van De Bogart

MORE TIPS ON WILD GAME

¶ Never give deer bones to dogs—they will be likely to chase deer especially if they are wounded. Packs of dogs running deer is unfair and illegal. In most states dogs can be shot on suspicion of running deer.

¶ Venison makes good mincemeat. If you have an old or tough deer, do like so:

¶ Remove muscles along grain, removing sinews. Cut crosswise every inch or so, and hammer till you can see through it—no piece of meat being more than ¼ inch thick. Dip in seasoned flour and "chicken-fry." This is good for sandwiches, too.

¶ Do not use rabbits until after the first killing frost—tularemia bacteria live on their fur, and are picked up by humans through abrasions or openings on the skin. They manifest themselves as swollen lymph glands and are very painful. When cleaning game, avoid contact of hair or fur on meat, as it causes spoilage and bad flavor. Game does not have the same kind of fatty tissues as commercial meat—it cooks faster, and if overcooked . . . bleah. Serve it as *hot* as possible, because the fat globulizes as it cools (see section about how fat tastes like mutton fat). If you live near clay, loose-pluck game birds, and coat in clay-based mud. Bury in hot coals. When clay is hard to dry, break it open. The pinfeathers stay in the clay, and the bird is cooked. This is an old Indian trick, and is useful for out in the field as well as at home in the kitchen.

¶ *Porcupine:* Soak overnight in salt, baking soda, and water, changing every 3–4 hours. This will draw out the gamy taste. Roast it with garlic, sage, or other strong herbs.

¶ Nonherbivorous game (skunk, raccoon, bear, etc.) should be cooked as well as you would cook pork, to get rid of parasites in the flesh. To soften old squirrels, parboil them.

WOODCHUCKS

¶ Among experienced foragers and woodsmen, the woodchuck has always been considered a delicacy. The woodchuck is one of the cleanest-living animals around; more so, for instance, than chicken. Cleaned and cooked properly, woodchuck tastes better than chicken.

¶ Cleaning and skinning a woodchuck can be done very easily. You will need a good knife, a hatchet, and a chopping block. Any wood surface that can be chopped on will do. Start by chopping off the head, and simply continue on around, chopping off all four feet and the tail as well. Now, using the knife, make one cut in the hide from side to side across the back. To do this, just hold up a fold of the loose hide with the left hand while you slice with the right (or vice versa if you're left-handed). A three-inch cut is sufficient. Now put the fingers of each hand into the cut in the hide. Gripping well, pull hard in opposite directions. If all goes well, you should have skinned the woodchuck. All it takes is 30 seconds: six chops with the hatchet, one cut with the knife, one strong tug with your hands.

¶ Now that the carcass is skinned, you should proceed to clean it much as you would a chicken. (A rule of thumb for cleaning and cutting game is: Anything deer-size or larger should be treated like beef, anything smaller than deer should be treated like poultry.) Old folk myths say that the glands in the pit of the front legs of a chuck ("kernels") should be cut out and thrown away, and that all fat must be removed. If you see them, and want to remove them, go ahead; however, they're just small accumulations of brown fat, and will do you no harm. With mature woodchucks, especially those shot in the autumn, it's usually advisable to remove whatever fat you can. Then again, leaving it does no harm. It just gives a more muttony taste to the meat.

¶ Woodchuck can be cooked in many ways, but there is one preliminary step that should always be taken: parboiling. Put the meat into a kettle, and cover it with salted water. Young woodchucks should be boiled for about ½ hour; an hour should be enough time for even the oldest chuck. After the preliminary parboiling, the meat should be drained. Then you're ready to cook it.

¶ Now the meat can be roasted, fried, broiled, or made into stew by substituting the woodchuck for the regular meat in your recipe. If you have an outdoor grill or fireplace, try barbecuing the woodchuck. Cut the carcass into handy-sized pieces, as you would a chicken, and grill over charcoal, brushing often with spiced butter or barbecue sauce to keep them from drying out. Because of the parboiling, the meat will be done in about 10 minutes. Serve fast, and prepare to receive compliments.

"Plants have a sensitive nervous system and a varied emotional life. Love, hate, joy, fear, pleasure, pain, excitability, stupor, and countless other appropriate responses to stimuli are as universal in plants as in animals."

J. C. Bose, India's great scientist

BERRY PICKING IN THE WILD

Awareness of the seasons becomes so acute as to become awareness of what berries are ripening in what meadow, on what slope, under what bridge, at what time. Nature still provides enormous quantities of wild berries: strawberries in late June, early July; blueberries in July; red raspberries early in August; blackberries late in August. To gather the berries, you should know where to look for them, then keep constant watch on the spot for the moment of ripening.

¶ Last summer was one stoned venture after another into meadows, checking out the main blackberry patch every three days to see if those red ones last week were black yet. We often raced against storms, bears, and birds to get to the berries, and in time, developed some pretty sophisticated, and *very* stoned, gathering techniques.

¶ Meadow picking is pretty easy—if you can get there before the bear and deer do. Late afternoon is a nice time to go berrying. It ends the day nicely and means that the berries have had a full day of sunlight to aid in ripening. When we pick, we go to the meadow first, picking the ripe berries, and making mental notes of berry bushes still to ripen. At the height of the blackberry season, we hit the same meadow every three days, getting at least 10 quarts of berries in just 2 hours of picking each time. But that's not the half of it. Meadow picking is merely an introduction into the pleasures of berrying. To the intrepid picker, there are *many ways* of getting to those hidden berries at the sides of roads or down slopes.

¶ Susan is our champion road picker. Driving up to and down from the meadow on the dirt road, Susan spies a bush here, another bush there of ripening berries. "Stop the car," she shouts excitedly, "we really can't pass over that bush." Hence begins Susan's road trip—a slow drive up and down the three miles of dirt road, with stops every few minutes to gather the fruit from solitary bushes that eagle-eye Susan has seen off in the woods. No one can match Susan's eyesight, nor the speed with which she bounds out of and back into the car. Nor can anyone ridicule her favorite method of gathering berries, because it, too, yields berries by the gallon.

¶ Colleen's theory is that if you look for berries in the most difficult-to-reach spot, you'll find them in great abundance. "After all," she reasons, "there isn't an animal in the forest stupid or brave enough to go through what I go through to get to those berries." Dressed in long pants, hiking boots, and a leather shirt, hair tied back, Colleen climbs down impossibly steep slopes and works her way into the bushes going up the slopes. This means numerous falls and incredible hangups in bushes that snag and tear at any available piece of loose clothing or hair, but it also means getting at bushes that haven't been touched all summer and are consequently overloaded with berries.

¶ Whatever way you dig doing berries, do it. It helps, though, to wear clothes that will protect you from scratches and at the same time won't get

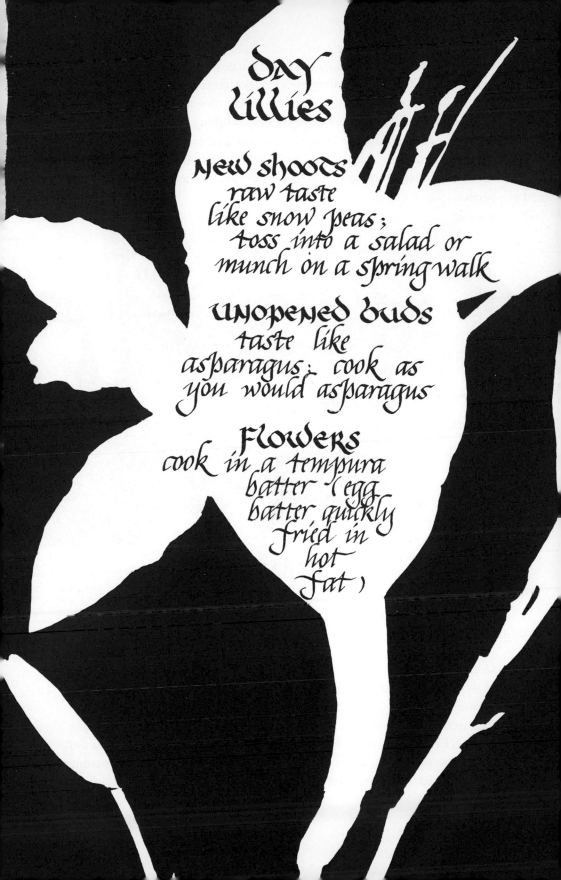

DAY LiLLiES

NEW SHOOTS
raw taste
like snow peas;
toss into a salad or
munch on a spring walk

UNOPENED BUDS
taste like
asparagus; cook as
you would asparagus

FLOWERS
cook in a tempura
batter (egg
batter quickly
fried in
hot
fat)

snagged. Long denim pants, long-sleeved shirts, leather jackets, and maybe even gloves are good protective articles of clothing; scarves, hats, bound-up hair, keep thorns from tearing at your hair. It's nice to have both hands free, either for getting at berries, or for disentangling yourself from bushes. So punch a couple of holes in some coffee cans, thread some string through the holes, and tie the cans around your waist. Get stoned, climb hills, work your way through meadows, and dig on the sun, grasses, bees, flowers, and berries.

FEATURE INSTALLMENT:

PORNOGRAPHY OF THE PALATE

During that long and excruciating experience called Americanization, most of us have lost the ability to deal with the full sensuality of the eating experience. It is certain that when the crazed, frozen pioneers at Donner Pass were gnawing away at human spleens and fingers in horror, someone said: "Hmmm . . . tastes like chicken. . . ." It is surprising that this dull perception of food should persist in an age when sexual experience becomes more savored, described, and explored.

¶ For example, there are no low-budget, fly-by-night *food*-exploitation films playing in the Bronx tonight; while on the hump front, the local JDL members and Rheingold guzzlers have a choice between *Alex's Stallions, Dry-ice Fetish,* and Dorothy Provine in *Feminine Hygiene.* Worse, from an old-line Western Civ point of view, there exists no written pornography for the palate.

¶ Pornography itself is both appetite and the satisfaction of appetite. When the United States starved a group of conscientious objectors during World War II to simulate concentration camp conditions, to its great amazement it found that the shirkers were interested in reading only . . . cookbooks. Yes, they dropped Proust and Kierkegaard like a ton of kishka and spent whole dazed days stirring phantom fondues, spearing marinated shrimp, and in general contributing nothing to the war cause.

¶ But cookbooks themselves are like photographic sex manuals. Loveless. They appeal to the technician in us but leave the esthete unsatisfied. And so it is with the same horny wonder felt by the first pornographer-caveman when the first two-foot phallus was carved into stone that *Feast* presents a morsel from the world's premier work of palate porno:

IT STUCK TO THE ROOF OF MY MOUTH

The Situation So Far:

Hedda, the fresh-faced farmgirl from East McKeesport, has finally made her way to the Continent, where she has been befriended by her father's aging, mysterious pen pal, Signore Suino. He has taken her to his windswept castle overlooking the Bay of Naples.

As we join the odd pair, Suino has just dispatched all his servants for the evening save his sultry, ample-bosomed cook Mangia. As the wind fondles the jacaranda trees the first pulsings of forbidden desire turn Hedda's sleek body into a maelstrom of burning need.

. . . . . .

Suino sat Hedda down before the velvet-covered table. Her blue eyes opened with suppressed lust as the old Count, snickering softly, reached into a delicate silver box and extracted two long Cuban cigars.

"These," he whispered cruelly, "are for *later,* mio bambino . . . much, much later!"

Hedda blushed beef-red and stared down at her clogs.

"I—I'm sure I don't know what you mean," she stammered.

Suino laughed a horrible laugh, a laugh covered with spurs and forks.

"Let the festivities begin!" he bellowed.

And with that ancient invocation Mangia the Cook materialized in the doorway, cradling two huge plates. Lying on each plate were five long, thin noodle shells dripping with meat-tomato sauce and stuffed to bursting with ground meat, spices, cheese, and onions.

Hedda's face contorted in agonized excitement.

"No!" she shrieked. "No! You demon Suino!" Beads of impassioned saliva streamed from her bee-stung lips as her mouth formed the terrible foreign word: "PAS-TA!!!"

The beautiful girl's stomach and palate beat a staccato song of blind raw desire against her inflamed brain. Suino's face was distorted but so seductive as he dangled it before her.

"Yes, *mio caro,*" he was intoning, "you will eat the huge, stuffed noodle!"

"Like fun I will, Suino," she cried, while every fiber in her mouth yearned for the taut tube.

"Oh, you will eat it," murmured Mangia, waddling up toward the helpless Hedda with chunky gravy pouring lasciviously down her chin and naked neck and forming a delicious, scented pool in her cleavage. She held the steaming, yearning plate up to Hedda's quivering lips. In fact, the entire scene teemed with adjectives meaning "excited."

Suino was already shoveling masses of the *cannelloni* into his brutal mouth, which made it difficult (but not impossible) for him to keep up his breathless dialogue with the pristine virgin.

"You will—blurp—take the hot staff in your—tlurg," he smiled open-mouthed, revealing an entire unchewed portion. "Tell her, Mangia."

"Darling," Mangia oozed, "first you will worry the edge of the *cannelloni* with your tongue, as each assault of hysterical flavor batters your drooling mouth. Slowly your mouth will move down to engulf the whole stick of pasta, receiving all its maddened messages of joy . . ."

"No!" the girl whimpered at last. "It's too . . . *big!*"

(*Continued on page 106*)

From Chicks to Soup

Thinking of raising chickens? Great idea. Just think of all the eggs you'll get
. . . fresh and/or fertile. And the meat (if you're into it), the meat is free
from poisons and cancers. And think of how nice it will be to go out into the
chicken yard in the early morning, to throw your chickens scratch from a
big old hopper of grain. You may, however, be a bit overwhelmed when
you receive your first batch of day-old chicks and are faced with the flesh
of what was, up till then, a very pleasant fantasy of true life in the country.
But don't let it throw you. It's easy. Just remember, chicks, like baby
humans, are healthy and hearty creatures who need to be taken care of
with love and common sense. You feed them, shelter them, keep them warm
and treat them kindly, and they reciprocate by growing and maturing. It
is helpful, though, to go about a new project such as chicken raising with
the advice and suggestions of someone who has already done it and been
successful at it. Here, then, are some (hopefully) helpful hints to those of
you who are about to undertake raising chickens for fun and food.
¶ You can order your chicks by mail from any number of chicken
hatcheries around the country. There should be a hatchery near you. Try,
when ordering your chicks, to stay within a radius of 200 miles around
your home. This will make the mailing of the chicks a safer, healthier
proposition. When you order your chicks will probably be determined by

your local climate. If you live in a section of the country where you get winter and spring snows, you'd probably be better off ordering your chicks in the spring (spring-hatched chicks—March, April, May). They can then spend the first few weeks of their life indoors and will be ready to go outside when the weather gets warm. As a 5–6-month growing period is required before a chick is able to lay eggs, the spring-hatched chick will have matured by fall and be producing eggs before the snow falls. If your climate remains consistently warm the year round, then you can start your chicken flock any time, and can probably even avoid having to keep your chicks indoors the first few weeks.

¶ When ordering day-old chicks, it's cheaper to order a straight run (pullets and cockerels randomly mixed) than it is to order a sexed run. Most poultrymen will tell you, in ordering a straight run, to order three chicks for every laying hen that you want. According to their thinking, out of every three chicks ordered, one will die, one will be a cockerel, and one will be a pullet. We ordered 50 chicks (we paid 22¢ each, but I've heard prices as low as 7½¢ each) and got an even split between pullets and cockerels. One pullet was squashed under the food dish on the second day. One rooster got sick and died. But that was it for casualties. As we were sent one extra pullet by mistake, we then ended up with 25 good layers and 24 good roosters (all but one or two of the roosters to be slaughtered for food). A good layer can be expected to lay one egg at least every other day. So, evaluate your needs and your food philosophy, feel out the honesty of the hatchery with which you're dealing, and order your chicks accordingly.

¶ When you receive your chicks, place them in a brooder box. The brooder box can be any wooden box with a wire screen over the top. For 50 chicks, we built a box 4×5×2 feet deep; this was sufficient, but tended to be crowded during the last week of brooding. Your box should be placed in a room that is free from drafts and equipped with an electrical outlet. (We put our brooder in the dining room for the first month. It was fine except that we couldn't eat in there—not because of the smell, but because of the dust generated by 100 little chick feet running around and around and around.) Hang above the box one or two infrared lamps, which will be kept burning at all times. The temperature under the lamp for the first week of the chicks' lives should be kept at 90°. This will mean that for the first day or two you'll have to adjust the height of the lamp until the temperature stabilizes. Don't worry if the fluctuations in temperature are a bit severe at first. The chicks are hearty little creatures and can withstand quite a bit. If you have trouble stabilizing the temperature, just remember that it's better for the temperature to be a bit too high than too low. If the box is big enough, that means that the chicks will be able to move out of the direct light when it gets too hot for them. Lower the temperature under the lights by 5° each week by raising the height of the light over the box.

¶ The most important thing in the health of your chicks is to keep them dry, well fed, and away from drafts. The bottom of the brooder box should be covered with a litter of dry straw or wood chips (not cedar chips) 3–5 inches deep. You can make feeders for your chicks by constructing a V-shaped trough, or, if you don't mind a lot of dust and quite a bit of waste, by laying pie tins of food on the floor of the brooder. Whatever your feeder, it should be kept full of food at all times. A special watering bowl may be made out of any quart jar and flat dish or bowl. Fill a quart mayonnaise or mason jar ¾ full with cool water. Place on top of the jar a flat plate or bowl that has a piece of clay on it. The height of the clay shouldn't exceed the height of the edge of the plate or bowl. Place the lip of the jar on the clay, then turn the jar upside down with the plate underneath it. If your clay is the right height, the water will flow out of the jar and out to the edge of the plate and then stop. When the water level drops, the plate will fill automatically again. Make sure that the plate isn't so large as to allow the chicks to walk in the water. If you don't want to bother with the jar-plate waterer, simple plastic watering dishes to fit over the tops of quart jars can be purchased for about 25¢ to 50¢ at a feed or hardware store.

¶ Feed your chicks chick mash or growing mash until they are full-grown. You may feed your chicks and grown chickens commercial feeds, being careful to avoid any medicated feeds that contain arsenic (to sharpen your chickens' appetites). Beware any feeds which contain the warning: "This feed should not be fed to chickens more than 10 days before butchering for human consumption." If you wish to mix your own mash and chick grain, you may use the following recipes:

Chick and Growing Mash

20 pounds yellow cornmeal
20 pounds wheat bran
20 pounds flour middlings
20 pounds pulverized oats
15 pounds meat scraps
5 pounds alfalfa leaf meal

2 pounds oyster shell meal or lime
1 pound cod liver oil (can be omitted if chicks have access to greens)
1 pound salt

Grind all ingredients finely and mix together.

Chick Grain

2 parts finely cracked yellow corn
2 parts cracked wheat

1 part pinhead oats

By the time the chicks are a month and a half old, if the weather is warm, they should be able to be moved into the coop—earlier if the coop is warm and dry. If your chicks are in the coop, but you're worried about cool evenings or cold days, just keep the infrared lights on to keep the temperature up.

¶ The advantages of starting with your own chicks are many. One big advantage is that you can raise them from the very beginning on good food in a healthy environment. This is extremely important if you're going to slaughter your roosters. (Pullets can be slaughtered and eaten, too, as roasters, fryers, or broilers, or as stewers if they don't lay any more. At any rate, there's no difference in taste between pullet and cockerel.) Roosters can be killed as early as 2 months old. If you get them at 2 months straight from the hatchery, it's no better than getting store-bought chickens. Raise them from chicks, and you'll know that they are healthy and edible.

Broilers: Kill the chicken at 2–2½ months when they weigh 2–3 pounds.
Fryers (versatile age, can be used as broilers or roasters as well as fryers):
   Kill at three months, when they weigh 3–4 pounds.
Roasters: Kill at 4 months when they weigh 4–6 pounds.
Fowl: Kill at any age, but remember, if your chickens have been allowed to
   forage they might taste a bit gamy. Also, if they're very old, they might
   take a lot of stewing to become edible.

Any chicken, hen or rooster, can be eaten. There are, however, certain breeds of chickens that are developed with qualities that are desirable for either egg or meat producers. If you're into raising chickens for both eggs and meat, try Rhode Island Reds or the new sex-linked breeds. They are good, hearty (withstand cold well), all-around chickens. They lay well and make good meat birds. Leghorns are super layers, if you're not into chickens for meat. If you're into chickens only for meat, try Jersey Giant or Light Brahma; they're big birds that develop quickly.
¶ Another big advantage to starting from chicks is that it makes getting started on the chicken project a lot easier. Surprised? Listen. We decided in the winter that we were really into raising chickens. By spring, when we were ready to try it, though, we were also faced with getting a garden in (starting seeds indoors, at least), getting the land fixed up after winter, repairing outside pipes, and generally digging on the spring weather a lot. We had no chicken coop prepared, and no idea of how to go about raising chickens. We became less and less enthusiastic about our plan to raise our chickens, until a friend turned us on to the idea of raising the chicks for the first month in the house.
¶ Hooray! The first sunny day after the great turn-on, we put the brooder box together out of some old plank doors. This was late April, the weather was still cold, so we had no choice but to put the box indoors. The chicks arrived, and we spend the whole rainy months of April and May watching them grow and digging them. We received the chicks in two batches, one

batch four days earlier than the other. When the second batch arrived, they were a bit bullied by the chicks in the first batch, who were four days older than them. We could have separated them for a while by putting a board down the middle of the brooder, but instead we put in more plates of food and jars of water, and after a week (the second batch only had 4 days of 90° heat) they were all about the same size, and all was well. By May, the dust from the chicks forced us to move the brooder box to an outbuilding that had electricity (they could have been moved into the coop, still keeping the temperature stabilized by infrared light, but our coop was still not ready), and by the end of May, we were finally motivated to fix up the chicken coop.

¶ Our coop is 12×8 feet and was made by converting an old garden shed. The coop at present houses 50 chickens, but will eventually house only about 30 layers and a couple of roosters. The floor is cement, although I would prefer a dirt floor, to allow the litter and chicken shit to decompose right into the earth. The walls of the coop are free of holes (to keep out drafts but also raccoons and rats, who can get into anything once they have a good start). The roof is secure and free of leaks (dampness is very unhealthy for the chickens). For added protection from coons and cats, the roof has chicken wire laid over it. The windows of the coop take up the whole southern wall and are just screened. In the winter, they are covered from outside and inside with plastic. That's all you need. Your coop should be well ventilated without being drafty. We spiffed our coop up a bit by insulating the ceiling; this makes the coop warmer in the winter. (The decomposing litter should be kept in the coop all winter. Throw some dry litter on it when it gets damp or smelly, to provide heat for the chickens. If the chickens are warm enough, they'll lay more and longer during the winter months. Also, a light should be kept on during the winter days to make the chickens think it's summer.)

¶ Inside the coop, you'll need feeding troughs, nesting boxes, and roosts or dropping pits. We got all of our equipment from defunct chicken farms (there are a lot of them, so give it a try) around the area. But all of the things you need can be made almost as easily as they can be scrounged.

¶ Nesting boxes should be about 20×14 inches, and can be made from old wooden crates. The front of the box (the open end) should have a short wall at the bottom to keep the nest material and eggs from falling out. Put a stick across some extensions built out from the bottom front of the box, and you'll have roosts that the nesting chickens can go out to sit on. It gives

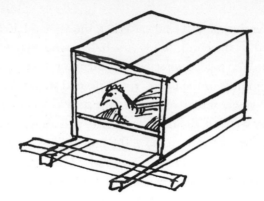

each nest a nice view, and keeps the hens from dirtying the nests. Place in the nests a nice bed of straw or sawdust.

¶ Feeding and watering troughs should be V- or U-shaped and should have some sort of a device running along the top of them to keep the chickens from walking in or dirtying their food and water. One way of keeping them out is to place curved thick wire across the top of the trough

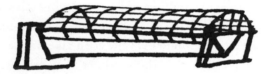

at intervals wide enough for a chicken to stick its head and neck through, and high and steep enough to keep the chickens from roosting on them or walking between them. An even simpler way of doing it is to fit loosely into slits at the end of each trough a dowel with a headless nail sticking out of each end. The dowel will run the length of the trough, right down the middle. A chicken can't stand in the small space between the dowel and the side of the trough, and when it tries to roost on the dowel, the dowel will swivel, and throw the chicken off.

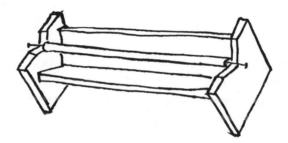

¶ Roosts can be made by turning an old table upside down and nailing pieces of wood about 2–3 inches wide in steps going up the table legs. An advantage to a diagonal roost is that it encourages early roosting (age-early, not in-the-day-early). Instead of a roost, however, you could build a dropping pit, which would consist of a box with 2×4-inch lumber running across it at intervals of 12–13 inches. Food and scratch should be kept in clean covered galvanized garbage cans inside the coop.

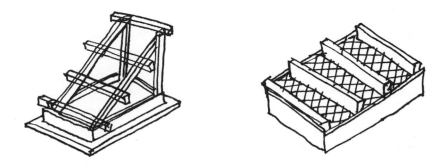

¶ The pens: Just string chicken wire around the area you want to use as the pen. Our pen is 6 feet high, and covers an area roughly three times the area of the coop. All we did to prepare the area for the chickens was to cut down any brambles which might have hurt the chickens, and string 2-inch-hole chicken wire (it's sufficient, and half the price of the 1-inch-hole kind) around trees and posts. You should make sure that the wire at ground level is secure from animals by staking it, much as you would a tent. If you're afraid that your chickens will fly out, cover the pen with more chicken wire, but I've heard that once a chicken flies the coop and discovers how hard it is to get back in, it won't do it any more.
¶ Let your chickens out of the coop in the morning when you feed them (you can now feed them laying mash, plus vegetable scraps—very important—scratch, and crushed oyster shells for calcium). Be sure to provide your chickens with fresh, cool water daily. Get your chickens into the habit of going back into the coop at sunset. They almost always head for the coop around dark, but if you have a strong rooster who can be taught that sunset means bedtime, he'll lead the rest of the flock right into the coop.
¶ The hens should start laying at about 5 months of age. You will need about 1 nesting box for every 4 laying birds, and these nesting boxes should

be kept clean and dry. If you want fertile eggs, you should have a rooster or two around. The laying hens will gladly give up their eggs for collecting. If they don't, perhaps you shouldn't force the issue. The hen might just be trying to tell you that she thinks it's time to add some new blood to the flock. A hen gets broody and will set on eggs from mid-April thru the summer. Any other time she won't set enough to hatch. Do what you want. Allow your hen to set on her own eggs to hatch them, or incubate them.

¶ The biggest things in the health of your chickens are cleanliness, plenty of space, and good food. If your chickens are too crowded, even as chicks, there is more chance for disease. Splotchy feathering (except during molting), thin, droopy chickens, bloated chests, are all signs of unhealthy chickens. If any of your chickens appear physically ill (loss of feathers is not usually contagious), they should be isolated from the rest of the flock immediately. Home treatment for various poultry diseases can be found in government publications, the closest local general store or feed store, and from a great old book called *Backyard Poultry Keeping*.

¶ The litter and the nesting boxes should be kept clean and dry. This does not mean that you'll have to clean the coop all the time. That job should be necessary only 4 or 6 times a year. Rather, if you start with a good foundation of 6 inches of dry straw or wood chips for litter, the chicken shit will settle in, decomposing instead of just sitting there getting wet and

smelly. The litter should be added to regularly, to prevent the formation of a damp and smelly surface. If the litter does become damp, your best bet is to remove it and replace it with dry litter.

¶ Don't forget, old litter from your chicken coop is excellent material for your compost heap. Don't use it directly on your garden right away, as it might be so strong as to burn out the soil.

¶ Make sure that your chickens get fresh, cool water daily, are fed a good diet, and get plenty of sunshine. Besides scratch and mash, your chickens should be getting crushed oyster shells for calcium (don't feed them eggshells for calcium; this encourages egg-eating cannibalism. If an outbreak of egg-eating occurs in your flock, feed them garden lime. It should stop it), and plenty of fresh greens daily. I can't overemphasize the importance of fresh greens in your chickens' diets. The greens provide them with plenty of energy and vitamin C, cause their feathers to be bright and full, and ensure regular laying of big, strong-shelled eggs.

¶ Most important, keep around the coop a source of inspiration to your chickens. From the time our chickens were just day-old chicks, we hung up a picture of the great Chicken Buddha above the brooder box. When the chicks were moved to the coop, the Chicken Buddha moved with them. His picture is there now, hanging above the food and watering troughs, in direct view of hens sitting in the nesting boxes. All the chickens of the coop can view his holy and radiant countenance at any time of the day. He's their Chicken Buddha . . . for Good Eggs.

¶ In this section, you will find a picture of the Chicken Buddha. Cut it out and hang it up . . . it's a good start to any good chicken flock.

Killing and Dressing Chickens

1. Don't allow the chickens to eat anything for 12–24 hours before they are killed, although you can give them water. This is so that their craw and intestines will be empty when you clean them.
2. Take the chicken and hold it under your arm, its head forward, its wings held close to its body. Talk to it, explaining what it is you're about to do, praising it for being your friend and food.
3. Hold tightly to the neck just below the head and swing the chicken around (as if warming up for a pitch) until the neck snaps. Let go.
4. Wait until the reflexes stop, then chop off the head, cutting the neck where the neck meets the body, and hang the bird upside down for ½ hour so the blood will drain.

5. In the kitchen:
   a. Put the chicken in a pot of boiling water for 30 seconds, allowing the water to get to every part of the chicken's body.
   b. Pluck the chicken, careful not to tear the skin. Pluck in the direction that the feathers go. If the feathers are hard to pluck, the water wasn't hot enough, or the chicken wasn't in long enough. If you're having real difficulty, put the chicken in boiling water a second time.
   c. Singe off the pinfeathers over the gas stove flame or any other clean-burning hot flame. If you're going to freeze the chicken before eating it, don't singe the pinfeathers; put it directly into the freezer unsinged, and singe just before cooking.
   d. **Clean the chicken:** Lay the chicken on its breast, its neck turned away from you. Above the cloaca, where the tail feathers were, there is a small oil gland, which you should cut out completely. Next, make a horizontal slash about $2\frac{1}{2}$ inches long and 2 inches down directly below the tail, and including the cloaca. Reach into the chicken and carefully remove the intestines. Attached to the intestines are edible parts, which should be removed. First, cut the liver away from the intestines, being careful not to puncture the green sac of bile it is also attached to. Next, remove the heart. Finally, cut the gizzard (the large hard round thing) away from the intestines. Cut all fat off of the gizzard, and make a slash all the way around it, but not through it. Pull it open, and remove the garbage (and that's all it is—grass, pebbles, sand, etc., that has been collected there). Peel the thick white film off the inside, and it's ready to eat. Put your hand back inside the chicken, and remove what look like two white kidney beans and all of the lung tissue. These last two things are the most difficult to get out, so to be sure you get them, you should put your hand deep into the breast cavity, almost up to the neck. Find the backbone. Scoop your hand along the back cavity in both directions, pulling out all the lung tissue. It's bright red, so you'll know when you've got it. The two white bean things lie a bit down from the lungs on the back. The windpipe lies at the top of the middle of the breast, and runs along the neck; you can pull it out now, or wait until your're cutting the chicken up to get it.
   e. **Cut the chicken:** Cut off the feet just below the knee joint (the narrow end of the drumstick), and set aside. Lay the chicken on the cutting block, breast down, with its legs pointing toward you. Pulling the leg away from the body, cut where the skin stretches. If you've cut in the

right spot, the thigh, and leg with it, should almost pull away from
the rest of the body. Cut until you reach the joint where the leg
joins the hip, and break or cut it off here. To remove the thigh
from the leg, feel for the joint where they meet, and where they
bend. Cut between the leg and thigh at that joint. To remove the
wings, cut between the wing and the breast, cutting toward the
neck. When you reach the joint, break the wing off, or cut through
the joint. You now have a body, with no wings or legs. Place the
chicken on its tail, and cut through the filament that connects
the breast to the back. Now turn the chicken and, placing the
knife in the holes where the wings were, cut up. The breast and back
should now be connected only by the bones at the neck. Snap these
bones till they break, and cut through the tissue and tendons that still
connect them. The breast and back are now separated from each other.

 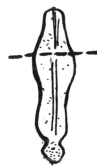 

Turn the back, skin side up, and feel along it until you find a slight dent about a third of the way down from the neck. Make a small cut there, and then break the back in two. To split the breast (if the windpipe is attached, remove it now), turn the breast, skin side down, with the tail part away from you. Make a small slit in the white gristle, parallel with the breast bone. Split the breast until the bone breaks, then, with your thumb, reach under the gristle, and pull the large breastbone out. With older chickens, the breastbone is very hard to pull out, so once the breast is split, you can just cut down it, leaving the breastbone attached to one side of the breast.

f. Rinse the chicken out, and cook, or freeze for later.

A note about all the goodies that can be gotten from a chicken:

Fat: When you cut up the chicken, reserve all the yellow fat that you find (especially prolific around the gizzard, around the breast, and under the neck skin). Place the fat and fatty skin (from around the neck, for example) in a fry pan, and cook down. Take all the yellow grease and put it into a jar. This is honest-to-goodness chicken fat and is good for many things (see Gribbiners).

Feet: Take the feet that you have cut from the leg, and hold in boiling water for 30 seconds. Peel the skin off the feet, and cut off the claws. Put in when you make chicken soup. They make the soup especially rich, and are a delicacy to eat, besides.

Gribbiners: The skin that the fat has been rendered from should be allowed to cook in the fat until it is crisp and brown. Then you can eat it as you would any good munchy thing.

CHICKEN FOR SUNDAY SUPPER

We went over to a neighbor's house yesterday, and he told us about his chickens. Talk to them, he drawled, and let them know what it is that you're 'bout to do. . . . It'll make the killin' easier. He killed one for us, and he and Bonita plucked it, telling us stories of chicken pluckers in Brooklyn who can pluck a chicken in one minute. One minute! And it takes us half an hour in the woods of Woodstock.

¶ We brought four of them home later and let them fast—a cleansing of their bodies to make a cleaning of their craws easier. *I* think more of a message to them that tomorrow is the day.

¶ In the afternoon, the Sunday after a visit with friends, we gathered behind the barn, and faced ourselves and our honesty: "If you eat meat, you should be able to kill it." Marty went first, and talked to his chicken all the way. Then, swinging it around and around, broke its neck. Another one . . . and we noticed that all of us were smiling—partly in embarrassment, but later just getting high off the fact that we were one with our food. That for the first time, we were actually doin' it: taking part in the food chain of the universe. No more A&P. No more biology textbook illustrations of grass, cow eating it, carton of milk, beefsteak in cellophane, all in a neat circular picture with arrows and the sun shining down on the whole thing. It was now us, and the chickens. No sun today: the trees bare, ready for winter, and blood dripping out of the chickens' necks.

¶ Later in the kitchen, we discovered that chickens are indeed remarkably adapted. We learned that the wings are just about all feathers, and that when a chicken preens to keep those feathers shining, he's getting all the oil from a little gland at the top of his ass. Beak to gland . . . oil to feathers . . . another circle. We all learned about the chicken, our food, and praised it all the time we were preparing it. Little Sarah didn't think the insides to be too soft or too sickening to touch. She pulled them out and saw them instead as intestines that looked an awful lot like the rubber worms that you buy in the bait shop. "I wonder if we could use them to catch fish." Sorry, no trout in the stream this late in the year.

¶ And all the while the chicken was in the oven, the smells and crackles coming from the cooking meat reminded us not that dinner was just about ready, but more: that we were, for the first time in our lives, about to enter a new level of consciousness . . . to become what we eat: the whole process of a relationship that was sacred.

CHICKEN BUDDHA
HANG IN CHICKEN COOP

¶ All through dinner, we talked of the sweetness of the meat, and gave freely to our children parts of the meat that we had never cooked before, fearing the poisons found in the store-plastic-chicken. We talked of Indians and pioneers and of waiting for the deer to come to you. Don't hunt it, but wait instead for it to give itself up to you. We talked of friends in the city and revolution. We talked of the day it had been and of how it felt to eat what we had killed. We talked of many things as we ate the chicken, and felt many emotions. We got up from the table and cleared away the bones, and were very thankful today of what we had learned.

CHICKEN

Chicken Soup

Serves 20+

2 chickens	**4 pounds carrots, sliced**
10 chicken feet	**Lots of salt**
3 onions, sliced	**Pepper**

Place all ingredients (gizzards, hearts, backs, necks, too, if you grow your own chickens) in a large pot. Cover with about 3 gallons of water. Add some salt and pepper (add more salt to taste as you cook) and bring to boil. Cook, simmering, until it tastes like chicken soup—about 2 hours. Skim bubbles and fat from the top as it cooks.

Sweet and Sour Chicken

Serves 8

1 chicken, cut in pieces
½ cup flour
½ teaspoon salt
Sprinkling of paprika
1 teaspoon marjoram
3–4 tablespoons butter

2 or 3 tomatoes
1 onion, sliced
2 tablespoons butter
4 cups cooked rice (preferably
    cooked with bouillon cubes)

Remove skin from chicken and debone. A *sharp* small scissors is good for deboning and quickly cutting chicken. Cut meat into bite-sized pieces. Shake pieces of chicken in paper bag containing flour, salt, paprika, and marjoram. Set aside. Cut up tomatoes and onion: sauté together in butter.

SAUCE:

Boil together:

½ cup water and juice from
    canned fruit
¼ cup white vinegar
¼ cup sugar
3 tablespoons tamari

Add:

2 tablespoons cornstarch in 4
    tablespoons water
4 tablespoons water

Stir into smooth paste.

Add:

⅓ cup apricot pulp

Sauté chicken in butter until lightly browned—barely 2 minutes. Add vegetables and sauce, and serve on rice.

Alan's Potted Chicken

Serves 10–20

Oil
3 fryers or stewing chickens
Seasoned flour
5 large onions, cut up
1 bunch celery, cut up
10 carrots, cut up

1 pound mushrooms, sliced
3 large cans whole tomatoes
Spices to taste: oregano, basil,
    thyme, cumin, pepper, salt,
    garlic powder, parsley

In the bottom of a large pot, heat ½ inch of oil. In hot oil, brown chicken that has been dredged in seasoned flour. Set aside. In same oil, brown onions. Then add celery and carrots, cover, and steam for 10 minutes. Add chicken and mushrooms and steam for 5 minutes. Add the tomatoes, stir, and cook for 5 minutes. Add enough hot water to cover chicken, add spices, cover, and simmer for at least 1 hour. This can be served over rice, and, after the meal, the leftover rice and leftover chicken mixture may be combined to make a dynamite leftover chicken rice soup. A True Light Beaver favorite!

Baked Chicken with Mushrooms, Bacon, and Onions

Serves 10–12

3 3-pound chickens, cut up
Butter
Flour
Chicken broth
½ pound bacon, cut into small
   pieces

3 medium onions, chopped
Salt and pepper
¾ pound mushrooms

Bake chicken at 350°, basting with butter until done. While the chicken is baking, melt some butter and add flour to make it a thick paste. Gradually stir in enough broth to make a thick soup. Set aside. In skillet, fry bacon and add to sauce. Pour off all bacon grease except just enough to sauté onions and add to sauce. Salt and pepper to taste. Brown sliced mushrooms in butter and add to sauce. Serve chicken with sauce poured over it.

Quick Chicken Feast for 10

¼ cup butter, or ½ cup olive oil
2 2–3-pound chickens, cut up
3 or 4 onions, chopped
3 cloves garlic, chopped fine
1 or 2 green peppers, chopped
1–2 large cans tomatoes
1–2 cans tomato paste (3-ounce
   cans)

1½ cups water
1 teaspoon salt
¼ teaspoon pepper
1 teaspoon oregano
1½ boxes elbow macaroni
Parmesan cheese

Heat oil or melt butter in very large skillet. Brown chicken until skin is golden brown. Remove chicken and set aside in bowl. Cook onions, garlic,

and green peppers until onions are transparent. Drain excess oil. Add
tomatoes, tomato paste, water, salt, pepper, and oregano. Bring to boil, add
a little sugar if bitter, cook for 5 minutes. Add chicken, cover with
aluminum foil, and simmer for 40 minutes. While this is cooking, cook
elbow macaroni. When done, pour chicken and sauce over macaroni.
Sprinkle heavily with Parmesan cheese.

(*Continued from page 84:*)

    need to worry, *bella,*" Suino grinned as he kissed the last tear away.
"This will rekindle your sagging appetite!"

    When Hedda had finished the thin lavender cigarette, she had
already begun a journey through fields of garlic waving in the summer
wind, cool forests of clove and cucumber housing herds of succulent
cows, and giant fruit trees hiding truffles in their center.

    She was, at last, ready for anything.

Arleen's Chicken with Almonds and Mushrooms

Serves 8–10

3 tablespoons oil	1 cup fresh peas
2 chicken breasts, or whole chicken	½ cup diced onions
with skin and bones removed;	1 cup chicken broth
dice raw meat	2 tablespoons cornstarch
1 teaspoon salt	3 tablespoons water
¼ teaspoon pepper	½ pound mushrooms, sliced
2 tablespoons soy sauce	½–1 cup blanched almonds
1 cup diced celery	

Heat oil in wok or deep skillet. Sauté chicken 3 minutes, stirring constantly.
Add salt, pepper, soy sauce, celery, peas, onions. Cook 2 minutes; stir in
broth. Cover and cook over low heat for 5 minutes. Mix cornstarch and
water. Stir into mixture. Bring to boil until thick. Add mushrooms and
almonds.

June's Chicken Sauté à la Toscana

Serves 12

2 2½-pound fryers, disjointed
1 pound fresh mushrooms, sliced
Butter
12 artichoke hearts
Lemon juice
6 small zucchini, halved

2 chopped shallots
Pinch of rosemary
12 ripe olives
1 cup white wine
1 cup demiglace (reduced canned
  bouillon)

Sauté chicken and mushrooms in butter until brown. Boil artichoke hearts
in water with lemon juice. In a separate pan, brown zucchini in a small

amount of butter. When the chicken and mushrooms have browned, add artichoke hearts, zucchini, shallots, rosemary, olives, and wine. Reduce the wine and add demiglace. Simmer for 5 minutes. Serve surrounding a mound of rice pilaf.

June's Chicken-Artichoke Casserole

Serves 12

1 tablespoon salt
½ teaspoon pepper
1 teaspoon paprika
2 3-pound fryers, cut up
¾ cup butter
½ pound mushrooms, cut large

4 tablespoons flour
1⅓ cups chicken bouillon
6 tablespoons sherry
2 12–15-ounce cans artichoke
    hearts

Salt, pepper, and paprika chicken. Brown in ½ cup of the butter and put in casserole. Sauté mushrooms in remaining butter for 5 minutes. Sprinkle flour over them and stir in chicken bouillon and sherry. Arrange artichokes between chicken pieces. Pour mushroom-sherry sauce over and bake in a 375° oven for 40 minutes.

Chicken Jardinière

Serves 10

2 large broiler-fryers, quartered
¼ cup vegetable oil
1 clove garlic, minced
1 teaspoon salt
⅛ teaspoon pepper
2 cups chopped celery
3 carrots, chipped

2 medium onions, sliced
1 pound mushrooms, sliced
1 15-ounce can tomato sauce
½ cup water
⅓ cup sherry or dry white wine
¼ teaspoon ground marjoram

Brown chicken in oil with garlic. Sprinkle with salt and pepper; place in a casserole. In the same skillet, brown celery, carrots, onions, and mushrooms. Pour off fat. Add tomato sauce, water, wine, and marjoram. Simmer 10 minutes. Pour over chicken. Cover and bake in a 350° oven 40–45 minutes.

Meat Cutting for the Beginner

In meal planning, one of the most important matters at hand is how to feed the most people for the least money. In buying meat, especially, the solution to this problem is to buy from the wholesaler in quantity. Wholesalers are generally honest, but to make you feel better, fresh meat is moist and light to medium red in color, while old meat is drier and dark red. Check yours when you buy. The larger the portion of a cow that is purchased, the less the price per pound. It is possible, of course, to buy sections trimmed of fat and bone and ready to be cut up and prepared; but the meat marketeer insists upon being rewarded for his efforts in a much higher price per pound for this meat. The key, then, is for our group to develop self-sufficiency in meat preparation so that we can purchase, for example, an entire hind of beef (see chart) and cut it into reasonable parts.

¶ At this point, to prevent any unnecessary panic at the thought of confronting the rear half of a cow and attempting to cut it into the appropriate parts for our dinner table, I should relate my limited personal experience to you. I recently graduated from college with a psychology degree, only to find that the Great Society no longer places much value upon these ornate pieces of paper. I then stumbled into meat cutting with the same amount of awe (grace?) as Alice falling through a hole in the earth in pursuit of the White Rabbit.

¶ I had visions of meat cutters as huge, bullish men, with a great deal of hair on their arms and none on their heads. I pictured a cow as a formidable foe who would be completely oblivious to reason. After about one month of practice, I now feel quite confident in cutting up the majority of an animal without professional assistance. A chart and common sense are invaluable tools. You will quickly see that cuts of meat are not artificially devised by man, but are (in most cases) natural divisions of muscle groups. (All red meat is muscle fiber.) There are, then, lines, usually thin layers of fat, separating the various cuts in many sections. The round is the best example of this. Many of the best roasts come from this section. They are clearly separated and may almost be pulled apart with a little luck.

¶ After discovering that you are not lucky at all, the best procedure is to separate the round section from the loin. The division runs from the base of the tail down through the hip joint (put that in your pipe and smoke it).

Then hang the round from a strong spike or hook by the muscle on the shank (ankle). (See chart.) Cut just below the knee cap (chart) and on down along the thigh bone (a natural seam serves as a guide on the inside of the leg) to the end of the round that was separated from the loin. You have just removed something closely resembling the top sirloin. This leaves the top round, bottom round, and eye round, which are separated en masse from the thigh bone in the same way that the top sirloin was. Then separate them on a table, following seams and the chart closely. You may discover that the original attempt at luck was more helpful than these instructions, but it is almost impossible to relate these things verbally. You will find it easier with practice than it appears from the B.S. that I just handed you.

¶ The next part of the animal, the loin, consists mainly of steaks, which are merely sliced off in the desired thickness. Two or three sharp boning knives of varying sizes are necessary for meat cutting, and the bones in the steaks require a meat saw. All of these and a steel (used to sharpen knives with flat strokes parallel to the surface of the steel) may be purchased in a restaurant supply store.

¶ The rear (hind) of the animal, then, contains the round (roasts—top sirloin, top round, bottom round, and eye round) and the loin (steaks— sirloin, porterhouse, T-bone, club). The front half of the animal contains other roasts (including two of the cheapest, pound for pound—chuck and brisket), but the rib cage makes cutting more complex (and there is more bone waste).

¶ No part of the animal need be wasted. Any small pieces of meat that cling to the bones after major cuts are removed may be cut up and ground for hamburger or added to stews or soups. Large pieces of fat may be hung by string from a tree branch and are greatly appreciated by wild birds in the winter. Fat may also be wrapped around roasts to seal in juices or boiled down into donut or frying grease. The skin is useful for durable clothing if one is willing to put forth a lot of effort for a small but worthwhile garment. The skin should first be scraped of all fat and tendons, then soaked in water and wood ashes for about 2 weeks to loosen the hair. The hair then must be scraped off by hand (with any convenient sharp object) and the skin soaked in alum or Krome-tan for varying amounts of time, depending upon what kind of skin you want. The Whole Earth Catalog lists sources for pamphlets and detailed instructions in this strenuous art. The work then begins, as skin must be rubbed by hand over a sharp piece of metal for a considerable number of hours (that may be stretched over a considerable number of

BEEF

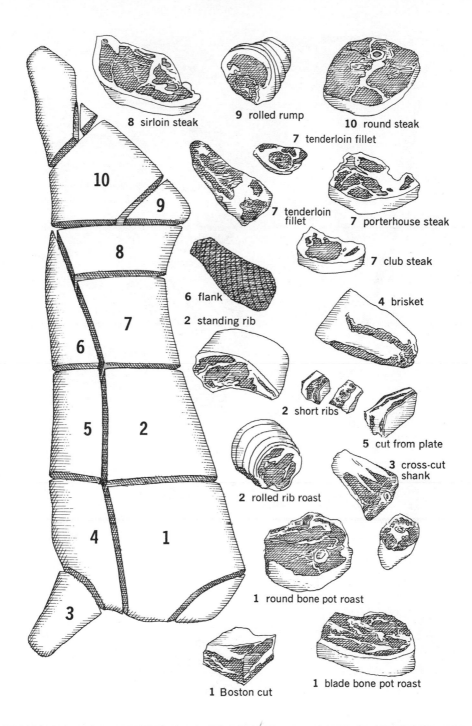

8 sirloin steak 9 rolled rump 10 round steak
7 tenderloin fillet
7 tenderloin fillet 7 porterhouse steak
7 club steak
6 flank 4 brisket
2 standing rib
2 short ribs
5 cut from plate
3 cross-cut shank
2 rolled rib roast
1 round bone pot roast
1 Boston cut 1 blade bone pot roast

VEAL

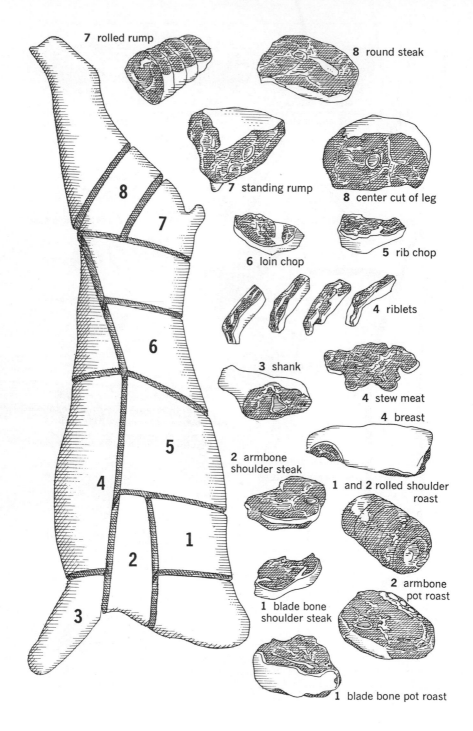

7 rolled rump

8 round steak

7 standing rump

8 center cut of leg

6 loin chop

5 rib chop

4 riblets

3 shank

4 stew meat

4 breast

2 armbone shoulder steak

1 and **2** rolled shoulder roast

1 blade bone shoulder steak

2 armbone pot roast

1 blade bone pot roast

PORK

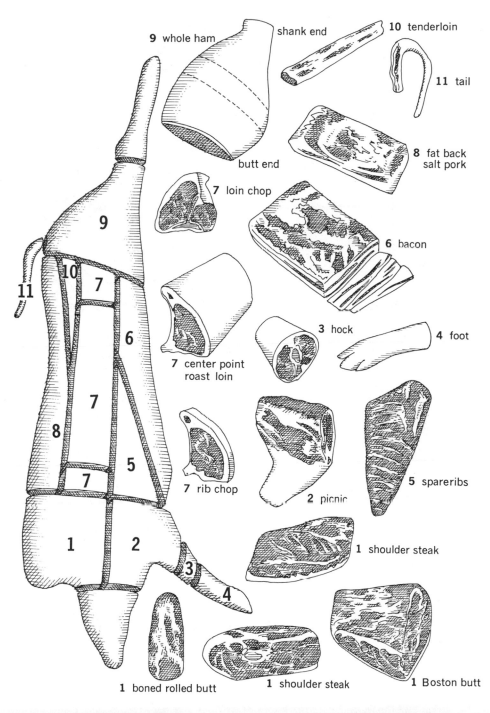

9 whole ham
shank end
10 tenderloin
butt end
11 tail
8 fat back salt pork
7 loin chop
6 bacon
7 center point roast loin
3 hock
4 foot
7 rib chop
5 spareribs
2 picnic
1 shoulder steak
1 boned rolled butt
1 shoulder steak
1 Boston butt

LAMB

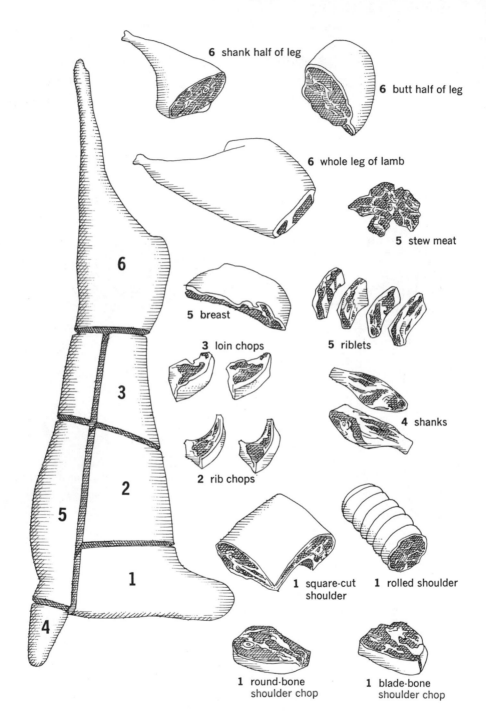

6 shank half of leg

6 butt half of leg

6 whole leg of lamb

5 stew meat

6

5 breast

3 loin chops

5 riblets

2 rib chops

4 shanks

5

2

1

4

1 square-cut shoulder

1 rolled shoulder

1 round-bone shoulder chop

1 blade-bone shoulder chop

days). I can tell you from personal experience that you will earn every square inch of leather that you make.

¶ In the event that you decide to get into steaks for special occasions, I'll try to explain the different cuts as well as I can. The steaks come from the loin portion of the animal. The flank should first be removed (see chart), and the rest is all steak. (All of these cuts should be done flat on a table or block.) The sirloin begins at the base of the tail and runs forward to the 7th disk in the spine. The next section is porterhouse. This has a large filet mignon, a tender round piece of meat that is very expensive if purchased by the pound separately. The next steak, the T-bone, is determined by meat cutters to be where the fillet is smaller (it tapers off) so it is no longer large enough to be used separately. The last section is the club steak. It goes forward to and includes the first rib. This is the end of the loin. The 2nd rib is in the rib roast section (2nd to 8th ribs) and from the 8th rib forward is chuck roast.

¶ I have explained the basic parts of a cow, but this pattern is fairly universal. Venison (deer meat) falls into basically the same pattern. Venison is a delicious meat, with a gamy taste all its own. It has steaks and roasts that you will develop quite a taste for. It may, however, be tougher (in the case of an older deer) than beef, but there are ways of solving this slight problem.

¶ The ultimate in self-sufficiency, though, for a commune, is the raising and slaughtering of animals (if anyone can manage to get it together enough to slaughter an animal . . . I suppose that I could if it were really necessary). Meat should be cut up and frozen within 1 day in warm weather, although it will keep about a week if the temperature is between 32° and 40°. The cuts should be wrapped in heavy wax paper or plastic bags for freezing. This, the raising and slaughtering of animals, combined with limited hunting and eating of wild animals, and the cultivation of a vegetable garden, is a means with which to achieve a remarkable degree of self-sufficiency. It is something to think about . . . and to do.

3–4-DAY TURKEY FEAST
OR: How to Spend Very Little and Eat Very Well

Turkey is our feast food. We buy it on sale (even 45¢ a pound is a good price), do a real job of cooking it to perfection, lay on all the extras, like thick gravy, cranberry relish, and stuffing, and for days we feast—lunch and dinner. Surprisingly, these feast meals work out to be some of the most inexpensive meals we ever have. Out of one 24-pound turkey (costing, with fixings, about $10) we get at least 3 days of good food for at least 10 people with never a complaint about repetitious taste. Each meal is different, and each taste a new rush. Here is our 3-day turkey feast plan. (This plan is for at least 10 people—more likely 12. If you have fewer people, of course, you can make the turkey last 4 days.)

First Day

Baked Stuffed Turkey

3 large cans sliced peaches
1¼ pounds butter or margarine
2 large bags (blue) Pepperidge Farm Herb Stuffing

1 pound mushrooms, sliced
1 24-pound turkey
1 large can frozen orange juice

To make the stuffing: Drain peaches, saving juice. To 4 cups of reserved peach juice (if not enough to make 4 cups, add water or other fruit juice), add 1 pound of the butter or margarine. Cook in saucepan over low heat until butter melts. Stir to blend and pour over stuffing crumbs. Add sliced peaches and mushrooms and blend until mixed and moist. Stuff turkey, putting any extra stuffing into a buttered casserole. Put the turkey into a baking pan, and pour water into the pan until it is ½ inch deep on the bottom. Dot the turkey with butter, and place in a slow (300°) oven. Baste the turkey every 20 minutes with ¼ pound butter melted with the frozen orange juice (don't add water) and with the pan drippings, once they become mixed with the basting liquid. When the turkey begins to get brown (usually after the first basting), cover it with tin foil, and remove the foil only when basting, then put it back again. Roast until the leg pulls away easily from the body, or until the juices run clear—about 5½ hours (13–15 minutes to the pound). For a moist turkey, baste often, and take out when the dark meat is still a little pink. Serve the turkey with stuffing and:

Gravy

Remove the turkey from the roasting pan and let sit 15 minutes before carving. Skim off most of the grease, and heat the meat drippings (there should be plenty, as they mixed with the water and basting mixture during cooking) till simmering. To thicken, make a paste out of turkey stock (the neck and giblets can have been cooked in water, making a rich stock. The stock is used in the gravy, as are the neck and giblets, cut up) and 2–4 tablespoons flour. Stir into meat drippings, alternating with plain turkey stock until you have gravy the thickness you like. For quantity, add more stock. Season with salt, pepper, and garlic powder. Also try throwing in some orange juice, apple juice, or peach ice cream. Add cut up giblets and neck meat, and serve hot over turkey and/or stuffing.

Note: Make lots, as it can be used on cold turkey and stuffing in the days to come.

Second Day

Lunch: Have stuffing, with gravy on it, cranberry relish, and salad . . . it's delicious, and not so heavy as to ruin your appetite for dinner.

Dinner: Hot turkey sandwiches, or cold turkey with hot gravy, stuffing, etc. Almost a repeat of yesterday's dinner, except that somehow, everything has gotten better by sitting overnight.

Third Day

Lunch: Make lunch a communal bone-picking meal. All extra meat can be cut and picked off bones, and wings and legs can be chewed on. The purpose of this communal bone-picking is to prepare the carcass for dinner's specialty:

Turkey Soup

Place turkey carcass and all other bones that are left in a large pot, and cover with water. Add 1 bunch celery, sliced (leaves included), 5 onions (sliced), lots of parsley, oregano, basil, and 3 teaspoons salt to start (as it cooks, you'll have to add more salt, to taste). Put in pepper, poultry seasonings, some garlic powder, thyme, a little bit of rosemary, and ½ bay leaf. Cook, covered, at a slightly rolling boil for 4–5 hours, adjusting seasoning as it cooks. When it's done to your taste, remove all bones (save them; with the meat taken off the carcass, they make a good side dish for the soup), strain out all vegetables and seasonings (save them, too), and bring soup to a boil again. When boiling, throw in some large egg noodles, and cook till done. Serve with fresh bread, bones, vegetables, salad.
Note: There'll probably be enough soup left over to go a fourth day. If you don't want to eat it the next day, just freeze it, or jar it and take it to a friend . . . it's a treat for anyone.

Meats

Hungarian Noodles and Veal

Serves 10–12

Noodles:

7½ cups flour
¾ teaspoon salt
6 eggs

1½ cups milk
1½ cups water

Mix above ingredients together with a spoon until smooth. Make sure that your batter is stiff, or you'll wind up with one very large non-Hungarian noodle. You should have 1 enormous or 2 large pots of boiling water ready to drop noodles into. If you have a spaetzle machine, there's no problem— just run batter through into boiling water. If not, scoop some batter onto a tablespoon and hold over boiling water. Take another empty tablespoon in the other hand, and scoop small chunks of batter from the first spoon into the water. You'll see the noodles drop and solidify in the water. If you don't like the size, either increase or decrease to the size you want. After a couple of tablespoons, you should arrive at a uniform size—otherwise the large noodles will be soggy, and the small ones overdone. Cook until done to taste—probably about 8 minutes. This may sound involved, but once you start dropping the batter into the water and watching all those delicious little spaetzle take shape, you'll realize how easy it really is.

Veal and Sauce:

2–3 large onions, sliced
Oil
Enough veal chunks for 10–12
    people

3 beef bouillon cubes
2 cups water

Brown onions in oil in large deep pan. Add veal and brown. Mix the bouillon and water and add to veal. Simmer for 1 hour. Add the noodles and cook another 10–15 minutes. This is not the type of meal that's easily overcooked, so don't hesitate to cook longer if you think necessary. Also feel free to add more bouillon and water if too much liquid seems to be evaporating.

The noodles are easily interchangeable with any number of dishes, one of my favorites being chicken paprika. Remember; when going hunkie, don't spare the paprika, and if possible, don't use the kind that comes in a can. Too many people think of paprika as a relatively tasteless spice, which it's not. If you get a chance to come into the city often (N.Y.C., that is), drop in at one of the many Yorkville stores (from about 79th to 90th streets, east of 3rd Ave.) and pick up some fresh hot, sweet, or mild paprika. Wait'll you smell 'em!

Debby's Super-good Pork Chops and Orange Sauce

(You'll love this, all you meat eaters)

Serves 10–12

12 pork chops
Flour seasoned with salt, pepper, and garlic powder
5 cups orange juice

5 teaspoons grated orange rind
5 teaspoons white vinegar
5 or 6 teaspoons brown sugar
2 teaspoons ground ginger

Coat pork chops in seasoned flour and fry 5 minutes on each side in your *very big fry pan*. Mix together the rest of the ingredients and add to the pan. Bring to boil. Lower heat, and cook for 50 minutes, turning chops once.

American Chop Suey

Serves 10–12

2 pounds round steak, cut in thin strips
¼ cup salad oil
3 cups sliced mushrooms
3 cups diagonally sliced celery
2 cups green pepper, cut into 1-inch squares

1 cup scallions cut in 1-inch pieces
2 cans beef broth
¼ cup soy sauce
¼ cup cornstarch
1 cup water
Cooked rice

Brown beef in oil. Add vegetables, broth, and soy sauce. Cover and cook over low heat until meat is tender—about 20 minutes. Stir now and then. Blend cornstarch and water; stir into sauce. Cook, stirring, until thickened. Serve with cooked rice.

Arab (Moroccan) Tajine

All daily meals are cooked out of a tajine, which one can make or have friends make. The tajine is a glazed ceramic bowl, varying in size according to family, about the depth of a frying pan. It is necessary to have a cone-shaped ceramic top fitting the lip of the dish so that little or no steam is released in the 2–3-hour slow-cooking process.

Small amount of meat or fish	**Beans**
Oil	**Paprika and/or red pepper**
Vegetables	

The Arab diet is largely a vegetable-bean one, almost always centering around a small piece of lamb or camel meat or fish. The meat is placed first in the tajine dish with a small amount of oil and left to cook over low heat or coals while the vegetables are being cut and cleaned. It is necessary, traditionally, to add first a small or large amount of chopped tomatoes and onions to simmer with the meat. Then, whatever vegetable is handy is added. On poor days, I've eaten largely potato and/or bean tajines. In general, though, pears, leeks, squashes, carrots, and any other fruits or vegetables are mixed together with a mild paprika to a hot pepper spicing (depending on taste) and left covered to cook in their own juices and meat for 2 to 3 hours. The tajine is then taken off the heat and left, covered, to sit for about 20 minutes to cool, for the Arabs eat the dish with their right hand and the help of a heavy pancakelike bread which acts as a marker and spoon. The tajine is eaten from the outside toward the center, and the meat is divided equally among the eaters and eaten last.

Polish Sausage and Lentils

Serves 10–12

2 cup lentils, rinsed	**4 pounds kielbasa**
Salt	**2 teaspoons sugar**
4 tablespoons vegetable oil	**1 teaspoon pepper**
4 medium onions, chopped	**2 bay leaves**
6 cloves garlic, crushed	
2 medium cans tomatoes, drained and chopped	

Put rinsed lentils in a large saucepan with salted water to cover. Bring to a boil, cover, and cook over low heat until tender but still holding their shape

—about 20 minutes. Drain and reserve cooking liquid.

Heat vegetable oil in a flameproof casserole. Stir in onions and garlic and cook until tender. Mix in tomatoes and cook over moderate heat until almost all the liquid has evaporated. Peel the casings from the kielbasa and cut into slices ½ inch thick. Toss sausage with tomato mixture. Add lentils, sugar, pepper, bay leaves, and salt to taste. Stir in a little of the lentil liquid and bake mixture for 30 minutes in a 350° oven. Add more liquid if the mixture looks dry during baking.

Sweet and Sour Pork for 8–12

4 eggs
1 teaspoon salt
Freshly ground pepper to taste
6 tablespoons flour
3 pounds pork, cut into ½-inch cubes
Oil
1½ cups chicken broth

6 large green peppers, sliced
2 cans diced pineapple (drain, reserving juice)
6 tablespoons cornstarch
4 tablespoons soy sauce
1½ cups pineapple juice
1½ cups sugar
6 tablespoons ketchup

Combine eggs, salt, pepper, and flour. Dip pork and fry in oil till batter is golden brown. Remove and place in warm oven.

In wok or skillet in 2 tablespoons hot oil, add 1 cup of the broth, green peppers, and pineapple. Cook, covered, for 10 minutes. Mix remaining ingredients and add to wok. Bring to boil till thickened. Add pork and serve over rice.

Greek Lamb

Serves 12

4 tablespoons olive oil
4 pounds lamb, cut in 1½-inch cubes
6 small onions, finely chopped
Chopped garlic to taste
2 cups canned tomatoes, or 6 fresh tomatoes, chopped

2 cups beef broth
3 teaspoons salt
½ teaspoon freshly ground pepper
1½ pounds green beans, sliced lengthwise
½ teaspoon thyme

Heat oil in heavy skillet; brown lamb on all sides. Add onions and garlic to taste; cook 5 minutes, stirring frequently. Add tomatoes, broth, salt, and pepper. Bring to boil, cover, and simmer till lamb is tender—about 1½ hours. Add beans and thyme and cook 20 minutes longer.

Gals! Why beg off when hubby calls to announce he's bringing home thirteen Satanists for dinner? Why, you might as well tattoo the word "ungroovy" across your forehead!
How to cope? Simple! Just start preparing—

Roast Duck à la Aleister Crowley

First, debone duck by breaking its back while alive. You'll know when you're done by the snap—similar to the more familiar sound of breaking chicken spine—and by the groovy rush you'll feel.
Simultaneously slaughter camel and store in cold, dark place.
Stuff uncooked duck with opiated chicken hearts (see page 47).
Lightly beat camel humps with *black* wall telephone receiver while chanting with party on the other end of the phone. Season with 2 tablespoons MSG, 1 tablespoon THC, 1 pinch sweet basil, and cocaine to taste.
Before serving, harangue the meat for 15 minutes. Pretend to be attacking with meat cleaver and heap abuse liberally on wing portions. Pound again until tender and repentant. Test with toothpick.

> LITTLE ROCK, ARKANSAS—Housewives are complaining of the low quality of the fresh oregano here. Much of it has been found to be cut with marijuana and some of it is little else.
> "It's gettin' ridiculous, fer crying out loud," complained Mrs. Yvonne DeColombo, "I've ruined two chickens this week. Nobody inna family likes it with that rope taste to it."

Jim and Jean's Smash

Let's say you've got a refrigeratorful of leftovers, then you can start making smash. Nothing short of a stove fire can ruin it . . . and the variables are infinite.

How to do it, our way:

The quantity will vary with the size of the family, so we won't bother with amounts. Use your own judgment.
Cook up some brown rice or pasta until nearly done. Fry ground beef,

drain off fat. Add any leftovers of sausage, bacon, chicken, salami, turkey, lamb. Onions can be sautéed along with the meat. Steam those raw vegetables that take a long time to cook, like carrots and celery, until they are not quite done. Don't forget to undercook the pasta or rice.

Put the cooked meat, cooked vegetables, and rice or pasta in a big pot or turkey pan and then add:

Parsley
Spinach
Kale—really great and healthy
Peas
Corn—good taste and health, and
   looks good
Anything else you want to
   experiment with

Black olives
Wild mushrooms
Tomatoes

Then add 2 large cans whole tomatoes, including the juice, and 1 or 2 small cans of tomato sauce. Mix with herbs and salt and pepper as you like them. Cover tightly and cook under low heat on top of stove for about 30 minutes. Or put in oven (350°) for about 30 minutes. Oven is best if you have one. About 10 minutes before done, add some lightly scrambled eggs and minced cheese, mix, and finish cooking.

Gloria's Quick, Easy, Delicious Beef Stroganoff

Serves 10

4 pounds round steak, cut into
   chunks ⅛ inch thick, or lean
   ground beef
Oil
4 tablespoons flour

4 packages onion soup mix
4 cups sour cream
2 6-ounce cans mushrooms, with
   liquid and enough water to
   make 4 cups

Quickly brown meat in oil. Set aside. Add flour to drippings; brown. Add mushroom liquid and soup mix, heating to a boil. Add sour cream, meat, and mushrooms. Serve over egg noodles or rice.

Joe's San Francisco Special

Serves 10–12

1 cup olive oil
¾ cup grated or chopped onions
6 cloves garlic, minced
3 pounds ground beef

3 cups cooked chopped spinach
Oregano, salt, and cumin to taste
12 eggs, lightly beaten

Heat oil, onion, garlic. Add beef, spinach, and seasonings. Cook slowly, thoroughly. Just before serving, add eggs. Cook till eggs are set, stirring. You may also add sautéed mushrooms.

June's Perfect Pot Roast

Serves 12

Select a boneless cut of rump, bottom round, rolled chuck, or beef brisket, figuring about 3 servings to the pound.

4–5 pounds beef
½ cup consommé, red wine,
  vegetable stock, or water
1 onion, sliced
Salt and pepper to taste

1 clove garlic and/or herbs such as
  thyme, rosemary, marjoram, or
  bouquet garni for beef
1½ tablespoons flour (optional)

In large heavy kettle or Dutch oven over medium heat, brown meat well on all sides in its own fat. (If there is not enough fat on the outside of the meat to brown well, add 1–2 tablespoons oil.) Remove meat and pour off fat. Put a trivet or crumpled piece of foil in kettle and set meat on it. Add liquid and onions, cover tightly, and simmer 1 hour. Set a cutting board in a jellyroll pan or other shallow pan with sides. Remove meat to cutting board in pan and cool 15–20 minutes. With a sharp knife, cut meat across grain in serving-sized pieces about ¼ inch thick. Remove trivet or foil, put meat back in kettle, and sprinkle each layer lightly with salt and pepper. Add garlic and sprinkle with herbs, if desired. Pour drippings in jellyroll pan into kettle with meat. Cover and simmer until fork-tender—1½–2 hours. Spoon a little liquid from bottom of kettle over top of meat 2 or 3 times during cooking. Broth may be thickened with flour if desired. Vegetables may be added to meat for last hour of cooking, if desired.

Marc's Steak and Peppers

Serves 12

7 pounds round steak, cut into
    strips
½ cup oil
Garlic salt, salt, and pepper to
    taste
6 green peppers, cut into strips

6 onions, sliced
Sliced celery (optional)
3 cups beef broth
1 pound mushrooms, sliced
½ cup cornstarch, mixed
    with 1 cup cold water

Brown strips of beef in oil; set aside, sprinkling cooked beef with garlic salt, salt, and pepper. In remaining oil, brown peppers, onions, celery. Add beef broth, mushrooms, and simmer for 45 minutes, adding beef strips at end. Thicken gravy with cornstarch-water mixture, and pour on top of cooked rice.

Marc's Shish Kebabs

Serves 12

½ cup salad oil
2 teaspoons salt
1 teaspoon pepper
1 cup cider vinegar
1 clove garlic, chopped fine
4 pounds boned shoulder of lamb,
    cut in 1-inch cubes

4 firm tomatoes, sliced ½ inch
    thick
4 large onions, sliced
4 large green peppers, cut in 1-inch
    squares
1 pound mushrooms
24 pineapple chunks

Combine all seasonings and pour over meat and vegetables. Let marinate in refrigerator overnight. String on skewers and broil until done. Serve with rice or rice pilaf.

June's Eggplant and Ground Beef Casserole

Serves 12

2 large onions, cut into small pieces
1 cup butter
2 pounds ground beef
1 cup tomato sauce

1 cup water
2 teaspoons salt
Pepper to taste
2 medium eggplants, sliced

Sauté onion pieces in butter, add ground beef, and cook until brown. Combine tomato sauce and water, salt and pepper, and pour over meat mixture. Bring to boil and cook for 5 minutes. Remove from fire, lift meat from sauce with perforated spoon. Slice eggplant and brown in remaining drippings. Place a layer of eggplant in 3-quart casserole. Then a layer of meat, repeating, ending with meat. Pour sauce over all. Bake, uncovered, in 350° oven for 30 minutes.

Johnnie Nacilli

Serves 16–20

1 cup chopped onions
1 cup chopped celery
1 cup chopped green peppers
3 cups sliced stuffed olives
3 cups sliced mushrooms
Butter
2 pounds ground beef

2 cloves garlic, minced
36 ounces wide egg noodles
2 cans tomato soup
2 cans tomato sauce
2 cans tomato paste
1 cup grated cheese

Sauté onions, celery, peppers, olives, and mushrooms in butter. Brown beef with garlic. Mix with cooked egg noodles and tomato soup, sauce, and paste. Top with grated cheese and bake in a moderate oven till brown.

Fast for Feast

In May 1970, I decided to take mescaline for the first time in about a year; the reason mainly being that I just wasn't feeling well, that is to say mentally, and only somewhat physically. I've always looked upon mescaline and peyote much in the same way as the American Indians do—as a sacrament being good medicine for the body and soul. It would take a volume of writing in itself to explain and describe what previous experiences had brought me to this way of seeing, but at this point, let it suffice to say that I believe with all my heart and soul that what I've gleaned from all this has been beneficial.

¶ In the midst of the aforementioned mescaline experience while my attention was focused internally, I saw very plainly that I was "clogged" up inside my body. My mental sphere was black and murky. I detected a very subtle stenchy odor emanating from the pit of my stomach. Only on rare occasion during normal consciousness did I have but a subtle sense of this feeling, only now it became more and more intense, and I became more and more nauseated. I began to realize what I had suspected for quite some time during the "normal" state, but never to such a great extent. I saw that I was unable to recover a once very beautiful and pure feeling that I had about eight years ago, during which time I ate only fruits and vegetables. I say dark heavy layers of consciousness that were the manifestations of different foods that I was eating since I stayed away from a vegetarian diet. Mind you, I didn't see this as a vague or flimsy idea, but felt it in great intensity.

¶ I began to vomit up a brown stenchy liquid, sort of a bile color. I felt a tremendous sense of relief and clarity returning with each upheaval. This continued for about an hour and I will spare you, the reader, from further gory details. But I can safely say that as I became cognizant of my inner being, I saw that this childlike purity that I was attempting to recover was lost to me, mainly because of a gross condition created by the food I had ingested over the years. As I spewed forth these poisons it became clearer to me that the dead flesh of cows, birds, and fish had left a residue within my body that had slowly built up over the years, and had created a veritable cesspool; a breeding ground for disease. No wonder that my thinking was messed up.

¶ This foul condition sent forth a toxic feeling throughout my body and mind, affecting me in every way. I then truly realized what I had read in the Bhagavad-Gita, the bible of India. The vibrations emanating from food most certainly determine states of consciousness to a tremendous extent. I am well aware of my point of view in relation to the normal concepts on health and well-being, and I know that this is not ordinary. I feel vibrant feelings are attainable only through clean and wholesome living. This may not be your way of seeing it, but I am certain that it is mine. I decided to follow this great healing that I was going through with a long fast, which I will describe briefly.

¶ I knew that I was going to return to a vegetarian diet, once and for all. In order to do this, I felt that my body should be purged of poison as much as possible. I had fasted in the past, sometimes 3 or 4 days, but never more. I decided that I would fast at least a week, and maybe more if necessary. I would let my intuitions guide me on the length of time.

¶ I purchased a gallon of distilled water, which was the only substance that I would ingest. In the past I had followed Arnold Ehret's guidance through his book, *Rational Fasting*. The whole purpose of a true fast is to stop digestion completely, giving all the body energy a chance to work on elimination. Even pure stream water has minerals in it, causing a subtle form of digestion, whereas distilled water contains nothing. It's kind of a "liquid air" so to speak, which flushes out the digestive system.

¶ The first 2 or 3 days of the fast are supposed to be the most difficult, but, for me, because of the momentum that I had gathered, they were quite easy. Normally, when one stops the everyday habit of eating, so-called hunger pains follow. What I think actually occurs is pain caused by the beginnings of toxic elimination. Once this is passed, usually no later than the 3rd day, there is a great feeling of peace. In my case I found that it was necessary to rest whenever I felt the need, which would occur at any given time of day. Sometimes I would get very dizzy and felt that I was "blacking out." I would then rest or sleep for a while, and then find

myself with a fresh surge of energy. I would work on my writings and everyday chores with heightened intensity and enthusiasm. I would drink water to appease any glimmering of hunger that I felt, and take half-mile walks to exercise my body. My heartbeat became very soft and much slower. I felt an enduring peace, and knew that this was truly one of the ancient methods toward self-realization.

¶ What really gets you when you fast is the tremendous amount of time you have. So much time is spent in our oral pleasure-oriented culture in cooking food, going and coming to eat, smoking, drinking, getting high, talking, etc. After a while all of this stopped, and here I was, like a quiet and peaceful lake, with a vast fountain of energy to draw upon whenever I needed it. I lost about a pound and a half each day, and this was most welcome. I decided to go to 9 days. This was long enough, only because of certain business and travel commitments that I had. I knew well of black comedian Dick Gregory's 40-day fast. He has evolved from a vegetarian up to pure fruits, nothing but foods growing above the ground. He runs 6 miles every morning, and really looks like a man in his early twenties, and he is more than twice that.

¶ The general word on fasting is that you shouldn't go too long at first, mainly because the body can overeliminate, causing great sickness. Some people have been known to die in their own stench. Nonetheless, I feel that intuition or instinct can best tell you when to stop. A year has passed since, and I'm happily a vegetarian again. All told, I've fasted about 16 more days since then, mostly 2 or 3 days at a time. Ehret calls fasting "nature's operating table" and I go along with it all the way. It's also the quickest and most time-honored way of getting and staying high that I know of. If you're hung up, fed up, whatever—fasting and natural eating can give you rebirth.

Betsye's Salad Game

Spinach
Bananas
Nuts
Mushrooms
Cucumbers
Onions

Dressing:

Lime juice
Good-tasting oil
Salt and pepper
Any spices you think of

Combine all or some of the above.

OR:

Spinach
Cucumbers
Onion
Pieces of bacon
Plain croutons
All fried in garlic and bacon
   grease
Mushrooms fried in bacon grease
Capers
Avocado
Artichokes
Tomato

Dressing:

Good-tasting oil
Cider vinegar
Garlic
Dill
Curry
Salt and pepper

Mix and match. Experiment. Blend. Eat.

Some Salad Dressings:

Oil and Vinegar

Mix and serve over lettuce, tomato, etc.:

2 tablespoons ketchup
½ teaspoon mustard
1 tablespoon Worcestershire sauce
1½–2 teaspoons garlic powder
♀ teaspoon salt

¼ teaspoon pepper
½ teaspoon sugar or honey
Dash of oregano
⅔ cup oil
¾ cup wine or white vinegar

Note: If you have dregs of ketchup in a bottle that you can't get out, just mix the dressing in the bottle, omitting the ketchup, as the ketchup in the bottle takes care of it. It cleans out the bottles, which, by the way, make attractive salad dressing servers.

Apple Cider Dressing

This dressing, being very sweet, is great over salads which include melon, apple, cabbage, peas, green beans, in addition to the regular lettuce and tomato.

Blend thoroughly:

½ cup cider vinegar
¾ cup sugar
1 teaspoon dry mustard

1 teaspoon salt
½–1 onion, minced
1 cup oil

Alan's Salad Dressing

Egg yolk, lightly beaten
½ teaspoon mustard
Oil

Vinegar
Salt and pepper
Chervil

Blend egg yolk and mustard. Add oil gradually so texture is smooth and thick, but not as thick as mayonnaise. Add vinegar, salt, pepper, and chervil to taste.

Mayonnaise

Makes 1 quart

½ tablespoon mustard
2 egg yolks
Oil

Salt and pepper
Wine vinegar

With a whisk, beat mustard into egg yolks. Slowly add oil so you keep a constant texture. Soon, as more oil gets in, it will begin to thicken. Do not overbeat, or else it will become rubbery. When you have about 1 quart, add salt and pepper to taste. Then add a little bit of vinegar and watch the mayonnaise turn white.

Joan's Caesar Salad

Serves 10–12

Pour enough olive oil to coat 2 heads of romaine lettuce into a salad bowl. Crush 3 or 4 cloves of garlic in the oil. Then put leaf-sized pieces of romaine in oil and toss until each piece is lightly coated. In a small bowl, chop 3 soft-boiled eggs with about 2 tablespoons Worcestershire sauce, and toss into salad. Add salt and juice from about 3 lemons to taste. Sprinkle with Parmesan cheese, add home-made croutons, give one last toss, and serve. Optional: Anchovies.

Joan's Tabbuleh Salad

Serves 10–12

2 cups boiling water	2 cups finely chopped parsley
1 cup uncooked bulgur	3 tomatoes, diced
2 cubes vegetable or chicken bouillon	⅓ cup lemon juice
	⅓ cup salad oil
½ cup finely chopped fresh mint, or 2 tablespoons dried mint	Salt, pepper, and garlic powder to taste
4 scallions, chopped	Romaine or grape leaves

Pour boiling water over bulgur and bouillon cubes. Stir and let stand 1–2 hours, or until light and fluffy. Add mint, scallions, parsley, and tomatoes. Beat lemon juice, oil, and salt and pepper and garlic powder together, and pour over bulgur mixture. Toss lightly and chill. To serve, place Tabbuleh in a mound in the center of a platter surrounded with romaine or grape leaves. Scoop salad onto leaves and eat, holding between 3 fingers.

Billie's Mayonnaise at Home (Garlicky)

Makes ½ pint

2 cloves garlic
1 teaspoon salt
1 egg yolk

½ teaspoon dry mustard
3 tablespoons lemon juice
1 cup olive oil

Peel and crush the garlic. Make a paste with garlic, salt, beaten egg yolk, mustard, and 1 tablespoon of the lemon juice. Adding it 1 teaspoon at a time, beat in ½ cup olive oil (no substitutes). Add slowly and alternately another ½ cup olive oil and 2 tablespoons lemon juice (bit by bit). Adding the oil very slowly is the most necessary thing and then beating thoroughly after each addition. This makes ½ pint of spicy, garlicky mayonnaise. Don't try to do it with a blender. It beats in too much air and the mayonnaise never thickens. We eat it on a salad of raw mushrooms and raw spinach, when we can get both.

Rachel's Diet Salads and Salad Dressings

Fruit Salad:

Pears
Apples
Bananas

Cantaloupe
Nuts
Currants or raisins

Pour juice of fresh orange over this and mix.

Variations: Sprinkle granola over fruit and/or add yogurt, apple juice, or a mixture of apple, lemon, and orange juices.

Vegetable Salad:
Cauliflower
Iceburg lettuce
Peas
Raisins

Nuts
Apples
Pears
Cantaloupe

Dressing:

Juice of an orange
Some apple juice

Some lemon juice (less than other juices) to taste

Toni's Refreshing 4-minute Salad

1½ cups fresh alfalfa sprouts
1 large cucumber, cut in half lengthwise and thinly (translucently) sliced
3 or 4 radishes, sliced very thin

1 box fresh, sweet blueberries
6–8 slices Munster cheese, torn into pieces the diameter of the radishes

Toss in a bowl and serve. It's good with rice and fish or chicken. No dressing or seasoning needed: nothing dominates.

Salad with Sour Cream

Serves 10

Slice 2 large sweet onions and 4 unpeeled cucumbers. In a bowl, mix the following dressing:

2 cups sour or cultured cream
4 tablespoons lemon or lime juice
½ teaspoon freshly ground pepper
2 teaspoons fresh or dried dill leaves

2 teaspoons chopped parsley
Salt

Line a bowl with lettuce or very young spinach. Next, place a layer of cucumber, then a layer of onion rings, then some dressing. Repeat this process. Keep in refrigerator at least 1 hour. Serve with dark bread.

Variations: Pickled gherkins replace cucumbers. Finely ground dill seed instead of fresh dill. Or caraway seeds, even.

Orange Salad for 20

16 large navel oranges
⅔ cup salad oil
¼ cup wine or cider vinegar
1 teaspoon salt

½ teaspoon freshly ground pepper
1 clove garlic, crushed
1 teaspoon oregano
Fresh mint leaves

Peel and section oranges. Place in a bowl and chill. Beat together oil, vinegar, salt, pepper, and garlic. Chill for 1 hour. Before serving, sprinkle oregano over oranges, and a little pepper. Remove garlic from dressing and pour over oranges; garnish with mint.

SPROUTS

Sprouts are great. You can eat them raw, in sandwiches, in soups, in salads, in eggs, in rice, as snacks—with anything. Sprouting is easy, and is one of the quickest and cheapest ways to have a steady supply of fresh greens throughout the year. While any seed that hasn't been chemically treated can be sprouted and eaten, those most commonly used are mung beans, alfalfa, soy beans, and wheat berries. Not only do all of these beans sprout easily, but they are also incredible sources of protein.

¶ If you're really into a lot of sprouting, the best thing for you to get is probably a commercial sprouter. The plastic ones are best, and although expensive (about $12), they seem to be worth it, as you can sprout many seeds at a time in plastic layers suspended over water. The seeds won't rot, nor will you be spending any time changing water. A much easier and simpler method than most home-sprouting techniques, the commercial sprouter is a useful tool.

¶ If, however, you don't have or don't want to get a sprouter, there are many ways of sprouting seeds. One way is to sprout seeds between layers of moist paper towels or tea towels. Simply place the seeds to be sprouted between the towels, and set the whole thing in a dish with water. Be sure to change the water—and, if you like, the towels—daily. Another way is to place the seeds in a large jar with water covering them. Cover the jar with cheesecloth or netting held in place with a rubber band, and set aside in a warm spot. Change the water 1 or 2 times daily by simply pouring the water out through the cheesecloth and adding new water the same way. Finally, a very primitive method may be used to sprout most seeds, but especially mung beans. Place the bean in a shallow pan, and cover with water. Change the water daily, and watch carefully for signs of rotting, a condition that occurs easily with this method.

¶ Most sprouts can be eaten as soon as they're about 1 inch long; they can also be allowed to grow until they are 3–4 inches long. They should be eaten as soon as they are ready, as they rot easily. Sprouts can be kept in the refrigerator for 2–3 days (be sure to drain the water off first, and to keep them in an airtight container), but, like most foods, lose their nutritive value the longer they are kept.

Jon's Bean Sprout Salad

Serves 10–12

¾ cup oil
6 tablespoons vinegar
6 tablespoons tamari
1½ teaspoons salt
1½ teaspoons black pepper
¾ cup chopped scallions

¾ cup chopped pimiento
6 tablespoons ground sesame seeds
3 cloves garlic, minced
6 cups fresh mung or alfalfa
    sprouts

Mix all ingredients but sprouts together and pour over sprouts. Chill 1 hour then serve. Delicious.

Save the Kids

I've never been much of a fanatic, food or otherwise, but when I gave birth to a baby, I was pretty certain that I didn't want to be responsible for polluting a perfect, brand-clean body with plastic formula or baby foods. The feeding program that I embarked on became one based on concern for good health, tempered by my reluctance to become fanatical, and forced into flexibility by a rather strong-willed Aries baby. It's easy to prepare healthy, quick meals for your baby. Just take it slow, don't be afraid to improvise, and try always to follow your baby's leads as to his likes and dislikes.

¶ Milk: I decided to breast-feed, although, today, even that decision may not be the best for a baby's health, in that most mother's milk contains amounts of DDT substantially higher than that found in cow's milk. I guess it just comes down to personal philosophy. In my case, it came down to blind faith: I believed that the immunities which I would be giving our baby in the first few months of life by feeding him breast milk would override the possible introduction of DDT into his system . . . somehow, I figured, one cancels the other out (our baby was breast-fed for 4½ months).

¶ If your baby is to be breast-fed, the mother should be sure to eat twice the amount of foods that supply essential vitamins and nutrients, especially vitamins C, D, and B. Plenty of protein, plenty of liquids: milk (or dried bone meal) for calcium, beer to build up her milk supply, and perhaps some brandy or scotch to pacify an unhappy, sleepless, or plain fussy infant (a little bit of anything like that won't hurt, but don't overdo).

¶ Any drug, stimulant, or strong food that the mother takes into her body will affect the nursing baby, too. My personal prejudice rules against a nursing mother smoking cigarettes, but finds nothing wrong with marijuana or hash. LSD I'm not sure about, but if the mother wants to take it, and doesn't want the baby to trip, too, she shouldn't breast-feed the baby from the time she ingests it until 3 days after she has tripped. By that time it should be pretty much out of her system, and shouldn't affect the baby. Chocolate, I've heard, makes mother's milk taste bitter, and eating anything from the cabbage family might give the baby gas. But the mother should try what she will: it'll probably be different with each mother-baby team.

¶ Finally, if she or the baby doesn't enjoy breast-feeding, or doesn't want to breast-feed, that's cool, too. No reason to feel unmotherly, unhip, or unhappy. Any well-fed, well-cuddled, well-loved baby is usually happy, no matter where the milk is coming from . . . and besides, fathers should be able to feel just as much a part of the miracle of feeding and caring for a brand-new growing person as the mothers do.

¶ So, if the mother decides not to breast-feed, or stops breast-feeding early, or wants to supplement breast-feeding with other milk, there are plenty of healthful foods that can be fed to an infant. For a basic formula recipe, consult Dr. Spock's section on formulas, or check with your pediatrician or health clinic. Once your baby reaches an age when formula isn't necessary (again, consult Dr. Spock, your doctor, or your own common sense), you can choose from a wide variety of milk or milk substitutes.

¶ All health food stores and many grocery stores sell powdered soy milk, which, when mixed with water, provides almost all of the essential nutrients found in cow's milk without the extra fats and antibiotics which most dairies find it necessary to add. To ensure a proper amount of calcium, however, a baby being fed soy milk should be given supplements of bone meal. Health food stores also carry goat's milk, either powdered or fresh. Goat's milk, it is said, is the animal milk which most closely resembles mother's milk. It is less likely than cow's milk to cause indigestion or diarrhea, and contains 10 times the amount of iron found in cow's milk. Finally, if you feed your baby cow's milk, you may be assured of getting a heathful, pretty uncontaminated variety by buying fresh farm milk. Farm milk is unhomogenized, and often unpasteurized, but as it's taken from cows who are regularly tested for TB and other diseases, it's pretty healthy.

¶ Other liquid foods that your baby receives early in life are water and juices. Until your baby reaches the age of 3 months, the water you give him/her to drink, and the water used in food preparation should be sterilized. To make the water more appealing (a lot of babies don't like water), try adding 1 teaspoon of sugar or honey per 8 ounces of water.

¶ Your baby will be getting a lot of energy and vitamin C from the juices you give him/her . . . and you don't have to get stuck feeding your baby small cans of special baby juices. Any good, smooth regular juice will do. Most babies start out on apple juice; just mix your regular apple juice (Red Cheek and Veryfine are both unsweetened, natural juices which are available in most grocery stores) in a ratio of 1 part juice, 3 parts water. Orange (Snowcrop has no sweeteners added), prune, grape, and pineapple (Dole is unsweetened) can be started later. Again, start off with a fairly diluted mixture, building up to pure juice as your baby's taste dictates. If the juice is too thick or pulpy, run it through a strainer; if you have a juicer, you can give your baby any type of juice you wish, vegetable included.

¶ Cereal is the first solid food most babies receive, some starting out on it as early as 1 week old. There are many alternatives to the jet-cooked instant-food-type cereals that are commonly used. Many babies I know were brought up on Koh-Koh, a cereal made of a combination of soy, wheat and rice flours—organic and healthy. Rice Cream is also good. Both can be found in any health food store. They both must be cooked for 20 minutes, so for the convenience that the instant stuff offers, you should make up a large batch at one time. Store it in the refrigerator, and heat it when necessary, or just warm it up by adding hot milk or water, or warm mother's milk. A type of infant oatmeal can be made using soy or oat flour. Just add water, and cook over medium high heat, stirring to avoid gooeyness. I know some babies who were fed macrobiotically from birth; the mother of one baby used to concoct a mixture of rolled oats (raw), apple juice, honey, sunflower seed, and soy powder in the blender. The consistency was good for even the tiniest of babies, and provided plenty of nourishment. The only problem was that it wasn't cooked, which, I have since heard, might not have been the healthiest of things. But if you're in doubt (I tend to be), mix it all up together in the blender, *then* cook it . . . it still remains one of the most nourishing, best-tasting baby cereal recipes. Once a baby reaches the age of 6 months, regular cereal can be given. Familia has a good baby cereal out (instant; can be eaten cold), or you can just do oatmeal, being sure to get it good and smooth.

¶ Now: solid foods. There is no reason in the world why you should have to feed your baby the solid foods that are offered to you by baby food companies. They are a large part starch (such a large part that a baby with celiac disease would die on a diet of commercial baby food), contain salt in unnecessarily large amounts, and, until recently, were perked up flavorwise with MSG. Add those things to the fact that baby food companies use the most inedible part of most foods (the necks, backs, and gizzards of meats, all of which have a higher concentration of DDT, antibiotics, hormones, and poisons than other parts; the skins of nonorganically raised vegetables and fruits, not necessarily fresh food, etc.), and the little extra work involved in making your own foods begins to seem like nothing.

¶ Ideally, you should try to work out a system whereby your baby foods can be made in large quantities and stored over a long period of time. This eliminates the hassle of preparing food when you have a hungry baby howling to be fed, and makes it easy for even a traveling family to feed their baby healthy, home-made food.

¶ Any food that you make for your baby can be preserved using regular canning techniques (see section on preserving food), or by freezing it. I prefer to freeze it: it's quicker, takes up little space, there's no fear of spoilage, and the frozen foods contain more vitamins and taste better. I learned a very quick and convenient way to freeze baby foods from the grandmother of a baby with celiac disease. She was forced to innovate quick, healthy foods without starch or salt.

¶ Prepare your foods in a blender or a strainer. Put the prepared food into an ice cube tray with the ice cube sections in it. Freeze immediately. Once the tray is frozen, pop out the cubes of frozen food, and place them in a plastic bag or freezer container. When you're ready to feed the baby, simply take out a cube of meat, a cube of fruit, and a cube of vegetable, and heat them, and serve. Old baby food jars are good to heat things up in, as are Pyrex dessert dishes. Simply place the dish or jar with the cube in it in a pan of water. As the water boils, the cube will melt, and you'll have instant baby food.

¶ For traveling, simply bag a couple of meals up in containers or plastic bags. Taken directly from the freezer and wrapped in several layers of newspaper, the meals will not defrost too quickly. As they do melt, however, the cold from the stuff that's still frozen will keep the rest of the stuff from spoiling too quickly. An added note: for teething babies there's nothing quite as soothing as an ice cube to chew on. Why not try a frozen cube of your baby's favorite fruit or vegetable?

¶ To prepare most foods, you almost always need a blender in combination with a strainer of some sort, although sometimes just a strainer can be used, if you have no electricity. In preparing your baby foods, keep in mind that the younger the baby, the more finely blended and strained the food has to be. As a baby gets older and is able to "gum" food, then the food doesn't have to be blended so smooth. It gives him something to work with if the food has a few lumps in it. At all times, any fruit, vegetable, or meat that appears too coarse, pulpy, or stringy can be strained through a sieve, becoming pretty smooth in the process.

FRUITS

Apples and pears: Wash and peel fruit. Place in pan and add water to cover. Boil until very soft. Drain, reserving water. Place fruit in blender, with honey to taste. (I use 1 teaspoon per 3 apples, but as apples vary in bitterness, you'll have to figure out what's best as you go along.) Blend, adding the water the fruit was cooked in, until the desired consistency is reached. Apples and pears, along with bananas, can be blended without cooking, but turn brown very quickly, and do not freeze as well as when they are cooked.

Peaches, apricots, prunes, plums: Any dried fruit can be used instead of fresh; it is remarkably high in vitamin C. When using dried fruits, soak them in water until soft, then process as you would fresh fruit, using water that the fruit was soaked in to cook it in.

¶ All fruits may be prepared without a blender, using a sieve instead. Prepare all fruits as if for the blender. Push the fruit through a sieve, adding the liquid and flavoring after straining.

MEAT AND FISH

Chicken and turkey: Place chicken in pot, covering chicken twice deep with water. (Chicken stock is invaluable—in preparing other meals, or as a clear liquid to have on hand for a sick baby. The more water you add to your chicken, the more stock you'll end up with. As you add water, however, the strength of the stock diminishes.) Add 1 onion, sliced, and some salt (onion, when cooked, is not bad for young digestive systems, and can be added to the diet as soon as the baby is able to eat meat. It's good flavoring and helps to cut cholesterol). Boil, as for chicken soup, until done— approximately 1 hour. Remove chicken, reserving stock. Debone, remove any skin or gristle, and cut into chunks. Place chicken in blender, adding enough stock to cover the chicken halfway. Blend, adding more liquid until the desired consistency is reached. If pulpy, strain through a sieve.

Note: Any chicken or turkey that you have around that has no liquid with it can be blended with water, reserved chicken stock, or chicken or vegetable bouillon.

Beef, lamb, pork: Prepare for blender by cutting cooked meat into chunks, removing any gristle or fat that might be too tough. Place in blender with a small amount of liquid. For beef, use beef bouillon or water. For lamb and pork, use chicken stock, bouillon, water, or milk. Blend, adding liquid until desired consistency is reached. Strain if too coarse.

Fish: Prepare for blender by skinning and deboning cooked fish. Place in blender with a small amount of water or milk. Add a few drops of lemon juice to taste. Blend, adding liquid until desired consistency is reached. Strain through a sieve if too coarse. Fish has always been a favorite of every baby I know. It is mild and not too heavy. Some fish that is not too bony can be prepared for the baby without the blender. Simply break it up by hand, and mix it with milk.

VEGETABLES

All vegetables: Steam or boil vegetable until soft, reserving water. Place in blender with enough water (use the water it was cooked in) to half cover the vegetable. Flavor with a few grains of salt or better, lemon juice. Blend, adding liquid until desired consistency is reached. Strain if too coarse.

Note: Squash, yams, carrots, can be flavored with honey. Spinach will require less water than other vegetables, and has a tendency to turn your baby's stools green, but don't worry, it's natural. Green beans will undoubtedly require straining; otherwise the strings, which don't get blended, will make the baby gag.

DESSERTS

Baby Food Pudding

1 cup milk	**2 teaspoons cornstarch**
Salt to taste	**¼ cup cold milk**
1 tablespoon sugar	**Flavoring**

Scald milk, salt, and sugar, stirring to dissolve sugar. Mix cornstarch and cold milk together until smooth, then stir into hot milk mixture. Over very low heat, cook and stir until thickened—at least 5 minutes. Don't stop stirring, or it will get lumpy. Remove from heat. Add ½ teaspoon vanilla or some puréed banana. You may use maple syrup instead of sugar. Kids under two shouldn't have chocolate.

Any time your baby is sick, you should consult a doctor or medical person. There are, however, some simple things that you can do at home for your baby to take care of minor ills, or to relieve the suffering until you can get to a doctor.

Colic: Babies are colicky for the first three months of their lives, so there really are not any foods that you can give them to relieve the pains of colic. You can, however, try these hints, they may work to help your baby:
¶ Booties: Some doctors feel that colic may simply be referred pain from cold feet. Try keeping your baby's feet as warm as possible.
¶ Pacifier: A colicky baby is often very comforted by sucking. Pacifiers are helpful tools.

¶ Holding: Hold your baby against your chest, one hand supporting the baby's back and neck, one hand holding the baby's feet up against his behind, with his knees up against his chest. This is a very good position for relieving the pains of colic; it is also very good for gas and stomach virus pains.

Diarrhea: Any bad diarrhea should be handled by a doctor. Minor diarrhea due to stomach digestion problems can be dealt with by feeding the baby milder foods, and some bananas (bananas that have ripened off the vine are good for diarrhea. Bananas that have ripened on the vine are terrible for diarrhea, good for constipation. All bananas found in the continental United States are ripened off the vine).

¶ Diarrhea as a reaction to antibiotics or other medication: Try feeding the baby yogurt.

¶ Diarrhea from a stomach virus: The virus is causing the diarrhea, and is probably causing a very sensitive stomach. If you suspect a virus, contact your doctor. To treat the sensitive stomach and at the same time deal with the diarrhea, start your baby immediately on clear fluids: water, apple juice, Jell-O water, clear, nonfatty chicken broth.

¶ All diarrhea: It is dehydrating, so you should replace the lost fluid by stepping up the intake of fluid in your baby's diet.

Colds, croup: Again, at the first sign of a serious cold or croup condition, you should get in touch with a doctor. Here are some things that can be done to relieve the suffering:

¶ Stuffed nose: If the baby's nose is so stuffed as to make feeding and sleeping difficult, you can clear it by suctioning the mucus out with an aspirator. You can get an aspirator at any pharmacy, and the use of it is simple: follow the directions.

¶ If the mucus in your baby's nose is solid and not liquidy enough to allow you to aspirate it, you may loosen it and often clear it with a simple saline solution: To 8 ounces of sterile water, add ⅛ teaspoon of salt. Mix until dissolved and cooled. Then apply a few drops to each nostril.

¶ Wheezing: A cold-mist aspirator in a tight, small area works very well in aiding a child with a congested chest or nose in breathing easier. For severe breathing problems (you should contact the doctor immediately for any breathing problem), place a blanket over the crib, leaving small open spaces for ventilation, and put the vaporizer under this "tent." Remember to leave breathing spaces in the blanket.

¶ Congestion: It is sometimes lessened by placing the sufferer in a semisitting position. This can be done for the infant by allowing him to sleep sitting up in an infant seat or similar device. You should place the seat in your bed at night so you can keep the baby covered, and make sure that the baby doesn't wiggle into an uncomfortable position. For an older baby, and for infants, place pillows under the mattress to elevate the baby's head.

Teething: For teething pain, rub a little alcoholic beverage such as rum, whiskey, or wine, on the baby's gums. This can be used even with small babies. Just use a couple of drops. Let your baby chew on ice cubes, hard bread, hard, nonbrittle bone from which all gristle and meat has been removed.

Diaper rash: On-the-spot cure: Zinc oxide cream makes an excellent diaper rash ointment, and can be purchased in any pharmacy.

¶ Overall measure: Diaper rash is often caused by very strong urine. Try giving your baby sugar water to dilute the potency of the urine. Or, your baby may be irritated by detergents or bleach residue in the diapers. Try using soap and washing soda instead. Rinse diapers well before washing, then wash in hot water. This should get rid of any residual bacteria.

¶ Sweet-smelling diaper pail: In a diaper pail, put 1 cup borax, ½ cup Ivory Snow, and water. Stir. It will soak your diapers, and the smell won't be too bad. In place of Ivory Snow, you might try Dr. Bronner's Castile Soap.

POISON SOUP kitchin tested
BY Jason and Nathan sullivan
½ Pot water
shugar
salt
ANGOSTURA bitters
Make some dough as you wold make a pie.
put green leavs in. stur it up.
6 Hand fulls of lentil Beans
Pepper and cinnamon and stir it a little.
matzo meall - taBasco sauce
4 roten chernies
1. slice of Bred and you are done.
Keep it - it will dry.

When you're thinking about eating less food, or changing your eating
ways, first get in touch with how your body feels. When you sit down to
a meal that's too big, or you polish off your stash of potato chips, you're
bound to feel miserable soon afterward.

¶ Awareness is the first step. Once you start questioning the necessity of
another helping, you'll pick up on the true needs of your body. Dieting is
really a matter of deciding to be straight with yourself—which isn't easy.
No one wants to admit he's overeating because he's nervous or angry.

¶ Instead of getting into an intricate calorie trip at first, use that time
to evaluate the way you relate to eating. Your stomach has had enough
about 15 minutes before your brain perceives it consciously. So if you stop
eating sooner than usual (even if you still feel hungry), just hang on and
you'll feel satisfied momentarily. It's a genuine rush.

¶ If you're eating too much, chances are you're eating too much of the
wrong foods. Unfortunately, starches and carbohydrates are usually easy
to eat; you don't need much muscle power to shovel in some mashed
potatoes or a dish of ice cream. We've all gone through the "I'll just have
this much" routine, adding a little bit more to the plate until . . . Yow!
It's all gone! How did that happen? . . . Most of us are conditioned to
enjoy food which is not necessarily nutritious, but tastes good and makes
us feel good. If you want to change, throw out all your shit food and buy
lots of fresh fruit and vegetables.

¶ Start the day with a big breakfast—eggs or cereal, juice, toast, and a
hot drink or milk—and you won't feel hungry until lunch. Don't rush;
eat slowly and chew. Savor your food.

Country Doctors

¶ If you find yourself feeling weak and hungry before midday, you're probably not eating a nutritious breakfast, and your blood sugar is low. In order to maintain a consistent level of energy all morning, breakfast should be balanced but high in protein. This high protein input will be gradually converted to sugar for energy as it is needed over the next several hours.

¶ A salad and/or sandwich with juice, milk, or a hot drink is good for lunch. Once you're eating less, you may find even this is too much. I used to have a cup of soup each day, and never felt hungry until evening.

¶ For dinner, cut out starches whenever possible. Eat only lean meats, and get into fresh fruit desserts. If you'd rather not eat meat, be sure you're substituting high-protein foods like soy beans. Remember that fish is filling, very nutritious, and practically all protein.

¶ If you need to lose weight, you can give up all fats and carbohydrates for a while. Your liver will convert its stored fat to sugar for its energy needs, and you'll see and feel results quickly. My wife and I went camping for 4 months and decided to substitute yogurt and fresh fruit for pastry, ice cream, and other sweets. One night after dinner in Missoula, Montana, we fondly reminisced about various cookies we had known. Believe it or not, talking about food can be just as delightful a trip as eating.

¶ Seriously, changing your diet is like giving up smoking. After the first crucial days, you find that your only source of satisfaction is in knowing you did it. You don't feel better yet; you're just proud of yourself for sticking to it. But after about a week or two, you'll really start feeling lighter and healthier. The foods you've substituted will be supplying the emotional satisfaction that junk food once did. The mere thought of eating food you once craved may make you shudder (a reformed soda freak I know has cold sweats each time he passes a soda machine).

¶ There are a number of good books to read on diet and nutrition. Read them if you like, but keep in mind that eating should always be a pleasurable and sensual experience. Don't get into a diet because it's "healthy"; brown rice has more calcium and phosphorus than white rice, but eating it exclusively won't provide adequate nourishment.

¶ Certain foods liberate the vitamins and minerals in other foods and should be eaten together. Reading *Let's Eat Right to Keep Fit* by Adelle Davis will help you understand the dynamics of nutrition.

¶ If you're living and working in a city, you probably dig the idea of eating healthier food, but the candy machines and hot dog stands just sneak up on you wherever you go. Conquer them! If you're working under heavy pressure, lunchtime may be the only relaxed part of your day. If it is—what are you doing? Leave. If not, get it together to make your own lunch. Items like white bread, packaged deli meat, and prepared salads have little nutritional value and are full of preservatives, starch, and animal fats. Save your money and be healthier by keeping away from processed foods.

¶ Zap Comics immortalized our masochistic eating tendencies in a recent story. The scene opens on a morose Zap character aimlessly walking the dark, dirty streets. Spotting a local eatery, he cheers up, dashes in, and smiles knowingly at the cook. "You know what I want," he says. "One shitburger coming up," the cook gleefully calls out as he gets to work. Our friend proceeds to devour the shitburger, which consequently nearly poisons him. After a fitful struggle with much gasping and groaning, he finds his way back to the diner, and orders a . . . you guessed it.

P.S.: Vitamins are naturally occurring organic catalysts which help the body perform its biochemical reactions. In medical school we are taught that a well-balanced diet with good supplies of green vegetables, citrus fruits, dairy, and a source of protein will supply all the necessary vitamins and minerals for a normal adult and that only children and pregnant and lactating women should take supplemental vitamins. No one, however, is really sure about vitamins. There is no government minimal daily requirements for vitamin E, for example, and yet it appears to help keep the arteries clear of blood clots, increase sexual competency, and aid the skin to heal itself. It is probably a good idea to take a good multiple vitamin every day, including A, the B vitamins, C, D, and E. It doesn't have to be "organic"—almost any multiple vitamin preparation will do, and one a day is enough.

Rusty's Earth People's Applesauce

Put whole apples, right off the tree, in a pot, covered with water and generously spread with cinnamon. Cook until apples are soft and breaking up. Put mixture in blender. Delicious.

Rusty's Good Medicine Tea

Osha root, mint from right outside near the walk, *cinnamon, rose hips, cloves.* Brew in a pot.

Pine Needle Tea

Steep a handful of fresh pine needles in boiling water. Magic! Bitterness disappears. High in vitamin C.

Perk-Up

(Hint: Add cinnamon to coffee before brewing)

Spicy Lebanese Coffee

1 pint very strong coffee	1 cup thick whipped cream
Dark brown sugar or honey	Nutmeg or mace
2 tablespoons grated orange peel	Cinnamon

Make coffee twice as strong as you usually do, then sweeten it with plenty of dark brown (raw) sugar or honey. While coffee is still hot, stir in the grated orange peel and allow to cool. Stir in ¾ of the thick whipped cream, a little nutmeg or mace, and ½ teaspoon cinnamon. Chill well, then pour into individual glasses and serve with a spoonful of thick cream.

FISH

Ockene Sauce

Serves 10–12

4 or 5 pounds shrimp   5 or 6 onions, sliced thin
3 sticks butter, or ½ butter, ½ oil

Shell and devein shrimp. Set aside. Melt butter, add onions, and simmer slowly, adding to taste:

Powdered mustard   Chopped parsley
Ginger, powdered or minced White wine
Lemon juice   Pignola nuts
Garlic, minced or pressed   Almonds
Chives   Sesame seeds

Add shrimp and cook slowly in sauce until they turn pink. Serve with rice.

Kathy's Salmon Bisque

Serves 10–12

2 pounds cooked (or canned; not   8 tablespoons butter
   as tasty) salmon   8 tablespoons flour
2 cups peeled tomatoes   6 cups milk
2 medium onions, chopped   Salt to taste
4 tablespoons chopped parsley   1 teaspoon paprika
4 tablespoons chopped celery leaves Chopped chives

If fresh salmon (steaks) is used, bake in small amount of milk dotted liberally with butter. Retain sauce. If canned salmon is used, retain oil. Combine salmon, its oil or sauce, tomatoes, onions, parsley, and celery in a saucepan with enough water to cover. In another, larger, saucepan, prepare a cream sauce of butter, flour, and milk. (Melt butter, blend in flour, and add milk gradually, stirring constantly.) Blend with wire whisk until smooth; heat until thick. Allow to boil. Season with salt and paprika. Remove from heat and stir in salmon mixture. Serve at once garnished with chives.

Fish Creole

Serves 10–12

6 pounds fish fillets
3 teaspoons salt
10 tablespoons butter
2 cups chopped onions
1 cup chopped celery
1 cup chopped zucchini
4 tablespoons flour

¼ teaspoon pepper
2 1-pound cans tomatoes
2 tablespoons chopped parsley
2 cups bread crumbs
½ teaspoon oregano
Grated Parmesan cheese

Wash fish and dry; cut into serving pieces. Arrange in baking dish and sprinkle with 1 teaspoon of the salt.

In 6 tablespoons of the butter, sauté onions, celery, and zucchini until tender—about 7 minutes. Remove from heat and stir in flour, 1 teaspoon salt, and the pepper. Stir in tomatoes and parsley. Bring to boil, stirring constantly. Simmer for 1 minute. Spoon over fish and bake, covered, in 375° oven for 25 minutes. Melt remaining butter (4 tablespoons) with bread crumbs and oregano, sprinkle over fish, and bake, uncovered, for 10 minutes longer. Sprinkle with Parmesan cheese before serving.

Love,
Judy

Fillet of Sole with Onions, Tomatoes, and Sour Cream

Serves 16

2 Spanish onions, sliced very thin
6 tablespoons butter or margarine
8 fresh tomatoes, minced

Flour, salt, and pepper
16 fillets of sole
2 pints sour cream

Brown onions in butter until golden. Place onion slices in bottom of casserole. Place minced tomatoes on top of onions. Put flour, salt, and pepper in a bag and shake fish to coat. Then place fish on top of onions and tomatoes. Pour melted butter over the fish, put the whole dish under the broiler, and leave until brown. Remove dish from broiler, pour on sour cream, and put in a 400° oven until brown.

Alan's Fabulous Flounder Dish

Serves 10–12

2 pounds fillet of flounder
Milk
Bread crumbs
Oranges
Walnuts
Lemons
Soy sauce

1 can minced clams
Salt and pepper
Garlic powder
Oregano
Parsley flakes
Onions

Grease enough baking dishes for all the fish to fit into single layers. Dip fillets in milk, then in bread crumbs, and lay them in baking dishes. Peel oranges and separate into slices, laying the slices on top of fish—at least 3 slices per piece of fish. Any juice should be poured over fish. Sprinkle walnuts over fish. Squeeze enough lemon juice mixed with soy sauce to make contact with fish when it is lightly sprinkled on. Drain clams and throw them in. Add spices and onions. Bake at 325° until done. Serve with white wine. Everyone flips out on this!

Peruvian Ceviche (Raw Fish Salad)

Serves 8–10

2 pounds fillet of sole,
   flounder, halibut, or
   any dry white fish
Juice of 8 lemons
2 medium onions, chopped

6 medium tomatoes, chopped
2 cloves garlic, minced
2 tablespoons ground chilies
1 teaspoon oregano
Salt and pepper to taste

Cut raw fish into 1-inch strips. Lay on a shallow nonmetal dish; cover with lemon juice. Let it sit till white and opaque (looks pretty much cooked)— about ½–1 hour. Drain, mix with remaining ingredients. Serve ice-cold on lettuce.

Broiled Fish

Make a mixture of tamari and ginger to taste. Marinate fish steak in this for a couple of hours, then broil, spooning liquid over cooking fish from time to time to keep it moist.

Susan's Stuffing for Baked Fish

(For big or little fish)

In a skillet, melt lots of butter or margarine. Sauté sliced onions in butter till soft. Add bread crumbs, garlic powder, and lemon juice, adding more butter or lemon to moisten. Mix until it tastes nice and lemony-garlicky. Spoon into cavity of cleaned fish (can also stuff zucchini with it). Dot fish with butter, sprinkle with lemon juice, and bake, turning midway in the cooking time, and dotting second side with butter and lemon juice.

True Light Beaver Salmon Patties

Serves 8–10

2 cans red salmon	¾ cup bread crumbs
1 can pink salmon	1 grated onion (optional)
4 eggs	

Mix all ingredients together; form into patties. Put enough oil in skillet to cover bottom about ¼ inch deep. Fry patties till crisp. Cut upon, put pat of butter in middle, drip lemon juice on top, and eat.

June's Shrimp in Creole Sauce

Serves 10–12

2 pounds shrimp, peeled and
   deveined
1 bay leaf
4 tablespoons butter

4 cups June's Creole Sauce
½ cup dry white wine
Salt and pepper to taste
Few grains cayenne

Boil shrimp for 3 minutes in boiling water with a bay leaf. Melt butter in skillet. Add shrimp and cook, stirring, over a hot fire for 2 minutes. Add Creole Sauce and wine. Simmer, covered, for 5 minutes. Add seasonings to taste. Serve with steamed rice.

June's Creole Sauce

4 tablespoons butter
2 tablespoons chopped onions
3 cups tomatoes, or 1 cup tomatoes
   and 2 cups brown sauce
1 green pepper, chopped
⅔ teaspoon salt

Few grains cayenne
2 teaspoons brown sugar
½ cup chili sauce

Melt butter over low heat. Add onions and cook for 2 minutes. Add remaining ingredients, and cook, stirring, until sauce is thick.

MUSHROOMS

Marinated Mushrooms

Waste not, want not—there is still some good after peyote.

1 pound mushrooms, sliced
¼ cup oil
½ cup vinegar
2 tablespoons sugar
1 medium onion, sliced
¼ cup ketchup

1 teaspoon salt
1 teaspoon ground pepper
¼ teaspoon thyme
1 bay leaf
¼ teaspoon garlic powder

Simmer mushrooms in salted water for 3–5 minutes. Mix together all other ingredients and add to drained mushrooms. Let sit for several days.
For mushroom freaks, multiply all ingredients severalfold.

Stuffed Mushroom Scampi

Use at least 2 pounds mushrooms to serve 10–12.

Some leftover grains—rice, bread, noodles, kasha—chop it up fine.

In the meantime, soak the mushrooms; remove the stems, cutting them finely. Sauté in oil: onions, garlic, mushroom stems, celery, the leftover grains, raisins, apple bits, parsley, salt, and pepper. When this is mixed together, fill the mushroom caps.

Now take ½ to ¾ cup olive oil. Sauté a lot of finely chopped garlic in the oil, plus some parsley and oregano. Pour this over the stuffed mushrooms. Bake at 375° until the mushrooms have absorbed the garlic sauce—about 15 minutes. Then top with grated cheese—your favorite. Bake 5–10 minutes longer.

Billie's Mushrooms à la Grecque

Serves 10–12

2 pounds fresh whole mushrooms
1 cup water
1 cup olive oil
Juice of 3 fresh lemons, or
    4 tablespoons cider vinegar
½ teaspoon thyme
1 bay leaf, crushed
1 teaspoon coriander
1 teaspoon chives

1 teaspoon parsley
2 cloves garlic, minced
Salt to taste
1 teaspoon black pepper
2 stalks celery, chopped
1 small carrot, chopped fine or
    shredded
1 sweet pepper, chopped
1 small onion, minced

Remove and chop stems of mushrooms, leaving tops whole. Combine water, oil, lemon juice, herbs, chopped mushroom stems, garlic, salt, and pepper, and bring to a boil. Reduce the flame immediately and let simmer 3 minutes. Pour the cooked mixture over the mushroom caps, celery, carrots, peppers, and onions. Marinate in a bowl, unrefrigerated, for 1 hour. Chill before eating.

Food for Thought

"If a person eats with anger, the food turns to poison."

Sufi saying

. . . . . .

"I was about six years old and was watching my little sister in her high chair drinking milk. Suddenly I saw it was like pouring God into God if you know what I mean."

J. D. Salinger in Teddy

. . . . . .

A woman once came to Mahatma Gandhi with her little boy. She asked, "Mahatma-ji, tell my little boy to stop eating sugar."

"Come back in three days," said Gandhi.

In three days the woman and the little boy returned and Mahatma Gandhi said to the little boy, "Stop eating sugar."

The woman asked, "Why was it necessary for us to return only after three days for you to tell my little boy that?"

The Mahatma replied, "Three days ago I had not stopped eating sugar."

. . . . . .

"People in general are more fond of Jala Yoga (union with food) than of Dhyana Yoga (union with God)."

Bhaduri Mahasata

. . . . . .

Ancient Vedic Recipe for a Person's Life

½ the time to study and do everyday chores and duties
  ½ the time to contemplation and meditating practices

Continue lifelong under the direction of a guru.

. . . . . .

"Cooking is tasting."

. . . . . .

. . . . . .

Among the levitating saints of the Christian world was the 17th-century St. Joseph of Cupertino. His monastery brothers wouldn't allow him to serve at the table, fearing he would ascend to the ceiling with the food and crockery.

The Staffordshire Goose Pie

Stuff a large goose with a medium-sized turkey, which has been stuffed with a duck, which has been stuffed with a capon, which has been stuffed with a small chicken or pigeon, which have been stuffed or surrounded with a stuffing of:

Currants　　　　　　　　　　**Flour**
The livers of all the birds　　**Herbs**

My old cookbook says this was covered with a pastry crust that had a pastry crust knob in the middle in the shape of a flower. You pulled the knob to lift the crust to reveal all the stuffings.

I've heard another version of the Staffordshire roast that put all the birds into a still larger animal for spit-roasting!

. . . . . .

Pine Needle Pillow: Make a pillow stuffed with pine needles. It is good for headaches. It makes them go away, go away.

. . . . . .

Watercress: The dried leaves of watercress contain 3 times as much vitamin E as do dried lettuce leaves. Watercress grows abundantly in the spring.

. . . . . .

Household Hint: For stains on tea and coffee cups, put a little salt in the cup and let it sit for a while. Then rub the damp salt into the stain. Clean!

. . . . . .

To refresh a stale bagel: Dunk in hot water for a second and eat.

. . . . . .

Other stale bread: Make it into bread crumbs, give it to the birds, or cut into cubes, roll in melted butter, parsley, and garlic mixture, and use as croutons for soups or salads. Or, to eat stale bread, place bread in foil. Sprinkle a few drops of water on it, and wrap tightly. Warm in oven or over fire for a few minutes, and you'll have soft, warm bread again.

. . . . . .

Fat man: "I suppose your advice is don't eat fast.
Doctor: "No, my advice is don't eat. Fast."

Basic Survival Manual (daily eating)

Dairy Products: Protein, vitamin D, calcium, B vitamins (if not skimmed
   product)
Parsley or Watercress: Vitamin E, vitamin A, vitamin C. Some B. Iron.
Wheat Germ: B vitamins, protein, heavy vitamin E.
Missing: Trace minerals (magnesium, zinc, etc.).

Marie Antoinette and the Peasant

Marie Antoinette is strolling through her sumptuous palace gardens,
fantasizing herself as a romantic shepherdess walking with her bleating
beasts across sun-dappled fields. Suddenly, a tattered, foul-smelling peasant
woman crosses her royal path.

"Your highness," says the peasant woman, revealing that she has only
two teeth left, "your highness, I haven't eaten in three days."

"But madame," replies Marie Antoinette, "you must force yourself."

.   .   .   .   .   .

The Unfed Dervish

When I see the poor dervish unfed
My own food is pain and poison to me.

Saadi of Shiraz

.   .   .   .   .   .

About the Strawberry

Doubtless, God could have made a better berry, but doubtless, God never
did

Dr. Boteler

.   .   .   .   .   .

Only a fool argues with a skunk, a mule, or a cook.

Old Western saying

Fiesta

The *slap-slap* sound of tortillas being made is one of the earliest recollections I have of my Mexican grandmother's kitchen. Before holidays or special occasions, the aunts would gather at my grandmother's to help prepare various Mexican dishes. In Mexican cooking, the corn tortilla is the building block. When I was a child, tortillas were made by hand, one by one. The corn flour was mixed with water, rolled into small balls, and then patted between the hands until it became a large flat pancake shape. Then it was quickly cooked on a hot griddle, deftly turned several times by careful fingers. Today, however, both corn and flour tortillas are machine-made and available in most markets.

¶ The tortilla itself is delicious just heated and eaten. To heat, place a tortilla over a gas flame or electric grid; turn frequently to prevent scorching; when hot, spread with butter, peanut butter, hot sauce, or cheese. Roll it up, and enjoy! There is even a special way to hold a rolled tortilla so that what is inside won't drip out. Simply place the rolled tortilla over the thumb and little finger, gently press down the other three fingers—no drips. To heat a quantity of tortillas at one time, wrap 8–10 tightly in foil and heat about 20 minutes in a warm oven.

¶ Flour tortillas have a more limited use than corn tortillas, and I don't remember seeing them used in Mexico. Here are a few things you can make with flour tortillas:

Quesadilla

Cover a flour tortilla with grated Cheddar cheese. Place on a cookie sheet in a 350° oven. Heat till the cheese is bubbly. To eat, tear or cut into pieces. Can be dipped into hot sauce.

Burritos

Place in center of a flour tortilla about ½ cup refried beans or cooked meat (or a combination of beans and meat—or if you're really brave, grated jack

cheese and chopped green chili). Add green chili or onion or hot sauce if
desired. Fold in 2 sides, secure ends with toothpicks, or fold them under.
Heat in a 350° oven for about 20 minutes. To prevent the tortilla from
cracking while cooking, brush the outside with oil.

Refried Beans

(For Burritos and Many Other Things)

Serves 10–12

1 package dried kidney beans	**Chili powder**
Garlic cloves, crushed	**Cayenne**
Grated Cheddar cheese	**Oil**
Salt	

Cook beans, following directions on package. When tender, drain, reserving
the liquid. Rice or mash beans until soft and lumpy. Add garlic, cheese, salt,
a dash of chili powder, and cayenne to taste. Continue to mash, adding bean
liquid until you have a smooth, thick paste.

In a fry pan, heat oil, turn beans into the oil, and fry. Add more cheese as
the beans fry, if desired. Turn the fried beans into a bowl, and let them sit
until you are ready to use them. When ready to use, fry the beans in oil
again. Toward the end, layer the top of the beans with cheese and cook,
without turning, until the cheese melts. Then serve the beans plain, or as
part of another dish.

Corn tortillas can be used in so many ways—and if they are left over or
dried out, cut them into small pieces, fry in hot oil till crisp, salt them, and
eat as you would corn chips. To soften a corn tortilla so it won't crack
while it is being rolled, dip it into hot oil (using tongs, not fingers) for just
a few seconds, then use.

Taquitos

Using any leftover meat, season the shredded, cooked meat slightly (I use
garlic powder and cumin). Lay a small amount of meat across the top edge
of a softened tortilla, then roll tightly, making a small cylinder. Carefully
lay the rolled tortilla fold down in hot oil, fry till crisp on all sides. Serve with
sour cream, hot sauce, or:

Guacamole

2 ripe medium-sized avocados	½ teaspoon salt
2 tablespoons lemon juice	¼ teaspoon fresh ground pepper
2 tablespoons grated onion	2–4 tablespoons chopped canned
2 cloves garlic, crushed	green chilies

Blend all ingredients together, cover (if left uncovered, it turns black), and chill. If you want it spicier, adjust ingredients accordingly.

Tacos

Packaged taco shells are really great for making tacos, and there is usually a recipe on the box. But I have an authentic Mexican recipe that I call "Greasy Tacos." (But *so* good.)
Spread a corn tortilla on one half of the circle with raw, seasoned (I use garlic powder and cumin powder) ground meat. Place in hot oil, allowing oil to flow over the center so the tortilla will then bend up and fold over. Cook till crisp on both sides, drain, and fill with lettuce, tomato, onions, radish. Top with grated cheese and hot sauce.

Or, you can try this variation, using fresh tortillas, making your shells separately, and filling them with a separate meat filling:

Colleen's Tacos

2–3 dozen tortillas	Cayenne pepper to taste
3 pounds ground beef	Chili powder to taste
2 onions, chopped fine	Shredded lettuce
2–3 12 ounce cans tomato paste	Chopped tomatoes, onions, and
2 teaspoons salt	radishes
3 teaspoons garlic powder	

Shells: Place tortilla in hot oil for about 10 seconds. Turn over, fold in half, and fry on each side until tortilla shell is crisp, but not so crisp as to shatter easily—about 30 seconds. Remove from oil, drain, and keep warm on top of stove.

Filling: Brown meat until done and remove from pan. Drain off all the oil from fried meat except just enough to sauté the onions in. Sauté onions and add the meat. Add tomato paste, salt, and garlic powder. Put in about ¼ teaspoon cayenne, and start adding chili powder to taste (I start with about 2 tablespoons chili powder and go from there).

To eat: Put meat into taco shell. Put in shredded lettuce, chopped tomatoes, onions, and radishes. Top with Cheddar cheese and hot sauce.

When aunts would gather in my grandmother's kitchen to prepare the "feast," the main dish was always enchiladas. It is always very easy to prepare enchiladas for many people way ahead of time, popping them into the oven just before they are to be served.

Cheese Enchiladas

Shredded Cheddar cheese
Chopped onions (for milder flavor, cook and drain first)
Sliced black olives

And: a little oil, vinegar, oregano (crushed between palms), salt, pepper, sage

Sauce: Sauté some crushed garlic in a little olive oil, add 1 or 2 tablespoons flour, and stir to brown. Add canned red chili sauce (or tomato sauce and chopped chilies) slowly to make the gravy.
Soften the corn tortillas in oil, then dip them in the enchilada sauce. Mix cheese, onions, and olives, season, and place a bit of mixture on the tortilla. Roll the tortilla up and place in a baking dish, until dish is full but not crowded. Pour a bit of sauce over, and garnish with leftover filling or shredded cheese. Bake 20–25 minutes in a 350° oven. Serve with leftover sauce.

Green Enchiladas No. 1

Sauce:
Green tomatos
Chicken stock
Garlic, minced
Green chilies, chopped

Cumin powder
Oregano
Salt

Filling:

Onion, sliced very thin
Monterey Jack or other white cheese, shredded

Chicken, if desired

To make sauce, peel and seed green tomatoes (or quarter and run through a food mill after they have been cooled). Cook in small pieces till mushy. Add to taste the rest of the ingredients called for, using more garlic and chilies if you want it especially piquant.

Dip corn tortilla in hot oil, then into green tomato sauce. Fill with cheese, onions, and chicken, if desired. Roll, place in a flat baking pan. Sprinkle with more cheese and sauce, and bake in a 325° oven until bubbly— about 30 minutes. Serve topped with more sauce and sour cream.

Green Enchiladas No. 2

Serves 8

1 3-ounce can green chilies
1 10-ounce can green tomatoes
2 or 3 sprigs fresh coriander, or
   cumin powder
1 cup heavy cream
1 egg, lightly beaten
Salt and pepper to taste

2 8-ounce packages cream cheese
4 chicken breasts,
   poached, boned, shredded
6 green onions, chopped
Oil
1 dozen corn tortillas

To make sauce, blend in blender chilies, tomatoes, coriander. To this add cream, egg, and salt and pepper. Mix well, and pour into saucepan. Heat slowly. Meanwhile, combine softened cream cheese with chicken and chopped onions to make filling. Dip tortilla in hot oil, then in warm sauce. Fill with about 3 tablespoons filling, roll, and fasten with a toothpick. Place rolled enchiladas in buttered baking dish, till full. Pour half of the sauce over, and heat in a slow oven till bubbly. Serve with the rest of the sauce, and top with sour cream.

An added note to cooking with tortillas: Any of the dishes mentioned above are good in combination. For example, a fried tortilla, held on the plate with refried beans underneath, and stacked with taco mixture (or leftover enchiladas) and salad condiments, makes a great dish called *tostada*. For a great leftover breakfast, scramble up some eggs with leftover enchiladas. Finally, for *huevos rancheros*, fry some corn tortillas in hot oil until they are between soft and crunchy in doneness. Fry up some eggs. Put the eggs on top of the tortillas on a warm plate and cover with warm chili sauce, or sautéed chilies, tomatoes, and peppers.

One of the traditions that have been carried down from my grandmother is

Albondigas Soup. Whenever a member of the family was sick in bed, a jar of grandmother's "miracle cure" was rushed over.

Albondigas Soup

Serves 10–12

Chicken stock (I boil a cut-up chicken or backs and wings in a large pot of water with onion, celery, bay leaf)

Chopped onions, celery, tomato, bell pepper, carrots
Salt and pepper to taste
Fresh mint (or dried, I guess)

For the soup, strain and chill the stock, remove the fat. Heat the stock to boiling and add the chopped vegetables and salt and pepper. Also add a sprig of mint (*hierba buena*—the good herb). Albondigas are little meatballs about the size of a walnut. To make, mix:

1 pound ground beef
3 tablespoons raw rice
¼ cup chopped parsley

6 mint leaves, chopped
1 egg, lightly beaten
Salt and pepper to taste

Roll into little balls and drop into the boiling soup. Cook about 30 minutes.

When we traveled in Mexico, we were introduced to another Mexican soup. We met some teen-age boys who were friends of our daughter, and they insisted that we have the Taxco specialty, which was Pozole.

Toño's Pozole

Serves 10–12

In a large kettle, put:

2 large fresh pork hocks, split in 2 or 3 pieces (or other fresh, fat pork)
2 quarts water

1 1-pound can tomatoes
2 1-pound cans hominy
2 medium onions, chopped
4 teaspoons salt

Simmer for 2–3 hours. Remove meat, cool, and cut into chunks. Skim fat from broth. Add meat back to soup, heat and serve with garnishes of chopped avocado, shredded lettuce, greens, onions, cubed Cheddar cheese, hot sauce, etc.

While in Mexico, we frequently went into "native" restaurants for authentic Mexican food. One of the great surprises to me was the color of the food. Accustomed to California-Mexican cooking, I associated it all with red sauce—from tomatoes or red chili. In southern Mexico, the sauces were either green or black. The green sauce is from green tomatoes or green chilies, and the black is from red chili and chocolate. The chocolate sauce is called mole and is delicious. I've been fortunate to find mole powder (in little cans in Mexican food stores: it simply needs to be mixed with chicken stock to make a thick dark gravy). But here is a recipe for mole sauce that is pretty easy:

Chicken Mole

Enough for 1 chicken

To prepare the chicken, either brown in olive oil or boil in water till tender. Set aside.
To make sauce, blend in blender (or grind or mince):

1 green chili	1 tablespoon chili powder
1 tablespoon sesame seed	¼ teaspoon pepper
2 cloves garlic	1 square unsweetened chocolate
1 slice dry toast	Pinch each of powdered cloves and
¼ cup almonds	cumin powder
¼ teaspoon cinnamon	

Cook with a little chicken stock till smooth. Pour over chicken, and bake in

My grandmother never fixed Chilies Rellenos, but I hope my children and grandchildren will fondly remember my specialty in the Mexican food area: 350° oven until done—20–30 minutes.

Chilies Rellenos

Serves 10–12

Monterey Jack cheese	Flour
Whole green chilies—1 for each serving	Oil—about 1½ inches deep in pan
Eggs—1 for each 2 chilies used	

Sauce:

Oil

1 onion, chopped

1 clove garlic, crushed

Green chili remnants

1 can tomatoes

1½ teaspoons salt

½ teaspoon pepper

1 teaspoon oregano, crushed in
  palms

Cut Jack cheese into oblongs about 1 inch wide, 2 inches long, and ½ inch thick. Put cheese into whole chili (or wrap strips of chili around cheese). Make a batter: Beat egg whites until quite stiff. Fold in 1 tablespoon flour for each egg used, and beaten egg yolks. Fold until well mixed. Drop the cheese-stuffed chilies into the batter. Pick up with a spoon, and place in hot oil. Brown on both sides. Drain on absorbent paper and let stand. Meanwhile, to make sauce: sauté onion, garlic, chili remnants (from cutting it open) in oil till soft. Add tomatoes, salt, pepper, oregano; simmer 5 minutes.

To serve, heat stuffed chilies in sauce, then serve the chilies with some sauce on them.

Aunt Theresa's Lemon-Garlic Dressing

4 large cloves garlic, minced

½–1 cup olive oil

½–1 teaspoon combination of salt,
  cayenne, paprika

Juice of 4–6 lemons, to taste

¾ cup grated Parmesan cheese

Combine garlic, oil, and seasonings in a large jar. Shake, and let sit in the refrigerator for 1–3 hours. Just before using, add lemon juice until dressing is a good balance of lemon and garlic, tending toward the lemon, with an aftertaste of garlic. Pour over a salad of chilled romaine or iceberg lettuce to which some croutons and perhaps some onions have been added. Toss and serve topped with Parmesan cheese.

True Light Beaver Spanish Rice

Serves 10–12

Oil
3 onions, sliced
2 green peppers (or chili peppers), diced
4 cups uncooked rice
3 15-ounce cans tomato sauce and enough water to make the amount of liquid needed to cook rice (1¾ cups liquid per cup brown rice, 2½ cups liquid per cup white rice)

6 dashes Tabasco sauce
2 (to start) teaspoons chili powder (if you use chili peppers, cut down a bit on the amount of chili powder and cayenne used)
¼ teaspoon cayenne
2–3 teaspoons salt
Garlic powder to taste
1½ cups grated Cheddar cheese

Cover bottom of skillet with enough oil to sauté the onions and peppers. When soft, add uncooked rice and sauté until it begins to turn brown. Add tomato sauce, liquid, and spices and stir until it begins to boil.

Cover and cook at a low boil, stirring occasionally, until done—about 20 minutes. Turn into a greased casserole, cover with grated cheese, and cook an additional 10–15 minutes in a 325° oven until cheese melts and bubbles.

Bobby's Tamale Pie

Serves 12

2 pounds ground beef
2 cups chopped onions
2 cups chopped green peppers
2 15-ounce cans tomato sauce
2 12-ounce cans (3 cups)
   whole-kernel corn
1 cup pitted ripe olives, chopped
2 cloves garlic, minced
2 tablespoons sugar

2 teaspoons salt
1–2 tablespoons chili powder
Dash of pepper
12 ounces sharp cheese, shredded
   (3 cups)
1½ cups yellow cornmeal
1 teaspoon salt
4 cups cold water
2 tablespoons butter or margarine

Cook meat, onion, and green pepper in large skillet till meat is lightly browned and vegetables are tender. Stir in tomato sauce, corn, olives, garlic, sugar, 2 teaspoons salt, chili powder, and pepper. Simmer until thick—20–25 minutes. Add cheese, stirring until melted. Turn into a greased 9×9×2-inch baking dish. To make cornmeal topper: stir cornmeal and 1 teaspoon salt into the cold water. Cook and stir till thick. Add butter; mix well. Spoon over hot meat mixture. Bake casserole in moderate oven (375°) above 40 minutes.

Chili Rice

Serves 16

1 can green chilies, minced or
   chopped, depending on texture
   you like
2 pints sour cream
6 cups cooked rice

2 teaspoons salt
2 teaspoons black pepper
1 pound Cheddar cheese, cut into
   strips
½ cup grated Cheddar cheese

Mix chilies and sour cream together. Butter a 4-quart casserole. Season the rice with salt and pepper. Layer rice, sour cream mixture, and cheese slices, in that order, ending with rice in casserole. Bake in a 350° oven for ½ hour. During the last few minutes of baking, sprinkle grated cheese on top and let melt. You can use macaroni or noodles instead of rice.

Enchilada Casserole

Serves 16

2 10-ounce cans Mexican
  enchilada sauce
2 8-ounce cans water
2 8-ounce cans tomato sauce
2 pounds ground beef
2 large onions, chopped
  (or 2 bunches scallions,
  chopped)

2 4½-ounce cans ripe olives,
  sliced
2 dozen corn tortillas
1 pound Jack cheese, grated, and
  ½ pound Cheddar cheese,
  grated (or 1½ pounds sharp
  white cheese)

Heat enchilada sauce, water, and tomato sauce. Brown meat with onions
and add olives and 1 cup of the sauce. Dip tortillas one at a time in sauce,
then layer in casserole with meat mixture and Jack cheese. Top with
tortillas and pour remaining sauce over all. Sprinkle with Cheddar cheese.
Bake 40 minutes in a 350° oven.

Chili Beans

Serves 12

1. Brown 4 slices of bacon. With it sauté 2 large onions, chopped; brown
   2 pounds hamburger.
   Add 2 15-ounce cans tomato sauce, 2 or 3 cans water.
2. Cook kidney beans according to directions on package. Add salt. Drain
   when cooked.
3. Add (1) to (2).

Mix in 3–4 tablespoons chili powder (or more to taste), some flour, dash
of cayenne, salt, pepper, dry mustard. Cook till savory, Eat.

Fiesta Bake Casserole

Serves 10–12

2 medium onions, sliced
¼ cup butter
2 8-ounce cans tomato sauce
2 4-ounce cans green chili peppers,
   chopped
Salt to taste
4 eggs

2 cups half and half
1½–2 doz. corn tortillas
1 pound Jack cheese, cubed
4 cups sour cream
2 cups Cheddar cheese, grated
Paprika

Sauté onions in butter; add tomato sauce, chili peppers, and salt. Simmer 5 minutes. Remove from heat. Beat eggs and mix with half and half. Add to sauce. Alternate layers of tortillas, jack cheese, and sauce. Cover with sour cream and Cheddar cheese. Sprinkle with paprika. Bake in 325° oven until bubbly—about 35 minutes. Let stand 5 minutes before serving.

Pat's Soy Bean Chili

Soak the soy beans overnight. Cook them for 2 or 3 hours until they are quite tender. Then grind them in a meat grinder.
Also cook up some other kind of bean; kidney or black beans are good.
Get a big pot. Sauté onions and garlic. This recipe is easier made in large amounts. You can use whatever amounts of things you want.
Add lots of tomatoes, canned or fresh—lots of them and stewed tomatoes, tomato paste—any kind of tomatoes to suit your taste.
Add green peppers, black olives, sliced mushrooms, the ground soy beans, the other whole beans, oregano, basil, chili powder, some hot chilies if you like, salt, pepper—any spices you like.
Let this keep cooking and keep tasting it. Season it to your taste. Then eat it when you think it's ready. Yummy.
The soy beans taste just like ground beef. It's great with a little grated cheese on top or a little fresh ground horseradish.

Face Stuffing

PUERTO RICAN–CHINESE SOUL

I'm not really certain why there isn't more Puerto Rican and Chinese food cooked in this country by white folks. Perhaps distrust of the former and fear of the difficulty of the latter are responsible; perhaps lack of information on both.

¶ The following recipes will not make you a Sino-Latin Escoffier, but they will provide an introduction to two very different styles of eating, of living.

¶ The solid earthiness of Puerto Rican food, the restraint and balance of Chinese, when added to the rest of this book may encourage a more daring approach to cooking.

Puerto Rican Food

On returning from a class trip to Philadelphia, I asked my mother why
the food I'd eaten there had had no discernible flavor.
¶ She laughed, of course, and said, "They're Americans, and Americans
are afraid of spices." Maybe, maybe not, but some may not want to risk
dermal-karmal poisoning by trying out these dishes. The Howard Johnson
Maya is powerful.
¶ For a Faustian few, however, here is our answer to the Christmas Goose.

Pernil

Serves 10–12

2–7 pounds uncooked pork
   shoulder
1 cup oregano
8–10 tablespoons salt
6 tablespoons pepper
3 tablespoons minced onions

2 tablespoons paprika
2 cloves garlic, minced
8–10 cloves garlic
2 small (3½-ounce) bottles
   Alcaparrado (capers and olives)
1 cup white vinegar

With a very sharp knife, puncture and gash the meat over its entire surface
including the thick skin on top. Gashes should be ¾ inch deep at 2-inch
intervals. Crush oregano in hands and mix it in a small bowl with salt,
pepper, onion, paprika, and 2 cloves garlic, minced. Place meat in large
bowl, and sprinkle oregano mixture over entire surface, rubbing well
into gashes. Coarsely chop 8–10 cloves garlic and stuff and rub into meat.
Drain capers and olives, chop, and press and stuff as with garlic. Pour
vinegar over meat and let stand at room temperature for 2 hours, turning
once. Cover bowl and place in refrigerator for 48–72 hours; turn once a
day. Remove meat from bowl, and roast on rack, fat side up, in shallow
pan in oven preheated to 300° for 4–4½ hours, or until internal
temperature is 180°. Do not cover; baste occasionally. When done, let stand
in open oven 5 minutes before carving.

. . . . . .

There were hot summer afternoons in Brooklyn, and I spent many of them
before the great window in the stairwell overlooking East New York. The
best of those days were those when the doors to apartments were propped
open with the galvanized insulated milk boxes used for deliveries, and by

3 in the afternoon the scent of cooking rolled from each doorway up and down the building.

¶ The staircase window faced southwest and the purple sunsets over the stone quarry were quietly, warmly spectacular. The light from those polluted skies was diffracted to greens and violets by the kitchen aromas, but it burst golden when my mother cooked beans.

Habichuelas

Serves 10–12

2 pounds red dry kidney beans	1 teaspoon paprika
½ pound salt pork	3 tablespoons oregano
2 large onions, sliced	2 small cans tomato sauce
2 small green peppers, finely diced	2 medium potatoes, peeled
4 cloves garlic	4 sprigs fresh coriander
6 tablespoons salt	2 bay leaves
4 tablespoons pepper	

Pick over beans, discarding any broken ones, stones, Wilkie buttons, etc. Soak overnight in water at room temperature, then change water and boil with oil for 10 minutes in water to barely cover. In Dutch oven or similar pan, heat salt pork till fat is rendered and pork is just beyond golden in color. Add onions and green peppers, and cook till onion is soft and translucent. Add garlic, salt, pepper, paprika, and oregano, stirring with wooden spoon till garlic is soft. Stir in tomato sauce and simmer gently for 3 minutes. Add beans and water to tomato mixture and stir well. Add potatoes, coriander, and bay, simmer till potatoes are soft, then remove potatoes, mash them, and stir back into beans. Simmer uncovered, till beans are of desired firmness (1¾–2 hours), maintaining level of water to just over top of beans by adding heated water as necessary. Serve with rice and Pernil.

Chinese Food

Chinese food is more than canned chop suey (invented, rumor has it, by a Greek in San Francisco) and deserves more stature than that afforded it by those cardboard containers used for delivery. "Hey, the gang's coming over, let's send out for Chinese food."

¶ The key word in its preparation, serving, and consumption is balance; it is best when several dishes are served at once, in large communal platters, each person having his own rice bowl. This system allows the great number of servings available from these recipes. (All the following dishes, served with rice, will easily satisfy 7 or so people.)

¶ Chinese food is, I think, best eaten with tea (not jasmine, that flavorless perfume served in many restaurants) and/or beer.

If you eat calmly and happily, hunger will not show its horrid self for well over 2 hours.

¶ John, by the way, now gorges himself every time we eat at our favorite Chinese restaurant and he's an excellent, if inscrutable, ping-pong player.

¶ The following is a selection of good dishes. There's a book called *The 1001 Chinese Recipe Cook Book* which is outstanding if you really want to get into it.

Spareribs

Serves 14

8 pounds lean spareribs
4 scallions
2 cans beer
Fresh ginger
Flour
½ cup sesame oil (or peanut, or
   mixture of both)

4 cloves garlic
1 cup soy sauce
2 sections Star anise (or 1 ball
   cardamom)
2 teaspoons sugar (optional)

Separate rack of ribs to individual ribs, leaving full length. Rinse scallions under running water and cut off root, leaving as much as possible of white bulb intact. Discard root. Cut scallions into ½-inch pieces. Set open beer to flatten at room temperature. From fresh ginger root, cut off a piece the size of the first joint of the left-hand pinky of a 17-year-old Gemini male. Dust ribs *very lightly* with flour. Heat oil in wok or Dutch oven; when hot, toss in garlic and half of soy sauce. (Oil will sputter angrily, so be careful.)

When garlic is brown and soft, and soy sauce is burning, brown ribs thoroughly, in shifts if necessary. When all the ribs are browned, add ginger to liquid, add anise to liquid, and sprinkle scallions over the ribs; sprinkle sugar over the ribs. Cover, reduce heat, simmer for 5 minutes. Meanwhile, mix remaining soy sauce with beer. Increase heat. Add beer mixture slowly to ribs, so that great billows of steam rise from the pan. Continue at intervals until the billowing ceases (the less liquid the better). Reduce heat, cover, let simmer 25 minutes more. Discard garlic and anise; serve very hot.

Bean Sprouts and Beef

Serves 14

4 pounds fresh soy bean sprouts
2 teaspoons cornstarch
2 ounces water
2 pounds lean beef (round, porterhouse)

Peanut oil
4 ounces soy sauce
2 teaspoons sugar

Pick over bean sprouts and discard any discolored beans; snap off threads from base. Soak bean sprouts in cold water for 30 minutes. Steam for 5 minutes; drain. Mix cornstarch in 2 ounces cold water to form smooth paste. Slice beef thinly. In wok or Dutch oven, heat oil, add beef, and stir till beef is gray. Add soy sauce and cornstarch paste; stir lightly. Remove meat mixture from pan; keep warm. Heat more oil in wok. Add bean sprouts and cook lightly, stirring and tossing. Sprinkle sugar over bean sprouts, stir again, raise heat. When sprouts are hot, add beef and toss together.

Steamed Shrimp

Serves 14

4 pounds large shrimp
2 scallions
12 ounces beer

6 ounces water
4 ounces soy sauce

Rinse and devein shrimp, but *do not shell*. Rinse scallions and cut off and discard root. Slice scallions in ½-inch pieces. In large pot, pour beer, water, and soy sauce. Suspend shrimp in steamer at least 2 inches over liquid (if no steamer is available, a collander in a large cauldron may be used). Sprinkle scallions over shrimp. Cover tightly. Bring liquid to a boil, cook till shrimps are opaque—about 3–5 minutes.

Rice

Serves 14

6 cups water
2 teaspoons salt

3 tablespoons oil or butter
4 cups long-grain white rice

Preheat oven to 250°. In heavy saucepan, bring water to boil over high flame. Add salt and oil. Add rice and reduce heat to medium, stirring to prevent sticking. Cook, uncovered, 3 minutes. Reduce heat to very low. Cover tightly and let rice simmer until rice is firm but tender (just past al dente)—20–25 minutes. Stir once to release excess moisture and place, uncovered, in oven until dry (10–12 minutes).

Marc's Veal Parmigiana (Lucky's Favorite)

Serves 10

Sauce:

6 cloves garlic, finely minced
2 onions, minced
6 tablespoons olive oil
2 No. 2 cans tomatoes (5 cups)
2½ teaspoons salt

½ teaspoon pepper
2 8-ounce cans tomato sauce
½ teaspoon dried thyme or
   oregano

In saucepan, sauté garlic, and onion in oil till golden. Add tomatoes, salt, and pepper; break up tomatoes with a spoon. Simmer, uncovered, 10 minutes. Then add tomato sauce and thyme. Simmer 20 minutes.

Veal: Breading, Sautéing:

2 pounds veal cutlets, cut thin	½ cup grated Parmesan cheese
2 eggs	Oil
½ cup finely sifted dried bread crumbs	

Ask your butcher to get 8 slices (about 4½×2 inches) out of 1 pound veal. While the sauce is cooking, fix veal. In a pie plate, beat eggs well with fork. Combine crumbs and cheese on piece of wax paper. Dip each piece of veal first in egg, then in crumbs. Sauté 3 pieces at a time in 1 tablespoon hot oil in skillet. When browned on bottom, loosen crumbs from skillet; turn with broad spatula. Set veal slices side by side in 12×8×2-inch baking dish. Repeat, twice, with rest of veal.

Finished Casserole:

1 pound mozzarella cheese	½–⅓ cup grated Parmesan cheese

Heat oven to 350°. Slice mozzarella thinly. Pour ⅔ of the tomato sauce over veal, straining sauce if desired. Arrange mozzarella on top. Spoon on rest of sauce. Sprinkle with Parmesan cheese. Bake for 30 minutes, and serve with spaghetti, if desired.

Ned's Baked Maraconi†

(It's really very good!)   *Serves 10–12*

2 pounds veal	4 cloves garlic, pressed
2 pounds beef	2 tablespoons sugar
2 pounds pork	2 pounds Ronzoni mezzani rigati
2 medium onions, chopped	No. 4
1 cup olive oil	Pinch saffron
6 cans tomato paste	2 cups water
8 tomato paste cans water	4 eggs
Salt and pepper	1 cup grated Romano cheese

Use cheapest cuts of meat. Sauté onion in olive oil until brown. Don't overheat oil—if it smokes, it's too hot. Add meat and brown on all sides. Add tomato paste and water, several pinches of salt and pepper, garlic, and sugar. Cook until meat separates and sauce is thick. Take off burner and let cool. Remove meat and chop finely. Cook macaroni, draining when done. Add saffron to 2 cups water, mixing well. Pour saffron water over macaroni and mix. Add about ⅓ of chopped meat to macaroni and mix. Place macaroni mixture in large baking dish or casserole, and top with remainder of chopped meat.

Top with sauce, pressing the sauce into the mixture. Beat eggs till fluffy, and pour on top of everything. Sprinkle with Romano cheese, and bake in 400° oven until browned.

Bobby's Special Spaghetti

1. Brown cubes of veal in olive oil with crushed garlic.
2. Add sliced peperoni and simmer.
3. Add sliced fresh mushrooms, sliced green peppers. Simmer till soft.
4. Serve over spaghetti with grated cheese.

Spaghetti and Clam Sauce

Serves 12–14

½–1 cup oil	2 12-ounce cans tomato paste
4 large onions, diced	3 cups clam juice (from cans)
6–8 cloves garlic, crushed	3 tablespoons wine vinegar
1 tablespoon parsley	3 dashes Tabasco
1 tablespoon oregano	3 teaspoons salt (or more, to taste)
4 8-ounce cans minced clams	3 teaspoons garlic powder
1 35-ounce can tomatoes	2–3 pounds spaghetti

In oil, sauté onions, garlic, parsley, oregano. Drain clams, retaining juice. Add clams to the sautéed onion mixture. Sauté clams a bit, then add tomatoes, tomato paste, and clam juice. Add vinegar, Tabasco, and seasonings to taste. Simmer for ½–1 hour. Serve hot over spaghetti. *Note:* Cook the spaghetti al dente in water with salt and a bit of oil in it.

When done, drain, and wash with cold water until cold. Return to pot with oil and ⅛ cup butter or margarine. Heat over low heat, adding oil if it is too dry. Add about 1 cup of sauce to spaghetti, or just enough to make it light pink in color. Mix and heat until hot. Turn out into large spaghetti bowl, and either pour sauce over it or allow each person to serve himself the sauce. Using this method, you'll be assured of having spaghetti that is free of a starchy, sticky taste, and to which the sauce will easily cling.

Bucatini with Broccoli Calabrian (*Jewish-Italian*) *Style*

Serves 6

1 large bunch broccoli
2 cloves garlic, minced
4 tablespoons olive oil
2 pounds ripe tomatoes, peeled, cut
  into strips

1 pound bucatini (thin macaroni)
2 tablespoons finely minced fresh
  parsley

Clean broccoli and rinse well. Boil in salted water until tender; drain. Remove flowerettes and place on warm platter. Sauté garlic in oil until brown. Add tomatoes and simmer 15 minutes. Cook bucatini al dente, drain, and place in large hot bowl. Add broccoli flowerettes; pour sauce over, and toss carefully with wooden forks. Serve immediately in hot soup bowls sprinkled with parsley.

Cold Italian Peasant Salad

Serves 12

1½ pounds stale country bread (or
  any dark bread)
⅜ cup olive oil
3 tablespoons vinegar
1½ teaspoons salt
¾ teaspoon pepper

6 or 7 spring onions or 2 large
  onions, sliced and ringed
1½ cucumbers, sliced
15 leaves sweet basil
6 ripe tomatoes, cut into wedges

Cut bread into thick, rough slices and trim away crusts. If in America, you'll probably use whole wheat or sour rye. Soak dry stale slices in ice-cold water. Crumble well with your hands until you get soggy pellets. Squeeze well in a clean cloth, extracting all the moisture; by now the bread is edible again. Place bundle in the refrigerator for several hours. This will dry bread out even more and make it cold. Make a dressing by mixing well the olive oil, vinegar, salt, and pepper. In a salad bowl, place onion rings, cucumber slices, basil, and bread. Right before serving, add the tomato wedges and dressing. Toss well. (Of course variations of this salad are possible and often delicious. Adding a little salami is usually a nice touch.)

Eggplant Rollatini

Serves 12–16

2 medium or 4 small eggplants
4 eggs, beaten
Seasoned bread crumbs
Butter or margarine
1 pound mozzarella cheese, thinly
  sliced

6 small fresh overripe tomatoes,
  minced (you can use canned)
2 teaspoons dried basil

Peel the eggplants and slice lengthwise into 28 thin slices. Dip into beaten eggs and then into the crumbs. Sauté in melted butter. Drain on absorbent paper (paper towels are fine). Cut cheese slices into fourths; place a piece of cheese, a sprinkling of tomatoes, and some basil down the center of each slice. Then roll up, jellyroll fashion. Arrange on cookie sheets and bake in 350° oven for about 15 minutes. Cover with foil. Serve hot. Makes a great snack or first course.

Servings: 28 individual eggplant rollantini. Everyone will want more than one.

True Light Beaver Manicotti

(To be cooked by many)

Serves 12

Susan's Sauce:

½–⅓ cup oil
5 medium onions, chopped
6 or more cloves garlic
4½ tablespoons chopped parsley
3 teaspoons sweet basil
2 35-ounce cans tomatoes

2 15-ounce cans tomato sauce
3 teaspoons salt
½ teaspoon pepper
4½ tablespoons sugar
2 teaspoons garlic powder (or
  more, to taste)

For sauce: In hot oil, sauté onions, garlic, parsley, and basil until onions are soft and clear. Add tomatoes, tomato sauce, salt, pepper, sugar, and garlic powder to taste. Simmer, uncovered, for 20 minutes.

(Continued on next page.)

Colleen's Filling:

45 ounces cottage or ricotta cheese
(6 very full cups)

12 ounces mozzarella cheese,
grated

12 tablespoons grated Parmesan
cheese

3 eggs, lightly beaten

9 tablespoons sugar

6 tablespoons parsley

Salt and pepper to taste

3 dozen manicotti shells

For filling: Mix everything but shells together until sweet cheesy mixture is obtained—you may have to adjust seasonings a bit. Stuff shells to bursting. On the bottom of a baking pan, put a thin layer of sauce, and lay stuffed manicotti shells on sauce, covering with remaining sauce. Cover pan with foil, pinching sides so that nothing can drip out. Place in preheated 400° oven until shells are tender, but not quite done—about 40 minutes. Remove from oven, remove tin foil, and let sit (the longer you let it sit, the better it tastes). Fifteen minutes before serving, sprinkle a liberal amount of Parmesan cheese over top, and return to 400° oven until cheese is brown and sauce is bubbly—about 10 minutes.

Pizza

Serves 12–14

Dough:

4 packages yeast

1½ cups water

2 cups milk

4 tablespoons shortening

4 tablespoons sugar

2 teaspoons salt

2 eggs, well beaten

10–14 cups flour

Put yeast in 1 cup lukewarm water and set aside for 10 minutes. In a bowl, put ½ cup water, milk, shortening, sugar, salt, eggs. Then add yeast. Mix. Gradually mix in flour, stirring, until dough is stiff but not dry. Cover and let rise 2 hours.

Sauce:

2 tablespoons oregano

3 cloves garlic

2 28-ounce cans tomatoes

2 12-ounce cans tomato paste

1–2 teaspoons salt

Garlic powder to taste

Sauté oregano and garlic cloves; add tomatoes, tomato paste, salt, and garlic powder. Simmer until ready to use.

To spread dough: Put handful of flour on board. Place dough on board and knead about 5 times, until dough is not too sticky. Take a small bit of dough (fist-sized) and spread on well-oiled pan. It helps to spread if your hands are oiled also. Place sauce on dough. Place cheese and whatever else you want on sauce. Place pizza in hot (450°) oven for 20 minutes. This recipe makes enough dough and sauce for 5 cookie sheet-sized pizzas.

Billie's Pan Bania

My mother-in law's super sandwich—only when tomatoes are in their true season.

Slice a long loaf of Italian bread and rub it well with fresh garlic; drizzle a little oil on one side after the rub-in.

On one side of the long loaf, arrange fresh tomato slices, thin cucumber slices, onion rings, cooked or smoked fish or boiled eggs (anchovies, whatever you've got—not meat usually), slices of Greek olives and sweet pepper rings. Cover it all with the other side of the loaf and weight it down with a substantial weight for ½ hour. Remove the weight and slice the loaf into servings. A long loaf can yield 8 servings. This can be infinitely expanded. A salad of romaine lettuce really goes well with it.

Lasagne with 4 Cheeses

Serves 8–10

2 pounds lasagne	1 cup grated **Parmesan cheese**
4 tablespoons butter	1 cup grated **pecorino cheese**
4 tablespoons flour	1 cup diced **mozzarella cheese**
8 cups milk	1 teaspoon salt
1 cup grated **Gruyère cheese**	2 teaspoons white pepper

Cook sheets of lasagne in large pot of furiously boiling salted water. The addition of 1 tablespoon oil to water will keep the pasta from sticking. When al dente, remove carefully with a pair of forceps and lay on paper towels to drain.

While lasagne is cooking, start preparing the sauce. Melt the butter and slowly stir in the flour, making a smooth, thick paste. Gradually add the milk, stirring over low heat until you obtain a smooth white sauce. Add the

Gruyère, the Parmesan, the pecorino, the mozzarella, and salt and pepper. Blend thoroughly. Cover the bottom of a buttered ovenware dish with sheets of lasagne. Pour over some of the sauce. Repeat until all the lasagne and all the sauce has been used. There should be at least 4 layers. Bake in a moderate oven until golden brown on top—about ¾ hour. When this comes out of the oven, it will be quite liquidy. But have no fear! As soon as it cools a bit, it all comes together. You are not going to believe the levels of taste.

June's Spaghetti Roast

Serves 10–12

Pot roast, 7-bone roast, or chuck roast, etc. (allow 3 servings to the pound)	¼ cup Worcestershire sauce
	¼ cup sugar
Oil	Salt and pepper
2 large cans tomatoes	4 medium onions, sliced
2 cans tomato sauce	2 pints sour cream
	1½ pounds spaghetti

Brown roast in oil in pan. Remove from pan and add all remaining ingredients except spaghetti. Return roast to pan, making sure to place it on a rack. Simmer slowly until meat is tender. Remove meat and rack from pan. Bring juice to a boil and add spaghetti. Stir frequently and cook until all the liquid is absorbed into the spaghetti. Serve spaghetti with sliced roast. Incidentally, my kids put away tremendous amounts of this, and to this day their favorite meal is spaghetti roast. Happy cooking!

Laurie's Spaghetti Carbonara

Serves 12

6–8 strips bacon, cut into small pieces	1½–2 pounds spaghetti, preferably green or whole wheat
2 large white onions, chopped	Salt and pepper to taste
14 eggs	
2 cups fresh grated Parmesan or pecorino cheese	

Cut bacon into small pieces, and fry. Set aside. Cook onions in bacon grease or olive oil. Beat the eggs in a large bowl to a foam. Add the onions, pieces of bacon, and half the Parmesan or pecorino cheese. Mix, and add hot, drained spaghetti. Mix well, adding salt, pepper, and the rest of the cheese, and serve.

Two Tucan Recipes

Spinach and Rice Soup

Serves 10–12

6 quarts broth
1½ cups uncooked rice
3 pounds fresh spinach

Fresh nutmeg
Salt and pepper
Grated cheese

Bring the broth to a boil. Lower heat, add the rice, and simmer till the rice is done. Turn off the heat. Add the spinach and cover. It's done in 3 minutes. Before eating, add the nutmeg, salt, pepper, and cheese.

Excruciating Pleasures

Serves 10–12

3 pounds spaghetti
Garlic and fresh parsley

3 cups olive oil
Grated cheese

You will cook the spaghetti and drain it. Ja! Take 6 or so cloves of garlic. Mince them finely. Chop about ½ cup of parsley. Warm the oil in a large saucepan. Don't make it hot. There is no frying involved in this little wonder. Add the garlic and parsley to the pot. Steep for 3 mintues. Add the pasta to the pot. Blow every synapse in your body.

Mama Mia Speecy Spicy Minestrone (makes hordes) — Lizzie

Serves 10–12

Make beef stock: In large kettle, add 9–10 cups water to several soup bones with meat. Bring to boil. Skim. Add 1 onion with 5 cloves stuck in it, 2 carrots, diced, celery leaves, cut, and bouquet garni: 1 bay leaf, few sprigs parsley, 1 teaspoon thyme, 2 peeled garlic cloves, ½ teaspoon basil. Salt and pepper. Simmer, with lid not quite covering pot, 1½–2 hours. Strain. Save meat.

Soak 1 cup dried kidney beans in 2 cups water overnight. Drain. Add 8–9 cups stock and bring slowly to a boil. In a skillet, fry 3 strips bacon till lightly browned; remove and save. In fat, sauté 2 large onions, chopped coarsely, till golden. Add to beans. Chop 5 garlic cloves with a little salt and add to beans. Simmer 1 hour.

Heat ⅓ cup olive oil and add 2 potatoes, peeled and diced, 2 small carrots (or more), scraped and diced, and 1 cup fresh zucchini, sliced; ½ cup chopped celery with leaves; ½ cup chopped broccoli. (Can add other vegetables too.) Add 2 tablespoons basil. Cook a few minutes and stick in 2 cups peeled, seeded tomatoes, and 1 cup shredded cabbage. Add to beans and cook for 1 hour. Add meat. Stir in ½ cup red wine, ½ cup raw pasta. Season to taste with oregano, thyme, etc. Simmer 15 minutes.

Serve with Parmesan and freshly grated lemon peel mixed with parsley.

Al Dente Debby-Susan-Arthur Fine Green Spaghetti

Serves 10–12

3 tablespoons olive oil **3 pounds spaghetti**
1 small bottle green food coloring

Bring appropriate amount of water for spaghetti to boil. Add olive oil, food coloring, and spaghetti. Cook al dente.

Al Dente Debby Fine Red Spaghetti

Serves 10–12

Same as above, only using red food coloring.

Al Dente Debby Fine Christmas Fete

Serves 20–24

Make both recipes above. When al dente, braid spaghetti into red and green braids. Serve at once.

CURRY ON CURRY

Curry is a blend of spices and herbs:

Coriander	**Cloves**
Cayenne	**Cinnamon**
Mustard seed	**Cardamom**
Turmeric	**Ginger**
Cumin	**Fenugreek**

Familiarity with the qualities of each will enable you to use them alone or together for a whole new range of exotic taste sensations. They are pretty easy to come by; worth any extra effort, for working from the basic ingredients will take you far beyond stale and repetitious prepared curry powder. Buy seeds rather than ground; most have medicinal properties and can be brewed as teas.

Basic Curry

This is a good place to start learning flavors and how they blend. Basic curry can be served over rice, as a soup, or as the beginning of a more exotic dish. Ghee, or clarified butter, is the preferred shortening in India; peanut oil will do fine.

¶ To 4 tablespoons of hot oil, add ½ teaspoon cumin seed, 1 teaspoon fenugreek, 4 cloves, 1 short cinnamon stick, ½ teaspoon mustard seed. Stir until mustard dances, then add, mixed together, 1 cup yogurt, 1 tablespoon chick-pea flour (substitute, it's O.K.), 2 cups water. Don't worry about lumping. Lower heat, add 1 teaspoon salt, 1 teaspoon turmeric, 1½ teaspoons coriander seed, 2 tablespoons sugar, ½ teaspoon cayenne. Let simmer 20 minutes—it's done. Watch out for the cayenne; it's easy to add too much. Be cautious at first until you're sure of the flavors.

Banana Curry

Getting right down to a really far-out dish, all you do is add an extra tablespoon or so of flour and seeds from 4 cardamom pods to the basic curry. Simmer 5 minutes, add a bunch of sliced bananas, cook another 15 minutes. Add raisins or other fruits as you wish. The combination of flavors is surprising.

Crunchy Vegetable Curry

Prepare basic curry, adding all spices without yogurt liquid. Stir-fry your vegetables for a few minutes (don't forget onions), then add yogurt liquid and simmer for 10–20 minutes. Try eggplant and okra by themselves; try potatoes, but cook them a while longer.

Soft Vegetable Curry

Boil vegetables in salted water—don't drain. Prepare basic curry spices in oil, add vegetables with their juices, add yogurt and flour (if you wish), simmer 10–20 minutes. Spinach and carrots are good this way.

Two Vegetable Flashes

Very quick and easy, and good flashes on how to use curry spices individually:

→ Add 1 teaspoon mustard seed to 3 tablespoons hot peanut oil, then add a finely chopped cauliflower with 1 teaspoon salt. Stir-fry for 3 minutes; serve hot or cold.

→ To 3 tablespoons peanut oil, add 1 teaspoon turmeric, 1 teaspoon mustard seed, 1 teaspoon salt, then 4 cups chopped cabbage, stir-fry for 5 minutes. Try cumin seed or coriander in either recipe, in addition to, or in place of.

Chapaties

Chapati is Indian flat bread. Mix 2 cups flour, 1 teaspoon salt, 2 tablespoons oil, add about ¾ cup hot water, mix until pliable and smooth, then knead. Roll a chunk of dough into a ball, then roll out flat in all directions with a rolling pin.
Cook on both sides on a hot surface (the top of an Ashley will do) for 20 seconds a side. Flip a few times for about 2 minutes total, until done. (Crunchy.)

In Conclusion

Keep experimenting. Add powdered milk if you can't get yogurt. A bit of leftover granola once enhanced a super banana curry, and it's hard to go wrong.

Curry

Note on curries: The whole trick seems to be in the slow and long cooking as each additional clump of ingredients gets added to the basic onion and marge. Paul Kashap insists that marge is better than butter, although his wife, who is from Flushing, told me that the girl Paul learned from when they were both Indian students at Cambridge always used butter. When we're rich, I'll use butter; until then I'll use marge.

Paul Kashap's Curry

Serves 8–10

1 large onion, chopped	1 teaspoon turmeric
4 tablespoons margarine	1 teaspoon curry powder
Big dash of garlic powder	1 teaspoon salt
Big dash of fresh coriander	30 ounces garbanzos, drained and
1 teaspoon cumin seeds	washed
1 teaspoon coriander powder	

Cook onions in margarine until translucent. Add spices and seasoning. Cook slowly for at least 5 minutes. Add and stir beans; cook slowly for at least 5 minutes. Add water until beans are almost covered, partly cover pan, and cook until water is almost absorbed. Add juice of 1 lemon.

Spinach Curry

Serves 8–10

3 pounds spinach
1 large onion, chopped
6 tablespoons margarine
1 teaspoon turmeric
1 teaspoon ground ginger
1 teaspoon cumin seeds

25 twists of the pepper mill
1/8 teaspoon cayenne
1/8 teaspoon ground California red
   pepper
1/4 teaspoon fenugreek
1 teaspoon salt

Cook onions in margarine until translucent. Add spices. Wash spinach, break off rough stems, and chop coarsely. Cook slowly for at least 5 minutes. Place almost dry spinach in a pot with a little water. Sprinkle 1 teaspoon salt on top of spinach and cook, covered tightly, until steam rises. Drain spinach and mix it into spice mixture. Re-cover, and cook 10 minutes. Partly uncover and cook until most of the liquid is absorbed.

Eggplant Curry

Serves 8–10

1 eggplant, peeled and chopped
1 small onion, chopped
6 tablespoons margarine
1/2-inch piece fresh ginger, peeled
   and chopped
2 tablespoons chopped fresh
   coriander

1/2 green pepper, finely chopped
1 good teaspoon turmeric
1/2 teaspoon ground cumin
1/2 teaspoon salt
1 tomato, cut up

Char eggplant under hot boiler. Cook onion in margarine until translucent. Add ginger, coriander, green pepper, turmeric, cumin, and salt. Simmer for 5 minutes. Add tomato and simmer until skin is wilted—about 5 minutes. Add chopped eggplant. Cover and simmer for 1/2 hour.

Lamb Curry

1½ pounds lamb, cut in chunks   ¼ pound margarine
2 large onions, chopped or crushed

Cook onions in margarine until all fat disappears. Add:

2½ cloves garlic, chopped fine   1 teaspoon ground cumin
1 full teaspoon turmeric   ¼ teaspoon cinnamon
2 teaspoons ground coriander   ¼ teaspoon ground cardamom
1½ teaspoons cumin seeds   2 tablespoons paprika

Simmer spices and onions very slowly for at least 7 minutes. Add:

1 teaspoon salt   **Lamb**

Simmer, uncovered, until lamb turns brown and shrinks. Add:

2 heaping tablespoons yogurt

Simmer, uncovered, until yogurt turns red. Add:

Approximately 1 cup cold water

Simmer, covered, about 1 hour.

Mushroom and Canned Potato Curry

Soak 1½ ounces dried mushrooms for 2 hours in hot water to cover. Retain water.

1 large onion, chopped   4 tablespoons margarine

Cook onion in margarine until translucent. Add:

¾ teaspoon turmeric   ⅛ teaspoon cayenne
¾ teaspoon cumin powder

Simmer at least 7 minutes. Add:

1 scant teaspoon salt   Sliced mushrooms

(*Continued on next page*)

Simmer uncovered, for 3 minutes. Add:

**1 15-ounce can small whole peeled
    potatoes, drained**

Simmer, uncovered, for 7 minutes. Add most of liquid from mushrooms.
Cover and simmer for 45 minutes.

Mai's Thoughts on Curries

Decide on spices to be used. For example: garlic, turmeric, thyme, cloves,
cinnamon, cayenne, coriander, pepper, etc. Heat cooking oil in a pan, and
add spices. Then add hard-boiled eggs (or meat). Then add vegetables and
a little water. Simmer.

Jim's Balduntum Curry

(Jim made this recipe up. It is good for a lot of people)

3 chicken breasts	**½ cup chopped onion**
Butter	**1 small can mushrooms**
Basil to taste	**Milk from 1 coconut**
Paprika to taste	**Patway's curry paste**
Rosemary to taste	**1 tablespoon flour**
Salt and pepper to taste	**1 cup uncooked rice**
1 bay leaf	**Pinch saffron**
½ cup chopped celery	

Braise chicken in butter, season with basil, paprika, rosemary, salt, pepper.
Remove from pan and simmer in pot with bay leaf till quite tender. In the
pan in which the chicken was fried, melt ½ stick (⅛ pound) butter.
Sauté celery and onions. Then add the mushrooms and coconut milk, and
simmer. Add 1½–2 heaping teaspoons curry paste to taste. After it has
cooked for 5–10 minutes, thicken with flour. Leave to simmer until the
celery is tender. When the chicken is tender, remove from pot, retaining
stock. Place chicken in sauce. Cook the rice, using stock from chicken, ½
stick butter, salt, and saffron. Serve the chicken and sauce over rice.
Beer and limeade are traditional to serve with this meal. Also Major Grey's
Chutney, olives, and dates.

Myth of the Deli=Llama

A FOOD FAIRYTALE FOR YOUNGSTERS
FROM 60 TO 85

Once upon a time, in a sylvan valley called Silver Hollow, in a fabulous land called Greene County . . . that's enough clauses and commas for you octogenarians to handle at first, so allow me to leave it a fragment and take it from there."

In any case, deep in this Silver Hollow lived a postbiological family of flaxen-haired trolls known outside the valley as a *community*. There were trolls who did visionary drawings, M.D. trolls, herb-ingesting trolls, tie-dying trolls. None of them lingered under bridges demanding money, and none could be hustled by billygoats gruff. It is time we buried that racist stereotype.

These trolls sung a happy song, they whistled while they worked, etc., you get the picture, they fiddled and diddled and shouted "HI-DE-HO" and so forth. They raised little trolls, and their consciousness.

One day one of the trolls quit diddling long enough to suggest:

"Say, fellows, why don't we invite our parents from their apartments where the settees grow heavy with dust and the fans complain of rheumatism and the doilies loathe each other, and bring them down into Silver Hollow?

"Far fucking out†," chorused the happy trolls.

"Why the h-e-double hockey stick *not!*" added an older troll.

And so it was that the parents of the trolls found themselves rubbing elbows with the beavers, chickens, and other celebrities who filled the Hollow in profusion.

But there was nervousness in the air. Some of the parents looked askance when one of the trolls launched into a "HI-DE-HO" routine.

"Mom, you're looking askance," said a troll.

"That's all right, darling," said his mother. "Just a little gallstone trouble . . ."

Many of the parents were of the Jewish persuasion, and since the trolls were one of the Lost Tribes there was very little friction there. But when it came time for dinner a terrible problem arose.

The trolls had forgotten that their great stocks of troll food—holly gathered under full moons, lime water, sprigs of mistletoe, ginger—were not their parents' style.

† Jargon from the youth culture employed solely for journalistic accuracy.

"Gevalt," the patriarchs and matriarchs gevalted in unison as they peered inside the cupboards.

This was real *tzuras.*

The trolls grew sad and cried out to Krishna, Christ, and Eugene V. Debs (a deity worshiped by their parents). The parents rocked unhappily on their chairs—but since they were not rocking chairs several found themselves sprawled on the lawn.

When it seemed the tragedy was at its deepest a cloud suddenly sheathed the sun and a tremendous (not that tremendous) roar of approaching hooves resounded through the valley.

Instantly, in what I believe young people refer to as a "flash," a bizarre goatlike animal appeared. Among the trolls and parents there were shouts of amazement (among them "Jeez!" "Yeah, right?" and "Clean jerseys!"), gnashing of teeth, leaping, and other reactions too numerous to mention here,† because:

Hanging from the neck of the rainbow-fleeced quasi goat were huge, glowing pastramis, bagels stuffed with lox and cream cheese, many-splendored Hebrew National salamis, singing slabs of gefilte fish, and the whole array of kosher cuisine, anything you can conjure up.

Tentatively the senior citizens reached out for the bounty. The beast reared up (nostrils spewing fire, bellowing mightily—see Blake's *Tiriel* for details), but it was all for show, and soon he was purring dazedly as the golden agers plucked the wonders from his neck. His eyes seemed to speak the East Side Inquiry: Did I make you a good sendvich?

But then the feast seemed over—everyone, even the trolls, rolling glutted on the sweet grass. One wizened, bold mother put her face next to the animal and said:

"Listen—you got challah?" (This being a Jewish bread more prized than Judas Maccabeus' hammer, and you can throw in some two byfours.)

There was a long silence as the crowd surveyed the soft animal. It deepened as the goat rose up, shuddered, and produced a huge golden loaf on the tip of a nose, as he did so saying:

"Fresh today!"

And as the woman snatched the challah from the magic horn of plenty the goat "split the scene," to use the hippie parlance again— never to be seen again, natch.

---

† Full catalogue sent on request.

And, to this day, in the midst of the fiddling, diddling, and whistling action that fills the Silver Hollow, the children fall asleep dreaming about it, the old folks (they stayed too, of course—never leave the scene of a miracle) trace its outline on their Etch-a-Sketches, and the singers chant the tale of the fabulous DELI-LLAMA.

FROM WARSAW TO WOODSTOCK

Beautiful, Bountiful Baked Bagels Lizzie

4 tablespoons oil

2 tablespoons sugar

½ teaspoon salt (or ¼ teaspoon
   salt and ¼ teaspoon garlic salt)

1 cup warm water

½ ounce dry yeast

1 egg

4 cups flour, sifted

Minced dried onions (optional)

Poppy seeds

Mix oil, sugar, salt, and warm water. When lukewarm, add yeast and stir. Beat egg till frothy and add. Mix in flour and onions. Knead till smooth (1 minute) and shape into donuts (12–15). Cover and set aside to rise (10 minutes). Drop one at a time into boiling water. Cook till they puff up and are light (2–3 minutes). Sprinkle with poppy seeds. Put on well-greased cookie sheet. Bake at 400° for 20–25 minutes.

Many Jewish "housewives" often run into "difficulty" cooking for discriminating Protestant in-laws. In this day of "intermarriage," I "often" counsel kosher hausfraus on the ins and outs of the sensitive WASP palate. ¶ My handy rule of thumb: When you talk *goyisch,* you're talking mayo. ¶ Mayonnaise is the magic key to so many of those tantalizing front-porch "dishes." Properly prepared with all the fixin's, a mayonnaise dinner can hit with all the impact of the financial pages of the *Christian Science Monitor.* ¶ I like to surprise my Kansas clan with a Mayo-Bone Soufflé. First, whip a half jar of Hellmann's VSOP in Osterizer. Then, pare beef bones of meat and polish until bare and gleaming. Then simply affix "colored" tassels to the bones and insert into deep dish filled with the whipped mayonnaise. For that exciting "picket fence" effect bones may be bleached under sunlamp for 12 hours.

Challah

3 cups milk	2 packages yeast
3 tablespoons sugar	2 eggs, lightly beaten
1 tablespoon salt	7½ cups all-purpose flour, sifted
¼ cup butter	1 egg yolk
¼ cup warm water	1 tablespoon water
1 teaspoon crumbled saffron	Poppy seeds

Heat milk till bubbles form at edge. Remove from heat, add sugar, salt, and butter, stirring till butter melts. Let cool.

Boil ¼ cup water with saffron. Let cool till semihot, add yeast, stir till dissolved; add milk mixture.

Add eggs and 3¼ cups of the flour, beating with wooden spoon till very smooth. Slowly add remaining flour, beating after each addition until too stiff, then mix rest with hands.

Turn out onto board and knead for 15–20 minutes. Place in greased bowl. Let rise till double in bulk—about 1 hour. Place in unheated oven, covered with towel. Punch down; turn onto board and braid. (Cut into 3 strips, pinch together at top, and braid, pinching at bottom.)

Place on cookie sheet, cover with towel, and let rise for 1 hour.

Brush with egg yolk beaten with 1 tablespoon water. Sprinkle with poppy seeds and bake in oven preheated to 400° until golden brown—about 40 minutes.

Gefilte Fish

3 pounds pike
1 pound whitefish
2 perch
2 medium onions
1 teaspoon salt
¼ teaspoon pepper

3 tablespoons matzoh meal
3 eggs
3½ cups water
1 large onion, sliced
1 large carrot, sliced

Fillet fish and save bones and skin. Grind onions and fish and put in bowl. Add salt, pepper, matzoh meal, and eggs, and chop, adding a little water, until ½ cup has been thoroughly chopped into the fish. Adjust seasonings. Put bones, skin, onion slices, carrot slices, and 3 cups water into a large pot. Bring to boil. Form fish mixture into balls, and drop into boiling water. Continue to boil slowly for 2 hours. Correct seasonings while it cooks, and add more water, so that there will be liquid enough to pour over the fish balls when they're done. When cold, the liquid will be jellied. It's delicious.

Shushi's Mock Chopped Liver

Serves 12

2 dozen hard-boiled eggs
Mayonnaise
½ pound mushrooms

2 small onions
Salt and pepper to taste

Chop the eggs with mayonnaise until you reach egg salad consistency. Chop the mushrooms and onions very fine. Add and blend to the egg mixture. Add salt and pepper to taste. Chill for about an hour. When you serve this dish, don't tell anyone what it is. Someone is bound to thank you enthusiastically for making chopped liver. Then tell everyone what it is and how easy it is to make.·

Marc's Noodle Pudding

Serves 20

1 pound noodles
½ pound butter, melted
1 pint sour cream
½ pound cream or cottage cheese

5 eggs
½ cup sugar
Corn flakes

Cook noodles, drain, and mix with melted butter. Combine sour cream and cream cheese or cottage cheese, and mix till smooth. Add to noodles. Separate eggs, beating the yolks and adding to noodle mixture. Beat whites till stiff. Add to egg whites the sugar, and fold whole thing carefully into the noodle mixture. Place in a greased dripping pan and sprinkle top with corn flakes. Bake for 30–45 minutes at 350°.

Meatless Tzimmes

Serves 10–12

3 cups soaked prunes
4 carrots
6 cups cubed sweet potatoes
2 6-ounce cans frozen orange juice

2 cans water
1 teaspoon salt
4 tablespoons brown sugar

Remove pits from prunes. Dice carrots and raw sweet potatoes into ½-inch cubes. Place in saucepan with prunes and pour orange juice and water over carrots and potatoes immediately to prevent discoloring. Add salt and sugar to taste and cook, covered, simmering until tender—1–1½ hours.

Cheese Blintzes

Serves 12

Batter:	Filling:
8 eggs	3 pounds cream cheese
2 cups water	1 pound cottage cheese
2 cups milk	4 eggs
2 cups flour	Salt, pepper, and sugar to taste
½ teaspoon salt	

Combine all batter ingredients thoroughly, until smooth. Pour batter into slightly greased, hot frying pan (about 6 inches). Fry on one side; invert on white paper or clean dish towel. Then make the filling. Blend all filling ingredients together. Place a tablespoon of filling in the center of the pancake. Fold the outer edge of the circle toward the center. Fry in butter with folded side down first, until golden brown on both sides. Serve with sour cream, jelly, applesauce, and other fruit.

Latkes

Serves 12–16

20 medium potatoes, peeled	5 teaspoons salt
5 onions	2½ cups flour
10 eggs	2½ teaspoons baking powder

Grate potatoes and drain off water. Grate onions into potatoes. Add remaining ingredients, stirring well. Drop batter by tablespoons into hot shortening. Fry as you would any pancake, until brown and crisp on both sides. Serve with sour cream, applesauce, sugar, fruit.

Mike's Jewish Breakfast for 1 or 1½

(Enlarge accordingly)

Sauté a 2-inch onion, diced, in butter till soft and sweet. Just before onion is brown throw in a 2×8-inch slice of lox, diced. After 2 minutes on hot flame, throw in 2 well-beat-up eggs, adding pepper and salt simultaneously. With free hand throw bagel into toaster. Stir lox, eggs, and onion, then get the cream cheese out. Remove eggs from frying pan. Cream cheese and eat.

Borscht

Serves 8

8 large beets
Lemon juice to taste

Sugar to taste
Salt to taste

Wash and peel beets. Cut up greens and put with beets into a large pot with water to cover. While beets are cooking, add lemon juice, sugar, and salt to taste. It takes a while to taste like borscht, but it's worth it. When the beets are done (poke with a fork), take them out and grate them or slice them into small slivers. The soup should taste like beets and be light red in color. Cool, then serve with sour cream, cukes, boiled potatoes, etc.

Helen's Pickled Herring

A snack for many

1 pint sour cream
2 tablespoons sugar

4 onions, sliced
2 pounds Vita herring (plain)

Mix sour cream, sugar, and all wine sauce from start together. Put in onions and herring. Refrigerate for 2–3 hours and eat.

Helen's Chopped Liver

Serves 75–100

10 pounds beef liver, sliced thin
Vegetable oil
50 small–medium onions, chopped

30 eggs
⅓ cup schmaltz (chicken fat)
Salt and pepper to taste

Fry liver strips in vegetable oil. Fry 4 onions in vegetable oil. Dice 10 raw onions. Hard-boil the eggs. In a meat grinder, grind eggs, liver. Mix in fried onions, diced onions, oil used in cooking, schmaltz (and/or more vegetable oil), salt, pepper.

Note: Chopped liver is a great new sculpturing medium. Become one with it and create masterpieces for the mind and stomach.

Mum's Noodle Pudding

For 16 or more

2 pounds fine noodles
2 pints sour cream
6 eggs, beaten

2 pounds cottage cheese
1 pound cream cheese
½–1 cup sugar (to taste)

Put all together; salt, raisins, cinnamon, sugar on top; also melted butter on top. Bake at 350° for 45 minutes.

Sour Cream Cake—"Iss Bery Good for You!"

Cake:

2 cups soft butter or margarine
4 cups sugar
6 eggs
8 cups sifted flour
2 teaspoons baking soda
1 teaspoon salt

2 cups dairy sour cream
2 teaspoons almond extract
2 cups coarsely chopped nuts
1 cup currants or chopped raisins
1 cup chopped citron or candied
   fruit

Topping:

·1 cup sugar
2 teaspoons cinnamon

8 tablespoons butter or margarine

Cream the butter in a bowl until fluffy. Gradually beat in the sugar until light and creamy. Add the eggs, one at a time, beating well after each addition. Add the sifted flour, soda, and salt alternately with combined sour cream and almond extract. Mix until well blended. Stir in the nuts, currants, and citron (optional). Pour into 2 greased and floured pans (13×9×2 inches). Sprinkle the mixed sugar and cinnamon over top of batter. Dot with butter. Bake in moderate oven (about 350°) until a cake tester inserted in the middle of cake comes back clean. Check after 25 minutes to be sure. Remove from rack and cut into pieces while still in pan.

Joel's Rolls

Makes 4 loaves or 24 rolls

3 tablespoons yeast
2 tablespoons sugar
1 cup warm water
4 teaspoons salt
4 cups water
⅓ cup oil

12–14 cups flour (you may use
  white, whole wheat, etc.; a great
  combination is ⅓ white, ⅔ rye,
  with ½ teaspoon ground
  caraway seeds to give it a good
  rye bread taste)
Optional (very good): 4 small
  onions, chopped, or 3 cloves
  garlic, chopped

Let yeast dissolve with sugar in 1 cup warm water. Let sit for 5 minutes,
then add salt. Mix with the 4 cups of water, oil, and flour until doughy
consistency is obtained. Mix in onions or garlic and knead and let rise until
doubled. Punch down and let rise ½ hour. Form into rolls on greased and
floured cookie sheets or place in greased loaf pans and let rise until doubled.
Bake at 350° for ½ hour for rolls, about 1 hour for bread.

Cheese-Onion Mushroom-style Bread

2 cups hot water
2 teaspoons salt
A big spoon of honey
A good pour of oil
2 cups rye flour

2 tablespoons active dry yeast,
  dissolved in ½ cup warm water
Caraway seeds, poppy seeds
Onions, chopped
1 cup grated Cheddar cheese

Mix first 5 ingredients together. Add yeast water. Add 3–4 cups more flour
(rye and whole wheat) and caraway seeds, poppy seeds. Knead. Let rise in
bowl for 1½ hours or till twice its size.
Punch down.
Now add sautéed onions and grated Cheddar cheese. Mix this well into the
bread. Make into 2 loaves. Place loaves in well-greased 1-pound coffee cans.
Let rise until the bread starts to look like a big mushroom. Caution—you
have to catch the bread before the top falls off, so don't let it rise too long

before baking. Bake in a 375° oven until done—somewhere between 45 minutes and 1 hour. The thing about bread is that it turns out different every time. You just have to experiment.

Carrot Bread

¾ cup vegetable oil
1 cup raw sugar, or ½ cup honey
2 cups whole wheat flour
1 teaspoon salt
1 cup grated raw carrots or
    carrot pulp

2 eggs, beaten
½ cup chopped nuts
½ teaspoon vanilla

Mix all ingredients. Put into well-greased loaf pan. Bake at 375° for 1 hour. Remove from pan and cool.

Pumpkin Bread

¾ cup sugar
1¾ cups flour
1 teaspoon cinnamon
½ teaspoon salt
½ cup oil
1 cup chopped pumpkin

⅓ cup water or orange juice
¾ cup brown sugar
1 teaspoon baking soda
½ teaspoon nutmeg
⅛ teaspoon ginger
1 egg

Mix all ingredients well. Add ¾ cup raisins and 1 cup chopped nuts. Bake 1 hour in loaf pan at 350°.

Shrimp Bread

2 cups lukewarm water
2 tablespoons yeast
1 teaspoon salt
2 tablespoons oil

6 cups white flour
½ cup flour mixed with ½ cup
    cornmeal

1. Mix water, yeast, salt, oil. Let yeast start working. Mix in 6 cups flour, knead. Let rise for 1 hour.
2. Knead; let rise for ½ hour under inverted bowl.
3. Cut into 6 portions. Dip in oil then into cornmeal-flour mixture. Cover thoroughly with mixture.

4. They are to be rolled into round flat loaves. Traditionally they should be very large and thin. Because my cookie tins weren't big enough I rolled them to about 9 inches' diameter so they are thicker. I like them better that way.
5. Bake in oven at 425° for about 15 minutes (till edges start to get brown).

Swedish Beer Rye Bread

1¾ cups beer
½ cup warmed molasses
2 cakes yeast, dissolved in ¼ cup warm water
⅓ cup butter

2 teaspoons salt
3 cups rye flour or meal
3 cups white flour, sifted
1 tablespoon caraway seeds

Combine beer and molasses; add dissolved yeast. Beat in rest of ingredients and blend well. Brush top of dough with melted butter, cover with light cloth, let rise till doubled, which is approximately 2 hours.

Punch dough down, turn it out onto a floured board, and knead thoroughly —8–10 minutes, using as much more white flour as is necessary to keep dough from sticking. Shape into 2 oval loaves.

Place on buttered cookie sheets. Cover and let rise until doubled—about 1½ hours.

Bake in 350° oven until done—35–45 minutes.

For a glossy crust, brush 3 times while baking with egg white diluted with water.

Oatmeal-Honey Loaf

1 cup steel-cut oats
1 cup boiling water
2¼ cups unsifted flour
2½ teaspoons baking powder
1 teaspoon salt

¼ cup melted butter
3 tablespoons honey
1 egg
⅔ cup milk

In large bowl, combine oatmeal and boiling water—stir till well mixed. Let stand till cool—about 2 hours.

Preheat oven to 350°; grease 9×5×3-inch loaf pan.

In medium bowl, sift flour, baking powder, and salt; add butter and honey to oatmeal. Mix well with wooden spoon.

In small bowl, beat egg with milk. Add flour mixture to oatmeal, then add egg mixture. Stir till combined.
Do not overmix. Turn into loaf pan. Bake 70 minutes.

Glazed Lemon-Nut Bread

Makes 2 loaves

½ cup butter or margarine
1½ cups sugar
4 eggs
4 teaspoons grated lemon peel
4 cups flour (mixed white and
  wheat)

5 teaspoons baking powder
2 teaspoons salt
1½ cups milk
1 cup chopped walnuts
4 teaspoons lemon juice
4 tablespoons sugar

Cream together butter and sugar; add eggs and lemon peel. Sift together dry ingredients and add to mixture with milk, beating until smooth. Add nuts; bake in greased bread pans, 50–55 minutes at 350°. Let cool. Spoon combination lemon juice and sugar over top, remove from pan, cool, wrap, store (ha!).

Corn Bread–Oyster Dressing

1 cup water
1½ cups butter
8 cups corn bread
2 cans oysters
½ cup chopped onions

½ cup chopped green peppers
½ cup chopped celery
1 teaspoon salt
½ teaspoon rosemary
¼ teaspoon pepper

In 6-quart Dutch oven heat 1 cup water and 1 cup butter until melted. Remove from heat, add corn bread, and toss. Drain oysters; cut in half. In remaining butter sauté oysters, onions, green peppers, and celery until onions are golden—5–7 minutes. Stir in salt, rosemary, and pepper. Add to bread. Can be used to fill turkey or baked in dish separately.
Really out of sight!

Mai's Unyeasted Sesame Bread

Makes 2 loaves

1 cup white sesame seeds (black
   have no nutritional value)
6 cups any combination flour
1½ tablespoons salt

1½ tablespoons oil
1 cup wheat germ
Water

Toast the sesame seeds in ungreased pan over medium heat until brown. Mix together the flour, salt, oil, and wheat germ. Add the sesame seeds. Add water until the mixture is doughy. Knead or shape into greased loaf pans. Bake 1–1½ hours in 350° oven.

Mai's Quick Muffins

2 cups whole wheat flour
2 teaspoons baking powder
½ teaspoon salt
3 tablespoons molasses
2 tablespoons cooking oil or
   melted butter

1 egg beaten (optional)
1 cup milk
¼ cup raisins, or ½ cup
   blueberries or dates or nuts (all
   optional)

Combine first 5 ingredients. Add egg and milk. Add nuts/dates/raisins. Mix to grainy texture. Beating is not necessary. Bake in greased muffin tins in 425° oven for 20–30 minutes.

Bread

I use this same basic bread recipe nearly every time I make bread, with variations.

2 tablespoons active yeast	2–3 wooden spoonfuls honey
¼ cup lukewarm water	A little salt (maybe 2 teaspoons)
2 cups hot water	5–6 cups flour
A good pour of oil	

Mix yeast in lukewarm water; set aside. To the hot water, add oil, honey, salt, and 2 cups of the flour (any kind you like; whole wheat and rye make a heavier loaf). Mix well. Now add the yeast water and mix well. Add 3–4 cups more flour, enough so that the bread doesn't stick to your hands.
Knead it until it feels like your earlobe.
Let rise until twice its size.
Punch down; knead for a few minutes. Put in loaf pans or coffee cans. We like to use coffee cans cause the bread comes out looking like big mushrooms.
Let rise till twice its size again.
Bake at 375° till done. Depending on the kind of bread, it will usually take from 45 minutes to an hour or more.
One way to test bread is to tap the top. If it is firm, take it out of the pan and see if the sides and bottom are brown. If the top gets too done while baking, cover with foil.
I bake bread with a pan in the bottom of the oven with ½ cup water in it. Keeps the bread moist and keeps it from burning.

Arleen's Soup

Serves 10

10 cups chicken broth
½ cup finely shredded pork
⅔ cup fresh green peas
½ cup shredded ham
⅔ cup fresh mung bean sprouts
⅔ cup shredded bamboo shoots
4 dried black mushrooms, soaked, drained, diced

12 tiny button mushrooms
3 teaspoons soy sauce
Freshly ground pepper to taste
3 tablespoons cornstarch
¼ cup water
2 eggs
2 tablespoons milk

Heat broth, add pork, peas. Cook gently till peas are tender—about 12 minutes. Add ham, bean sprouts, bamboo shoots, black mushrooms, button mushrooms, soy sauce, and pepper. Simmer 2 minutes. Mix cornstarch with water; add to soup. Bring to boil and thicken. Remove from heat. When ready to serve, heat again. Beat eggs with milk. Stir slowly into soup so that it forms ribbons. Serve at once.

Spinach-Clam Soup al Dente Debby

Serves 10–12

14 cups chicken broth
3 cups fresh minced clams
3 pounds fresh spinach, well washed

1 tablespoon garlic powder

Put broth in a very large pot with clams. Just before the third bubble, add spinach, and cook till soft. Add the garlic powder, too.

Pumpkin Soup

Serves 10

Boil pulp from 2 medium pumpkins in vegetable or chicken stock. Put through a sieve or food mill. Add finely chopped onion and 2 cloves garlic, crushed. Add 1 tablespoon butter, reheat, and serve.

Paul and Lisa's Cauliflower Soup

Serves 8–10

2 heads cauliflower   Ceres Veget-All powder
4 cups milk   2 quarts water
Chopped onions   8–10 cloves garlic, crushed
Butter   Fresh grated cheese, any kind

Steam cauliflower. Cut up, and put with milk in a pot. Sauté onions in butter, add Ceres powder, and add to chopped cauliflower. Add water, garlic, cheese, and a little butter, and simmer for 5 minutes. It's a whole meal.

Belgian (?) Stew

Serves 10–12

Why this is called Belgian stew no one knows. Literally, the Belgians have no cuisine to speak of. Asking a Belgian about Belgian food is like asking a Swiss about Swiss writers. Both will anxiously shift the conversation to the French.

¶ Anyhow, this is a cheap, simple, and unique dish. Serve it to family and unimportant visitors. Actually, the cooking odors alone make this dish worthwhile.

1 large onion, sliced   Salt and pepper to taste
½ cup diced carrots   Flour
1 clove garlic   1 tablespoon cooking oil
1 tablespoon butter   2 16-ounce cans beer
3 pounds lean stew meat

Sauté the onion, carrots, and garlic in butter until the onion turns pale gold in color. Season the meat with the salt and pepper and dredge in the flour. Brown the meat in a bit of oil. Now add the onions, etc. Open the beer and quickly drink half of one. You deserve it. Add the remaining beer to the pot. Turn up the heat and wait until the beer is just on the verge of boiling. Now cover the pot tightly and cook on the lowest possible heat for about an hour. You can make rice as you wait.

Jack's Tomato Soup Plus

2 large onions, sliced
4 cloves garlic
1 pound butter
2 tablespoons oregano
4 pounds fresh tomatoes, sliced

4 tablespoons flour
6 quarts hot beef broth
1½ cups rice
1 pound Swiss or Gruyère cheese

This is a particularly rich and sumptuous dish. The tartness of the tomato is set off perfectly by the creaminess of the butter . . . and all of this is forgotten in the gluttonous rapture that the melted cheese provides. It's totally, unbearably good. Serve this with freezing-cold beer and garlic bread. Get corrupted.

Basically, soups are a form of existential cookery. If you've more tomatoes, less broth, and a teaspoon of nutmeg you've been wondering what to do with, the soup will absorb it. Anything but a rough recipe is subversive to the concept of soup. Its nature is essentially fluid.

Place the onions and garlic in a large skillet in which 4 tablespoons butter have been melted. Add the oregano. (This spice tends to bring out the sweetness of the onion.) Cook over low heat for 5 minutes. Add the tomatoes and continue cooking over low heat for 10–15 minutes—until the tomatoes have become pulpy and completely unappetizing. You can hasten

this process by punishing the tomatoes with a wooden spoon while they are cooking.

When the tomatoes have been transformed, mix the flour into the pan and turn the heat up a bit. Brown slightly.

Empty the contents of the skillet into the broth. Add the rice. Cover and simmer for about 50 minutes. Stir occasionally.

Now you can relax and get high. Have a seat and either grate or thinly slice the cheese. Take care not to let friends whimpering with hunger get to the cheese. That is the most important advice I can give you. Ten minutes before you serve the soup add the cheese and the remaining butter to it. Your life will change.

Lizze's Luscious Lemon Soup

Serves 8–12

8 cups water	8 eggs, separated
Sugar	⅔–1 cup lemon juice
½ teaspoon salt	8 teaspoons grated lemon peel
2 cinnamon sticks	

To water, add 1 cup sugar, salt, and cinnamon. Bring to a boil. Cover and simmer for 15 minutes. Remove cinnamon sticks. Add ⅔ cup warm soup to 8 egg yolks, lightly beaten, beating fast. Add to soup. Cook, stirring, on low heat for 2–3 minutes and *don't* boil. Add, stirring, fresh lemon juice. Cover and keep warm. Beat 8 egg whites till foamy. Add 8 tablespoons sugar gradually and beat. Add freshly grated lemon peel—serve soup with dollop of meringue.

True Light Beaver Sweet and Sour Beef Stew

Serves at least 12

1 cup flour
1 teaspoon salt
⅛ teaspoon pepper
½ teaspoon garlic powder
6 pounds chuck steak or roast cut
   in 1-inch cubes
Oil

1 large head cabbage, cut into
   eighths
2 bottles ginger ale
2 bottles chili sauce
3 pounds sliced carrots
1 teaspoon ginger, or to taste

Combine first 4 ingredients in paper bag and shake up cubed meat in it. Brown meat in oil in a large pot or Dutch oven, and drain off excess oil. Then add cabbage, ginger ale, chili sauce, carrots, and ginger to meat in pot. Cook for 2 hours over low heat until almost done. We then add parboiled potatoes and finish cooking. Serve on a cold winter day with fresh baked bread. It is deelicious.

Note: This is also good using chicken instead of beef.

Bille's Flemish Stew in Beer

Serves 8–15

4 tablespoons flour mixed with:
½ teaspoon thyme
1 teaspoon sugar
2 teaspoons dry mustard
1 bay leaf, crushed
5–8 pounds chuck or other cheap
   beef, cubed

2 pounds onions, sliced
4 tablespoons oil
Salt and pepper or tamari to taste
1 pint ale, or 1½ pints beer

Mix together the flour, thyme, sugar, mustard, and bay. Put in plastic bag and cover meat with flour mixture by tossing it around. Cook the sliced onions in the oil to the point of soggy transparency. Add the floured meat cubes and brown them. Put in the salt, pepper, leftover flour-herb stuff from the bag, and the ale or beer. Bring it all to a boil. Then cover and simmer till the meat is tender—anywhere from 2 hours on up. This makes a heavy winter stew, even better when reheated a few days later.

Herb Soup—With or Without Shrimp

Serves 10

2 cups chopped onions
1 cup chopped green peppers
3 cups chopped mushrooms
8 tablespoons butter
4 tablespoons lemon juice
2 teaspoons basil
1 teaspoon tarragon
2 teaspoons powdered savory

2 teaspoons salt
½ teaspoon pepper
4 10½-ounce cans cream of
    mushroom soup
2 or more cups milk
4 10½-ounce cans consommé
1 cup cooked, shelled, deveined
    shrimp (optional)

Sauté the onions, green peppers, and mushrooms in butter till the onions are tender. Season with lemon juice, basil, tarragon, savory, salt, and pepper. Meanwhile heat the mushroom soup, milk, and consommé together. If desired, add the shrimp—whole, if small, cut in half if large. Add the sautéed onion mixture. Simmer for 5 minutes, stirring constantly so that flavors mingle and the shrimp are hot. Serve hot or cold. This soup is absolutely delicious, and really easy to make. Just make sure that you follow the exact measurements for the herbs and spices. It's a fantastic blending of many subtle flavors.

Marc's Beef Stew

Serves 12

6 pounds roast beef (chuck, rump,
    round)
¾ cup shortening
4 medium yellow onions, chopped
8 cups water
2 cups red wine
4 bouillon cubes
2 cloves garlic, finely chopped or
    crushed
Few sprigs parsley, chopped

2 bay leaves
Dash of thyme
3 tablespoons salt
½ teaspoon freshly ground pepper
12 medium potatoes
12 medium carrots
20 small white onions
6 stalks celery
4 medium green peppers
4 medium tomatoes

Cut beef in 1½-inch cubes. Heat shortening in a Dutch oven. Toss in meat; cook over high heat until brown on all sides. Meanwhile, chop yellow onions coarsely, set aside. When meat is brown, remove from Dutch oven; set aside. Toss in chopped onions, cooking over low heat until limp.

Now return meat, add water, wine, bouillon cubes, garlic, parsley, bay leaves, thyme, salt, and pepper. Bring to boil; then reduce heat, cover, and cook slowly for about 1½ hours.

While meat cooks, prepare vegetables. Peel potatoes and carrots (if too large, cut in half; otherwise, leave whole). Peel white onions; leave whole. Cut celery in 3-inch sections; cut peppers and tomatoes in chunks. Place all vegetables except peppers and tomatoes in beef liquid and cook gently another hour, till soft. Twenty minutes before the end of cooking time, add peppers and tomatoes. If the gravy is thin, thicken with flour, if desired. (Simply suspend flour in water so there are no lumps, and add flour liquid a bit at a time until desired thickness is obtained.)

DESSERTS

Cathy's Cheesecake au Plancher

Serves 2–10

A delightful invention of my mother's from her somewhat capricious youth.

Crust:

12 zweiback, crumbled with
    butter and sugar

Filling:

12 ounces cream cheese	2 eggs
½ cup sugar, or 3 tablespoons honey	2 tablespoons fine sherry

Make crust. Combine filling ingredients in bowl and beat until the consistency of sour cream. Bake for 20 minutes at 375°.

Topping:

½ pint sour cream	Few drops of same fine sherry
2–3 tablespoons sugar	Sprinkling of crust mixture

Spread on top of pie and bake for 5–7 minutes at 450°.

In those days my mother, a native Montrealer, was an ardent communist. Of course one of the duties of every respectable card-carrying communist was to recruit as many new people as possible. Now, what better way to seduce a potential party member (her ambition *may* have been twofold) than to ply him with sumptuous cheesecake. She did this with no meager amount of preparation. In a last-minute frenzy, arranging her vast assemblage of Lenin memorabilia, together with this regal repast, the hot cheesecake, on its way from stove to counter, mercilessly slipped from her grasp, plunging to the floor.

¶ Without a moment's hesitation, the creamy confusion of cheese and crumbs was scooped back into the plate, artistically rearranged, and duly served to her unwitting guest—a Midwesterner ignorant of cheesecake au plancher.

¶ The deceit was not unjustified—the party got a member and sometime shortly afterward, my mother, a husband.

Cathy's Lime Pie

4 eggs, separated	¼ teaspoon salt
½ cup lime juice	1 package gelatin
1 cup sugar	½ cup cold water

Beat yolks. Add lime juice, ½ cup sugar, salt, and beat a little more. Meanwhile, dissolve gelatin in cold water and let stand. Cook yolk-lime juice mixture until thick, stirring constantly (thick enough to coat wooden spoon). Remove from heat, let cool slightly and add the gelatin dissolved in water. Mix to thicken. Whip egg whites until stiff and add other ½ cup sugar 1 or 2 tablespoons at a time. Fold lime mixture into egg whites with a feathery gentleness, 1 tablespoon at a time.

Pour into a baked piecrust. Chill for at least an hour.

Serve with unsweetened whipped cream.

Strawberry Glaze Noodle Pie

Makes 2 pies

Pie:

6 cups broad egg noodles
2 teaspoons salt
1 cup butter, melted
⅔ cup sugar
1 teaspoon salt
2 teaspoons cinnamon
1 cup pecans
6 eggs, separated

Glaze:

2 10-ounce packages frozen strawberries, thawed
¼ cup cornstarch
Water
½ cup water or berry juice

Cook noodles for 20 minutes in 4 quarts boiling water and 2 teaspoons salt. Rinse under cold water, drain, and set aside, mixing with melted butter. Blend sugar, 1 teaspoon salt, cinnamon, pecans, and beaten egg yolks. Add to noodle-butter mixture. Beat egg whites till stiff and fold gently into noodle mixture. Place in 2 well-buttered 9-inch pie pans, and bake in a 350° oven for 30 minutes.

While the pies are baking, prepare glaze. Drain juice from strawberries, adding to it enough water to make 2 cups liquid. Place in saucepan and bring to boil. Mix cornstarch with water or berry juice and add gradually to hot juice, stirring until thick and clear—about 5 minutes. Cool slightly. If the glaze is too thick, thin with hot water. Add berries and spread on pie. Refrigerate until very cold. Decorate with whipped cream.

Rhubarb-Custard Pie

Makes 2 pies

2 cups sugar	4 cups milk
¼ cup flour	1 teaspoon vanilla extract
Salt	2 tablespoons butter
4 egg yolks	Rhubarb, raw, peeled

Mix sugar, flour, salt, and egg yolks. Then add milk, vanilla, and butter. Cover bottom of unbaked pie shells with rhubarb, baking in moderate oven till done. Pour custard mixture over cooked pie shell/rhubarb, cover with meringue, and bake 15 minutes in 400° oven. Lower to 325° and bake 45–50 minutes.

M-M-M Coffee Cake

½ cup shortening	1 teaspoon baking soda
¾ cup sugar	½ pint sour cream
1 teaspoon vanilla	1 cup brown sugar
3 eggs	6 tablespoons butter
2 cups sifted flour	2 tablespoons cinnamon
1 teaspoon baking powder	1 cup nuts

Cream shortening, sugar, and vanilla together thoroughly. Gradually add eggs, 1 at a time, beating well after each one. Sift together dry ingredients and add to mixture alternately with the sour cream. Mix brown sugar and butter with a fork till crumbly. In a greased tube pan lined with wax paper, put in a layer of batter, sprinkled with sugar-butter mixture, cinnamon, and nuts, then another layer of batter, etc. Repeat till full. Bake 50 minutes in 350° oven.

Kim's Carrot Cake

2½ cups grated carrots (for a
    special taste, add 1 cup grated
    apples and pears)
4 eggs
2 cups sugar
1 cup salad oil

2 cups flour
2 teaspoons soda
½ teaspoon salt
1½ teaspoons cinnamon
1 teaspoon vanilla extract
1 cup chopped almonds

Combine first 4 ingredients, then add the remaining ingredients. Pour into
a greased and floured 9×13×2-inch pan or 2 9-inch cake pans. Bake
45 minutes at 350°. To ice, mix 1 8-ounce package cream cheese with 1 box
powdered sugar.

Indian Pudding

⅔ cup cornmeal
½ cup molasses
½ cup brown sugar
1 teaspoon cinnamon

1 teaspoon vanilla extract
2 quarts milk
2 tablespoons butter

Mix everything together, and cook in a slow oven (325°) for 3 hours. Stir
during the first ½ hour. Serve warm or cold with cream or ice cream.

Gloria's Apple Crisp Pudding

4 cups peeled and sliced apples
½ cup water
1 teaspoon cinnamon
½ cup butter

1 cup sugar
¾ cup flour
1 cup cream, whipped, or ice
  cream

Turn apples into buttered casserole. Pour water and cinnamon over. Work butter, sugar, and flour to crumb consistency, and sprinkle over apples. Bake 35–40 minutes at 375°. Serve warm with cream or ice cream.

Gloria's Oatmeal Macaroons

They're good

½ cup shortening
1 cup sugar
1 tablespoon molasses (or more,
  maybe)
1 teaspoon vanilla
1 egg
1 cup sifted flour

1 teaspoon salt
1 teaspoon cinnamon
¾ teaspoon soda
1 cup oats
⅔ cup chopped dates
⅔ cup raisins

Cream shortening, sugar. Gradually add molasses, vanilla, egg. Sift together the dry ingredients, add oatmeal and the shortening mixture. Stir in dates and raisins. Drop from teaspoons onto a greased cookie sheet. Bake for 10–15 minutes at 350°.

Mum's Applesauce Cake

1 cup butter or shortening
2 cups sugar
2 eggs
3 cups sifted all-purpose flour
1 tablespoon baking soda
1½ teaspoons nutmeg
1 tablespoon cinnamon

½ teaspoon salt
1 teaspoon ground cloves
2½ cups applesauce
2 tablespoons corn syrup or honey
1 cup raisins
1 cup chopped walnuts

Cream butter and sugar; gradually add unbeaten eggs 1 at a time. Sift together flour, soda, spices. Add alternately with combined applesauce and syrup. Fold in raisins and nuts. Pour batter into greased tube pan and bake in slow oven (300°) for about 1¼ hours. Check at 1 hour, though, to see if it's done. It should be moist.

Sabayon

6 oranges	26 ounces sugar
21 egg yolks	1 tablespoon gelatin
4 ounces Grand Marnier orange liqueur	4 ounces hot water
	½ tablespoon cornstarch
28 ounces white wine	Whipped cream

Peel and separate oranges and lay them on the bottom of 12 bowls. Hand-mix with a whisk egg yolks, Grand Marnier, 24 ounces of the white wine, and the sugar. Then mix gelatin with hot water and add to mixture. Stir cornstarch in with rest of white wine and put into mixture. Stir entire batch with a whisk over a medium flame until it begins to set. Taste it as it gets warm and maybe add some more Grand Marnier. Remove from flame and stir for 5 more minutes. Scoop mixture into bowls with orange slices; refrigerate; serve with whipped cream. Pour yourself some Grand Marnier and drink slowly.

Pastry Cream

2 quarts milk	16 egg yolks
Vanilla extract	20 ounces sugar
Almond extract	10 ounces flour

Heat milk, but never let it come to a boil. Add a dash of both extracts. In a separate bowl, mix egg yolks with sugar, then add the flour. Over a low flame pour sugar mixture into milk and stir until it is all worked in. Great filling for pies, tarts, and finger-lickers.

Baba au Rhum

Makes 7 or 8 cakes

4 ounces flour
¼ ounce dry yeast
3 ounces warm milk
2 eggs
¼ ounce sugar

1⅔ ounces butter
Maple syrup
Rum
1 match

Put flour into a bowl and spread yeast on top. Pour warm milk over yeast and wait until the milk is absorbed. Add eggs and fold them in with your fingers. Cover bowl with a towel and set in a warm place to rise for about 45 minutes. Separately mix sugar and hand-mashed butter. When other mixture has risen, fold in sugar and butter to it and let it sit for 5 minutes. Line pastry cups or cupcake cups with butter and flour dough. Bake at 325° until brown and fully risen. Meanwhile, boil maple syrup and water, proportioned to taste, and add rum until it tastes even better. When cakes are baked, put them in syrup mixture to soak. For a good show, when cakes are warm, take 1 cake at a time in a pan with a little syrup. Heat the pan with a constant flame underneath. Put fresh rum over cake and set afire.

Crescents

1 cup margarine
¾ cup sugar
2¼ cups flour

¼ teaspoon salt
1½ cups nuts

Cream everything together and shape into crescents. Bake at 350° until brown, and loosen from pan immediately.

MINT

Ecstatic Housecleaning

SCENTS TO REMEMBER

Once upon a time there was a lady who lived in a clean house. And because she liked things clean and didn't like to do the cleaning, she hired help. Before long, she helped the help. Help, in those days, didn't stay long in homes where there was much to do.

The help taught the lady to clean well. Her fourteen rooms shone with well-cleanedness. Nevertheless, cleaning remained a chore and a bore to the lady.

One day, the lady got turned on. Wow ! ! ! ! !

Pretty soon the house with the fourteen rooms disappeared. It had been an illusion. She lived in one room now—no help. Also no bank account. And she kept pretty stoned.

She still liked it clean. More than she ever had before. For to her silent room a Presence came that looked out through her eyes. Her days were filled with preparations for this Presence. She courted it with all her heart. There must be nothing in the room to offend the sight of one so High, so Holy, so Divine!

And so her room became a shrine, a temple ever ready to receive the High Guest. Now cleaning it was no longer a chore. It was a prayer and a dance.

And as she cleaned the objects in the room, it seemed to her that dusting and polishing were ways in which the objects were caressed, and that they thanked her by gleaming prettily. Every thing now had its own meaning and uniqueness—yes, even the chairs . . . One day, as she was scrubbing the floor, the words "I'm scrubbing the face of God!" audibly came from her lips. Naturally, she was stoned. And luckily, her teen-age son and daughter were not home. (They don't turn on. Not that this justifies the stoned lady's heresy.) Still . . .

Isn't the face of God the visible world? And shouldn't we clean and beautify His face each moment that we are alive?

The last time I saw the stoned lady she was still cleaning away . . .

Nina Graboi

Memories are triggered by smells. You can save scents, and feast on them and the pictures they bring to mind all year round. It's easy. Pick your memories early in the morning, when the dew is still on the ground. Then spread the petals/buds/leaves/herbs/grasses flat out on a newspaper in a dry warm place away from direct heat or light until dry.

¶ Preserve any mixture made for scent with either orris root powder or cinnamon. With these things in mind, you may be creative with your favorite scents.

Recipes for Every Discriminating Nose

Shushi's Wild Weed Sachet

Gather weeds and wild grasses that smell good. Dry thoroughly.
Put them through a food mill, or chop coarsely.
Add 1 ounce orris root powder per 4 cups of mixture. Place in pretty
fabric covering and sew or embroider closed.

Pomander Ball

Poke whole cloves into the skin of an orange or lemon.
Roll ball in cinnamon, and hang up it in a clothe's closet for a surprise
whenever you open the door.

Fall Petal Potpourri

Equal amounts of dried:

Marigold petals	**Basil**
Thyme	**Peppermint**

Mix with an equal amount of kosher (coarse) salt, and store in a sealed
container for 6 weeks before using.

Spring Flower Potpourri

Dry:

1 cup lilac petals	1 cup carnation petals or any other
1 cup apple blossoms	dried white flower
1 cup lavender leaves	1 ounce orris root powder

Mix and store in tightly sealed container for 6 weeks before using.

Rose Scent Potpourri

Pick and dry:

Rose petals, blossoms and leaves

Layer in jar with:

1 teaspoon nutmeg	1 tablespoon cloves
1 teaspoon allspice	3 tablespoons cinnamon
2 tablespoons orris root	

Store sealed for a few weeks, longer if you want a stronger scent.

MARIGOLD

Earthworm Races

At Brighton, England, an 8-inch earthworm called Toy Token Tom captured the Brighton Worm Prix at the International Toy Fair.

Tom scooted across a 2-foot plate-glass course, polished to perfect condition, in a record-setting 1 minute, 7 seconds.

This figured out at 2/100 mile an hour, a pace that bettered the best time of the former champion, the late Wippie Willie Mark, who finished second.

Tom's owner, Gerald Masters, a toy company executive, said: "Tom was trained by Chessington Zoo, and fed a secret diet."

Could that secret diet have been an organically produced diet? I recall that years ago a man named Friend Sykes raised high-price champion race horses by feeding them an organically raised food. If it works with horses, why not with earthworms?

Youth of the land, here is a worthy hobby, much more socially significant than swallowing goldfish, which was done by a previous generation.

From Organic Gardening, *June 1971*

"Earthworm Races" taken from the June 1971 issue of *Organic Gardening and Farming,* Emmaus, Pennsylvania.

TWO CATS AND THE BEAR

IN THE PARK

I Freddie and Moms

Once upon a time in a delicatessen on West 72nd Street in New York City there lived two domestic tiger cats. You might think that being a cat in a big city wouldn't be much fun. But Freddie and Moms—for those were the cats' names—had a terrific time. In the world of New York City cats, they had the best deal possible.

In New York there are only two ways a cat can make out. He can be an inside cat who lives in an apartment and never goes out, or he can take his chances in the street. The inside cat sacrifices the freedom of the great outdoors for security. He can count on a steady, if occasionally boring, diet of warmth and comfort. He receives regular meals and a dry place to sleep and has close relationships with humans. He becomes sleek, fat, lazy, and dependent. He is taught not to use the Louis XVI dining-room chairs for scratching posts. He is expected to use his kitty box carefully, without kicking the absorbent litter all over the place. He learns to purr gratefully when scratched under his chin. The inside cat has names like Otis, Maggie (r.i.p.), Popcorn (r.i.p.), Fallenwell, Brandy, and LeRoi (r.i.p.).

The outside cat, the cat of the streets, reverts to its early instincts and becomes a panther in miniature. The outside cat must scheme, forage, and kill to live. He must learn to avoid the groups of mean little children who would torment him for sport, the speeding cars and trucks, and the city cat catcher. He must seek out and fight to hold shelters. The outside cat quickly becomes lean and tough. His eyes are narrow and hard. He is wary of everything that moves. He is grimy and usually well scarred. His compensation for such a rugged existence is his complete freedom to explore the city at will, and experience as many adventures as his nine lives will allow.

Most New York cats don't get to choose their life-style. They are simply born into the way of life. But a small percentage of New York cats are luckier, like Freddie and Moms, and are able to get hitched up with delicatessens. This is tricky business, because owners of delicatessens don't really love cats. To them, the presence of a cat in their store merely ensures that the mouse population will diminish, and the cat has to pay plenty of dues for the privilege of maintaining residence in such a place. He must, for instance, produce a dead mouse every so often. This is a tough assignment, considering that the mice move out, bag and baggage (contenting themselves with small hits, during cat-nap hours), when the cat moves in. Most delicatessen cats resort to underhanded dealings with some cat of the street who runs a dead mouse racket. The dead mouse dealer typically employs teams of second-story cats who knock over hospital research labs and pet shops on a regular basis.

Delicatessen cats must not drop a litter of kittens into the chopped liver. Or be caught napping on the casaba melons. Or get tough with stupid customers who pat them too hard and pull their tails. Such behavior would be cause for eviction.

The delicatessen cat endures all this without complaint, because his life combines the pleasures and adventures of the great outdoors with the comfort of regular meals and a dry place to sleep. On the one hand, deli cats can promote as close a relationship with humans as they wish. And since deli customers in New York tend to be regulars, deli cats can get to know a number of different people fairly well. Because of their worldliness, the deli cats are held in considerable awe by apartment-bound inside cats, many of whom spend long hours perched on their windowsills, watching the delicatessen door, wondering and daydreaming.

On the other hand, the deli cat can—if he moves with care—cultivate cool but workable relationships with cats of the street who frequent their neighborhood. The outside cat tends to be resentful—jealous would be a better word—of the deli cat, and would like nothing better than to give him a good thrashing just for the hell of it. The deli cat discourages such treatment by taking plenty of exercise, eating well, and keeping in shape. Moreover, deli cats have a good record of keeping outsiders in their neighborhood in life-saving food scraps during the lean winters. Then of course there is the annual Christmas party in the delicatessen storeroom, to which the whole neighborhood is invited—even the inside cats if they can find a way to make it.

Roger Vaughan

Fine-tasting Peyote Tea from Entropy Acres

Boil 1 quart of water and apple cider mixed half and half. Steep 3–6 buttons of peyote and a handful of fresh mint for 10–15 minutes. Serve. It's delicious and psychedelic.

. . . . .

When you live in a tepee and are foraging for food as a donkey would, eating what you find in the ground upon which you are walking, you stay high organically and continuously.

. . . . . .

Marjoome

Really gets you off   *Serves 16–20*

2–2½ cups peanut (or any good) oil	2 cups mashed roasted chick-peas
3 ounces poor-quality hash	½ pound finely ground almonds
	1 cup chopped dates

Bring oil to boil. Add hash. Simmer, covered, for 3–4 hours. Strain mixture through cheesecloth, squeezing. Retain hash/oil in bowl. (Throw away the dregs.) Add chick-pea flour, almonds, dates, making oily paste. Eat 1–2 teaspoons per person, **no more.** Keeps you high a long time, but it's very easy to get too much.

TIME TO PLANT

YOUR SEEDS

Note: The authentic Marjoome recipe above can be awfully thick, and a bit hard to take, taste and texturewise. Well-traveled sources now report a Europeanized version of the Marjoome which hides the taste of the hash, removes the oily taste of the paste, and, when made well (get stoned before you make it for *real* inspiration) makes a sweet fruitcake-type paste. Use:

3 ounces poor-quality hash
2–2½ cups oil
2 cups flour (or brownie or
    chocolate cake mix)

2 pounds mixed chopped raisins,
    dates, nuts, etc.

Cook as you would for authentic Marjoome, allowing again 1–2 teaspoons per person, **no more.**

. . . . . .

Pasta: A poor people's narcotic offering instant gratification. Before Mao, millions of Chinese ate clay as other peoples eat pasta.

. . . . . .

Sacred Honey

When you go to Lebanon to buy hash, and you finally hook up with a big dealer, he'll probably take you right to his farm/factory. All around you, in the fields of cannabis, you'll see bees flying back and forth, pollinating the plants and gathering nectar for their honey. Later, in the dealer's house, he'll offer you a smoke, and a cup of tea with his own private honey in it. This honey is very special: It is the honey gathered from the hives made by bees who fly through the pot fields. This honey is not for sale. It is called Sacred Honey.

AND DO YOUR DEEDS

Starting with a pound of hash, reduce hash to a liquid by mixing it with pure grain alcohol in the proportions of 3 parts alcohol, 1 part hash. Cook this mixture over a very low flame until it is dissolved. Render as in cooking. Strain the remains through a coffee filter (laboratory filters are better; the resin gets so thick that you will use hundreds of the coffee filters, not at all as many of the laboratory filters) into a clean pot. Keep returning mud to original pot and cooking and straining until a clean black liquid (like black lacquer or like 30- or 40-weight motor oil) is obtained. You will continue to add alcohol as it is needed (it evaporates).

To test: Smoke cooking mixture. If it gets you stoned, keep (if you can) cooking; it's not done yet. When it's done, heat up the honey you are going to use and drop the hash mixture (70 drops hash to 1 pound honey) into it, and mix until it is mixed throughout. Honey being predigested sugar, this mixture will get you stoned in 20 minutes.

Some special notes on Sacred Honey:

In preparation, everything in the kitchen should be wiped clean of even
a drop of the mixture, put into alcohol, and used in the preparation.
Cook your filters in alcohol, and use the remains in the mixture. Wash
your hands in alcohol, and use the alcohol to add to the cooking sacredness.
In short, this stuff is so potent that even the cooking fumes will get you
stoned. The mixture can be injected into all kinds of things—candy, any
drink; you can baste food with it, soak dried fruit in it. Don't forget:
It's a powerful and long (10–12-hour) high. To make YIPPIE tobacco:
thin the original hash mixture with alcohol until it is thin enough to spray
(cooking all the time over low heat—if it gets too hot, it'll burn and be
destroyed). Spray on grass for supergrass.

.　.　.　.　.　.

Sacred Ghee

In Lebanon (country of a thousand del-high-ts) vegetable butter is spread
in the sun and sprinkled with hash pieces. Resin is draw into the butter
to make ghee. To make it at home: use 3 parts butter to 1 part hash, or
3 parts butter to 3 parts grass. Put lots of water in a pot. Add butter and
hash. Cook over a slow flame for 6–8 hours. Remove from heat and let
sit overnight. Carefully use the butter in any cooking, or:
In India there's a yoga sect that uses the Sacred Ghee in anointing their
bodies at the breathing points (temples, inside of arm, wrist, etc.). They
really get off on it and carry on. You can too. Carry on.

.　.　.　.　.　.

Morning Glory Seeds

Use only *Heavenly Blues* or *Pearly Gates* (as you might expect) and only use them from an organic source that can guarantee that they have not been treated with poison. Each person should use about 500 seeds. Grind them up and put them in gelatin capsules. Swallow the capsules. You will vomit. It is important, though, to try to keep it down as it will keep you up.

Note: Yams belong to the same family as the Morning Glories.

. . . . . .

Yoga Sun and Moon Exercises: Get a good yoga book or a good yoga teacher, and try these exercises. They are also good for natural childbirth, as you cannot hyperventilate.

. . . . . .

Eating yogurt only for 5–7 days.

. . . . . .

Eating only honey or honey and nectar will give you quite a
BUZZZZZZZZZZZZZZ . . .

. . . . . .

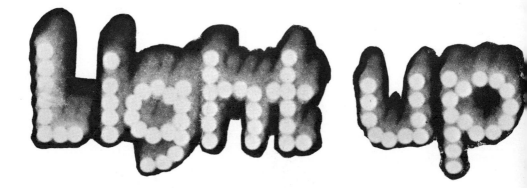

Li Chung-yun and Ginseng (1929):

¶ Li Chung-yun of China was born in 1677. In the year 1827 the Chinese government sent official felicitations to him on attaining his 150th birthday. In 1877 the government again congratulated him on attaining his 200th birthday. He has married and outlived 23 wives and is now living with his 24th wife at the age of 252 years.

¶ Li has recently given in a Chinese university a course of 28 lectures on longevity. Each lecture was 3 hours long. For 200 years ginseng root has been a part of his diet every day. He advocates an herb diet and disbelieves in any exercise that tires. He seems not older than a man of 52, according to those who have met him.

. . . . . .

To choose ginseng root: Look for one that resembles a male with sex organs and one that resembles a female with sex organs. Soak for 10 days in water and honey. Remove. Make a new mixture of water and honey. Dip in new mixture and enjoy. It is an aphrodisiac and gets you high.

AFTER HOKUSAI

Compost Casserole

THE REMAINS

To get through a day of cooking without accumulating five pounds of waste is a problem. Today, when food processors and distributors insist on overpackaging items, after each feast we have a load of garbage on our hands. Or is it garbage?

¶ Beware the great garbage rip-off! Are you just throwing out all the remains, all the containers, all the valuable kitchen scraps?

¶ Reclaim your waste. There is a growing list of uses for what we used to consider just garbage.

¶ The most obvious use of aftermeal refuse is the building of compost from organic matter. Save your vegetable scraps and other organic items (everything except bones and fat) from the meal. Place these, together with some ground limestone, in a large plastic garbage pail with a secure lid. This can remain outdoors (even in winter) to begin decomposing, while you gather the other items for your compost heap.

¶ If you are into eating, you should be into growing your own. And the organic method is the only way to ensure chemical-free, nutritious food. The compost you make as an integral part of the organic gardening method will enrich your soil and help it provide food for your table. And it will accommodate your remains.

¶ Materials needed for the compost heap are manure, earth, hay or leaves or grass cuttings for bulk, sawdust, coffee grounds, peanut shells, limestone, weeds, garden leftovers, and those ever-present kitchen scraps. Almost anything that was once alive is fair game for the compost heap.

Compost Recipe:

Take a flat piece of land near the garden. Enclose the area to mark it off. The spot should be about 6 feet wide; and allow the heap to grow about 5 feet in height.

¶ Clear the ground, and place brush and stalks over the bare spot. This will allow air to circulate up through the pile, ensuring more rapid decomposition of the materials.

> Layer hay or straw on the brush.
> Add garbage (vegetable scraps).
> Add 2 inches of manure and animal bedding.
> Add a covering of topsoil (don't be afraid to take the earth from the garden; you'll only put it back enriched when the compost is finished.
> Sprinkle lime, wood ashes, or granite dust, if you need an alkaline compost.

Water each layer as you build the pile. Water until the layers are moist, like a damp sponge (not running with water when squeezed).

¶ Continue the layering until the 5-foot height is reached. Don't stomp or mat down the heap. Place large vertical poles at intervals (2 or 3 feet apart) throughout the heap. These too will allow for passage of air into and through the pile.

¶ The heap will begin to heat up in a few days. The temperature will soar (if sufficient nitrogen is present from adequate animal manure). It may reach 150° inside in a week. After a few weeks, the pile will need turning, to ensure that the outside parts are getting heated enough to break down. After about 3 months (and turnings at 3-week intervals), the compost should be done, and ready for use on the garden.

¶ If the compost is rough with large coarse materials still throughout it, you can put it on the garden in the fall, and by the following spring it

will have decomposed into the soil, enriching and fertilizing the earth.
¶ If the materials were chopped and cut small before adding to the pile, you can get a finished compost in as little as 14 days. This method requires turning after the first 3 days, and then every few days to ensure even decomposition.

Now that the organic matter has been ecologically dealt with, we still have all the other garbage.
¶ Most products sold today reach us in overwrapped or no-deposit, no-return containers. This leaves us with growing mounds of waste, and depleted natural resources. Remember that as citizens of the United States we make up less than 6% of the world's population, and yet we use more than 50% of the planet's natural resources.
¶ It is imperative that consumers who purchase items in glass containers and aluminum cans deal with these resources in a responsible way. That is not to say that we shouldn't strive for an economy that delivers goods in returnable containers. But while we're stuck with handling large masses of glass and aluminum, we must be careful not to just dump it all in some hole in the ground and bury it like ancient treasure.
¶ Bottles can be rinsed and saved for preserving. Or they can be rinsed and saved for local recycling drives. Separate the glass by colors (different metal contents make the bottles different colors) and remove metal rings and caps. Glass can earn as much as $20 a ton, so if your area does not have a recycling campaign, help get one started. The glass is taken by manufacturers and remelted and formed into bottles or a new product called glassphalt, which is used for paving roads.
¶ Metals can be similarly separated and recycled. Aluminum brings $200 a ton, but it takes a lot of the light metal to make a ton. All cans without seams and that can be easily crushed by hand are aluminum. So are TV-dinner trays, pie plates, aluminum foil, etc. Most local recycling drives handle this valuable material. To reuse aluminum requires much less electricity than to make the metal from scratch. So it saves energy and causes less pollution to recycle the metal.
¶ Combined metals (tin cans, etc.) are less valuable and bring only about $5–$20 per ton. Many recycling drives are not interested in using them because of the large amounts needed to make it worth their energy.
¶ Paper: That's a big item. More than half our waste is in paper. Do you use paper napkins and throw them out? Try cloth instead. Instead of using paper bags from the supermarket, trying carrying a cloth or

wicker basket when shopping. Or take your bags back with you each week. There is a market for recycled paper. Currently less than 20% of our national paper needs are using recycled paper. This amount saves more than 200 million trees from destruction.

¶ Tie old newspapers and cardboard in bundles and save for paper drives. It sells for about $10 a ton.

¶ If half of our paper was recycled products, we would save a forest totaling all the square miles of New York, New Jersey, Pennsylvania, Maryland, and New England combined. Half a billion trees would be spared.

You say there is no local place to recycle these items? You say the only public facility for waste is the smoldering dump, or the yawning pit at the landfill?

¶ Demand a change, and work for it. Set up a recycling center where all the materials on hand (including vegetable matter) can be utilized and made available again. Get a community compost farm started. Get places set aside for separation and storage of vital resources. Income gained from sales of the collected items could be earmarked for environmental projects, such as cleaning the local water supplies or dealing with air pollution.

¶ Other uses of recycled materials are coming with fresh looks at technology. If you are planning on building a structure, you might want to consider using reinforced, compacted metals and glass as part of the building. Used with various coverings, materials for low cost housing could be salvaged from our junk yards. The Japanese are already using their garbage to build with.

¶ So before you add your daily total of 5.3 pounds of personal garbage to the earth, stop and think. Then act out of a rational decision: make the materials on hand work for you. Don't just treat the remains as garbage.

Tobe Carey

Chicken Shit!

Garbage is in Our Minds

GARBAGE OR NOTHING

I. The recent death of capitalism has everybody fucked around and confused.

Private-enterprise laissez-faire legally murderous piracy **gone,** already buried, to be replaced by what?

>If it doesn't have a name, how can you talk about it?

>And what about the garbage?

>>**WHO'S GOING TO COLLECT THE GARBAGE?**

>>Now there's something you can talk about . . .

II. America so incredibly wealthy that the local spiritual crisis is what are we going to do about the garbage?

>>The economic crisis how to distribute the garbage,

>>>The political crisis who's going to collect the garbage

>>>And why should anyone want the job,

while in the oblivious streets attention has suddenly exploded into flesh bodies & the various ways of rubbing them together.

¶ The Evolutionary Credit & Loan Association has terminated our contract, stamped it PAID IN FULL, & the planet is ours at last.

>Sudden flashes that maybe those five thousand years of time payments

>>*—all those payments ON THE DOT—*

>>>>>>>>>>all those

food wars & social cipher contracts were gestures of empty anxiety.

¶ Now that it's ours & we can take a casual look around, well there's so much **GARBAGE.**

¶ 4 billion people camped in the planetary wilderness & somehow

>**WE FORGOT ABOUT THE GARBAGE.**

>>Our wilderness is turning sour.

>>**IT STINKS!**

>>>No place in the cosmology of planetary physics for garbage.

>>>What?

What an astounding oversight!

What were our ancestors **thinking** about?

*III. America a nation so wealthy that all morality is based
on the problems of EXCESS:*

Fantasy executives & government spies running wild-eyed down the
corridors of control:

> "There's too fucking much of it!"
>> "It's completely out of control!"
>>> "Power leak! Power leak!"

The cells of power grow wild: undisciplined freedom cancer.

¶ Sudden flashes that the future of bureaucracy spy systems lies in
garbage control.

¶ People are **using** it, picking it up **free** on the streets, living on it, they
no longer respond to the seduction of the state, there's no way to get a
HOLD on them.

¶ Pomposity suicided & rigidity machines put to work at a furious clip:
all this garbage must be catalogued and filed, garbage-destruction teams
trained, parking lots on the rillable land, thousands of well-programed
garbage experts march to work each day to GET IT DOWN ON PAPER,
enormous factories hastily tooled for garbage conversion.

> "By God, we'll make napalm out of it."
>> Youngsters who don't understand it's all been paid for already
>>> are given guns!
>>> given napalm!
>>>> & shipped to parts of the planet where there **may** be people
who **might** be hip to **our** garbage & **MIGHT WANT SOME OF IT FOR
THEMSELVES.**

¶ The situation complicates itself incredibly.

¶ Computer engineers make it worse: the machines don't **understand**
power, sex & control: the machines program usable garbage & forbidden
fantasies of **FREE.**

¶ The Secretary of Garbage Control considers dropping acid & getting
it over with.

Systems of control grow schizophrenic . . . they writhe & contort in
involute paranoia.

SYSTEMICIDE MAKES HEADLINES.

*IV. America a nation so incredibly wealthy that all morality is based
on Excess:*

> True American career counselors now ask only one question.

"Do you want to produce garbage or do you want to collect garbage?"

Industrialist or politician?

Fishfarm or junkyard?

The young people want no part of it, of course, what with garbage their natural matrix & medium.

Produce it?

Collect it.

They want to fuck in it!

The career counselors build marvelous constructions of seduction & mystery, they transsubstantiate symbol money

into sex

into power

into death insurance

into pleasure

But it's just **things,** it's garbage, it's overflow & the young people know it. They throw the career counselor out the window.

Who's going to collect the garbage?

Who knows?

Who cares?

Let's use it to act out our fantasies, use it for unimaginable gratifications.

V. We were sitting around the other night talking about garbage, making screaming intuitive leaps through each other's arguments, when Wm. Fritsch suddenly woke up and shouted, "What I gotta do is learn to do nothing."

And of course that's it

& it's not surprising that the solution came from a man who sometimes arrives at the compulsion to visit all his friends & empty the garbage for them.

VI. Garbage crises cannot be SOLVED:

they must be ALLOWED TO DISAPPEAR.

The alternative to the garbage collection production box is to do just exactly nothin . . . no more & no less.

¶ Sudden flash of the invisible network w/ the individual spine planted squarely on it,

organic units in the planetary ecology,

DOING NOTHING.

Ecological systems have no garbage in them, contain nothing that is
alien to them.

*VII. Invisible networks of nameless human connectives (names shed as
metaphysical garbage) can help each other to do nothing.*

That part of the psyche organism to which name is attached, that part
which **does** things in praise of the name,
that part withers in the flesh caress of the anonymous community.
> The galactic actor dows nothing in the NAME of anything:
> > he receives his direction from the silent spinal telegraph;
> > > his spine is planted square on the invisible network;
> > > **HE DOES NOTHING;**
his movements are not outside the process.

VIII. It's paid for, all of it.

A cellophane bag represents 5000 years of machine history, inventors
suicided by their inventions, eons of garbage dedication, paid for in cancer
wombs, in fallen cocks, in the crazy waste of our fathers.
> Generations dead of lacklove sold for 29¢.
> > Your birth certificate is your final credit card.
Stack the garbage in piles & people will live in among it, communities
of free parallel spines planted square on the invisible network.
They will do nothing to effect the celebratory transformation of garbage
into spinal food.
Their movements are not outside the process.

*IX. The invisible networks grow through the absent university of
nothingness, disguised as dopesellers.*

> > as sneakthieves
> > > as naked dripping 17-year-old American girls.
Doctors of garbage philosophy.
Doing nothing in **public** teaching nothing demonstrating nothing living
paradigms of nothing!
> The absent university is powered by social magic.
> > It has flesh classrooms
> > > It is the university of the spine
> > > > Tuition is paid in units of psychic bondage
> > > > > Its graduates are **FREE.**

Susan Carey

Colleen Carey

Marty Carey

Tobe Carey

Alan Carey

Ronnie Van Wagner

Allen Norman Gordon

Nina Graboi

YOU ARE THE INFORMATION

Susan Carey.   Sun in Cancer, moon in Gemini. Sagittarius rising: Feast
   Layout & Cover Design
Marty Carey.   Sun in Leo, moon in Cancer, Saggitarius rising. Life is Art,
   so let's get on with it. Feast Drawings
Colleen Carey.   Aries, Libra rising, moon in Leo. By nature, a practitioner of
   the Mud Flat Theory (the only way to get a stuck boat out of the mud is
   to rock it). Random Feast Writings
Tobe Carey.   Cancer, Gemini rising, moon in Taurus. In and out, up and
   down, slow and lazy, quick and fast. Feast Photographer
Alan Carey.   Is a dreamer. "Reality is more than I can see." Feast
   Photographer
Allen Norman Gordon.   Age 36, born December 25, 1934, in the Bronx,
   N.Y.C., stayed till 19 years old, into the army—I luved the streets and the
   ghettoes I grew up in—blacks and Puerto Ricans were hip. Latin music
   brought together first hip tribe that I know of. Mescalin and God in 1950
   —the whole world up to now in Woodstock.
Nina Graboi.   Born in Vienna in 1918, died for the first time in 1938 when
   Hitler came. Was reborn in England as a domestic servant, then died
   again under the bombs of World War II. Was reborn in the U.S.A.
   (1941) as a businesswoman, suburban housewife, mother, intellectual,
   student, actress, writer, scrubwoman, party-giver and nag. Was busy
   chasing the elusive rainbow of happiness and success, and died to the
   world when I had "everything." Was reborn when the first hint of a reality
   beyond the body penetrated behind iron curtain of my ignorance (1956).
   Read feverishly whatever I could find on ESP and Hinduism, then
   started meditation, guided by Patanjali's Yoga Sutras. Died again in
   1966 when I smoked Cannabis sativa for the first time, and was
   simultaneously reborn. Today I'm still constantly reborn and just as
   often die. . . .
Ronnie Van Wagner.   I was born in this place that seems to be where many
   of you are being reborn—Woodstock. I suppose that I did about the same
   things that you did and, like you, my only regret is that I didn't do them
   more often. I went to Longhair U. (New Palts College) and endured the
   proper number of courses to be awarded a degree in psychology. When
   this didn't get me a job, I started to learn meat cutting. (I'm now a
   social worker.)
   I hope that what I learned in the short time that I was doing meat will
   be of some help to you. This will make it all worthwhile.

Lynn Anderson

Shushi Young and Steve Young

Aaron Van De Bogart *Gloria Ballerino Roberts*

Mitchell Rivera Woo *Bryn ("Cat Iron") Meehan and John ("Juke Boy") Eskow*

Shushi Young. Voted president of the girls' side of Camp Boiberick in 1958 and showers in the nude.

Steve Young. Dropped out after 5 years at Mount Sinai Hospital (3 years as an intern, 2 as a resident), Park Avenue coop, to become a country type.

Lynn Anderson. Cook at communal macrobiotic restaurant.

Aaron Van De Bogart. Head forest ranger, Catskill Mountains, Woodstock.

Gloria Ballerino Roberts. 4th-generation Californian. By nature and talent, a great Mexican cook.

Mitchell Rivera Woo. Recently OD'd on Liberal Nookie while attending the Mickey Bitsko Correspondence School of Scholarship Acceptance and Tokenism from which he was graduated summa cum laude for filling 5 quotas: black, tall, Chinese, Puerto Rican, and radical. His hobbies include Frisbee playing, honky baiting, and domino stacking when he's not working as a free-lance depilatory agent.

Bryn ("Cat Iron") Meehan and John ("Juke Boy") Eskow. Miss Meehan was born to an itinerant tattoo remover in mid-1951 when the sun was in Aquarius and the Olympics were laying down the final harmony on "Big Boy Pete." She is presently at work on an epic prose poem entitled "Damaged Hair" and is completing a thesis on the influence of the lithographs of Albrecht Dürer on the work of Rod McKuen.

Juke Boy Eskow, last reported running Kaopectate in Cuernavaca, Mexico, is a figure of near-mythical proportions in the North Bergen Shopping Mall in Hohokus, New Jersey. In his too-brief life he reports he has been "abused, 'buked, and vilified, made to hear Donovan albums till I moaned and cried." His last significant work was the country-and-western hit "All I Needed Was One Lousy Dime (But the Ones I Was Offered Were Spotless").

Roger Vaughan   *Pam Wilson*

Roger Vaughan.   In the beginning was a good Eastern prep school followed
by an ivory league college. Married early. Moving fast at 21. Success in
the mass media was to be mine for the taking. Bright light at 25. Divorced
early. Then? Maybe it was something I ate. Right now I am listening to
the Rolling Stones ("me I'm just trying to do this jigsaw puzzle"). I help
with the dishes, sometimes I vacuum the rugs, and do the heavy work in
the garden. I work for the local commercial fishing company. In the
winter I chop wood. Physically I feel wonderful. I take pictures and print
them. I am crazy about the Possum, my wife. For fun my friends and I
talk about the search for meaningful work. In the meantime Dylan says
it—we watch the river flow (the ocean roll).

Pam Wilson.   A 1949 Virgo, knowing the way to the Peaceable Kingdom;
learning to live it; and studying how water fills the hollows. Someday I
hope to ride the clouds, keep bugs off the cabbage, and go swimming
and eat strawberries the rest of the time.